W9-CCB-469

GREAT MARQUES OF ITALY

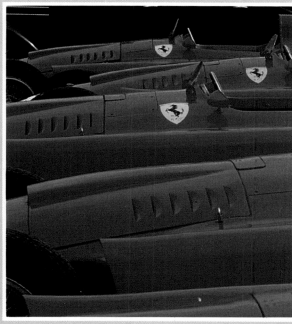

GREAT MARQUES OF ITALY

Jonathan Wood
With a foreword by Giovanni Agnelli, Chairman of FIAT

VISCOUNT BOOKS

This edition published 1989 by
Viscount Books
an imprint of the Octopus Publishing Group
Michelin House
81 Fulham Road
London SW3 6RB

© Octopus Books Limited 1987

ISBN 1 600 56444 4

Produced by Mandarin Offset
22a Westlands Road
Quarry Bay
Hong Kong

Printed and Bound in Hong Kong

The chapters on Alfa Romeo and Ferrari originally appeared in the Great Marques series published by Octopus Books Limited. These sections have been abridged and updated. The Alfa Romeo section was written by David Owen, Ferrari by Godfrey Eaton. They have been edited by Jonathan Wood. All other sections were written by Jonathan Wood.

PAGE 1 CLOCKWISE The badges of Fiat, Maserati, Alfa Romeo, Lamborghini, Lancia and Ferrari.
PAGE 2 TOP LEFT Lancia Stratos, TOP RIGHT Lamborghini Countach, MIDDLE Maserati Bora, BOTTOM Alfa Romeo Montreal.
PAGE 3 TOP Fiat Panda, BOTTOM Ferrari Testarossa.
PAGE 4 TOP LEFT Fiat 500, BOTTOM LEFT Lamborghini Silouette, RIGHT Lancia Rallye.
PAGE 5 TOP LEFT Ferrari Daytona, BOTTOM LEFT Maserati Mexico, RIGHT Alfa Romeo Arna.

The publishers would like to thank Alfa Romeo, Fiat, Lamborghini, Lancia and Maserati for permission to reproduce their logos. The Ferrari logo is reproduced with the kind permission of Maranello Concessionnaires Ltd, who are the sole concessionnaires for Ferrari in the United Kingdom.

CONTENTS

SWITZERLAND

AUSTRIA

FRANCE

● BOLZANO

● FOBELLO
● VARALLO

● LECCO

MONZA
● **MILAN**
Alfa Romeo

YUGOSLAVIA

CHIVASSO
●

PINEROLO
● **TURIN**
Fiat, Lancia

● PADERNO

● PADUA ●

● VOGHERA

● CUNEO

GENOA

MODENA
Maserati

**SANT'AGATA
BOLOGNESE**
Lamborghini

MARANELLO
Ferrari

BOLOGNA
Maserati (1926-1939)

LIGURIAN SEA

ADRIATIC SEA

● LUCCA

*The map shows the headquarters of the
principal Italian car makers. Although
first established in the north they are
now spread throughout the country.
Locations mentioned in the text are
also indicated.*

● LIVORNO

● PANICAROLA

MEDITERRANEAN SEA

ROME

ROME

Scale in miles

| 0 | 50 | 100 |

Scale in kms

| 0 | 50 | 100 | 150 |

FOREWORD

Fiat, founded in Turin in 1899 and 88 years old this year, is Italy's largest company and one of Europe's most successful car makers. My grandfather, Giovanni Agnelli, was Fiat's first company secretary though he subsequently became its president and ran it until his death in 1945.

The real growth of Fiat occurred in the inter-war years when production rose from 173 cars in 1919 to nearly 53,000 cars in 1939. This growth was matched by an increase in manufacturing capacity with the building of a huge factory in the Lingotto district of Turin and the Mirafiori plant, which is now our main manufacturing centre, in 1938.

In 1936 Fiat introduced the 500, the smallest four-cylinder car in the world, which became affectionately known as 'Il Topolino' (Mickey Mouse). This car and its post-war successors, the 600 and the new 500, gave many Italians and drivers throughout the world the opportunity to own a car for the first time. Today the Panda and the Uno fulfil that role.

Through our ownership of Lancia, Ferrari and now Alfa Romeo, Fiat offers a broad range of vehicles that are not only some of the most popular in Italy and Europe, but are also manufactured by the most up-to-date production methods, and often by Fiat-designed robots.

These moves are the result of an intensive investment programme – initiated after the war – which I have continued since taking over the Fiat chairmanship in 1966. It ensures that Fiat is well equipped to meet the challenges of the 21st century, and beyond.

GIOVANNI AGNELLI

7

INTRODUCTION

The Italian motor industry is essentially a post-war phenomenon. In 1939 Italy produced a mere 55,533 cars and came a poor fourth behind Britain, Germany and France, whereas today, Italy has not only overtaken Britain, but also vehicle output has not dropped below the million mark since 1963. Italian styling and engineering has had an enormous impact on the motor industries of the world, Italy's racing cars have dominated the racing circuits, and Fiat, the country's largest car maker, is one of Europe's most successful businesses.

Yet, in 1886, when the motor car was born in Germany, Italy was a relatively poor and backward country. Inevitably, the first cars to be seen there were French and German imports. It was not until 1896 that the first all-Italian motor car was designed, by Enrico Bernardi, a former professor of physics, at Padua. One of his followers was Giovanni Agnelli, a young cavalry officer from Villar Perosa, who was one of the principal architects in the creation of Fabbrica Italiana Automobili Torino, the company that we know now by its Fiat acronym.

Fiat is unique in the European motor industry in that it was created by a group of socialist intellectuals and aristocrats. Because of the founding fathers' political beliefs, a factor in the company's birth was a desire to provide employment in Turin – capital of the province of Piedmont, and rich both in engineering talent and stylistic flair. Rather than create a new car from scratch, the company decided to buy an existing design which was on the point of being marketed by Giovanni Battista Ceirano, a Turin bicycle maker. His Welleyes car formed the basis of the first F.I.A.T. (as the make was known until 1906). The firm's growth was so rapid that, by the outbreak of World War 1, Fiat was easily Italy's largest car maker and had already diversified by moving into commercial vehicles in 1903, marine engines two years later and, in 1908, aero-engines.

As the country is crucially short of natural resources, exports were, and still are, a prime requirement. Consequently, most of the foremost Italian makes of the day catered to the international carriage trade, selling across the Atlantic in America, and in Britain, France and Germany.

Ceirano's bicycle business was also the starting point of another of Italy's great marques, for young Vincenzo Lancia, although ostensibly Ceirano's bookkeeper, was in reality an enthusiastic driver and mechanic. When F.I.A.T. took over Ceirano's business, it inherited Lancia who became a pillar of its racing team, prior to his leaving in 1906 to form his own car company, which was also Turin-based.

ABOVE *Vincenzo Lancia's revolutionary Lambda, introduced in 1922, with unitary construction bodywork, independent front suspension and 2120 cc V4 overhead-camshaft engine. The* Autocar *test driver averaged 106.89 km/h (66.42 mph) 'with three passengers . . . and a stiff adverse wind' in this car.*

RIGHT *Italy's most illustrious racing car of the inter-war years was the Alfa Romeo P3 monoposto, by Vittorio Jano, initially with a 2.6-litre eight-cylinder supercharged engine. The P3 virtually wiped the board with the opposition from its 1932 arrival until the Mercedes-Benz and Auto Union challenge began to bite in 1934.*

8

Meanwhile, the rival city of Milan was spawning its own motor industry. Initially, the most significant firm was Isotta-Fraschini, established in 1900, but, in 1910, came Anonimà Lombarda Fabbrica Automobili, or ALFA, which followed an abortive attempt to produce French Darracq cars in Italy. The firm started by producing soundly designed, rather traditional cars but, in 1911, came a racing model, a *genre* with which the marque has been identified ever since. At Fiat, Giovanni Agnelli also recognized the publicity value of motor sport and, in the golden year of 1907, his cars won no less than three of Europe's premier races.

After World War 1, in which Italy fought with Britain and France against Germany and Austro-Hungary, Fiat continued racing, a commitment which culminated, in 1923, in the arrival of the Tipo 805, the first competition car in the world to use a supercharged engine. Although the company finally withdrew from racing in 1924, the Tipo 805's power unit was to influence racing-car design for the next 25 years.

During the war, in 1916, ALFA was taken over by industrialist Nicola Romeo and, when production re-started in 1920, the cars carried the new name of Alfa Romeo. After Fiat withdrew from racing, the Milan company took up the Grand Prix baton and wooed Vittorio Jano, one of Fiat's most able racing-car designers, to Milan. There he produced the supreme P2, which trounced the opposition and gave the firm the Automobile World Championship in 1925.

In 1926, yet another Italian marque made its appearance on the racing circuits: Maserati. Three Maserati brothers, Alfieri, Ernesto and Ettore, had all worked for Isotta-Fraschini and, in 1914, they opened a tuning shop in Bologna. After the war they produced racing cars for the Turin-based Diatto company and the first Maserati racing car had its genesis in this work.

Although Vincenzo Lancia's name was world-famous due to his success as a racing driver, paradoxically his cars seldom took part in competitive events. Until 1922 they had been well-built, competently executed designs, but all this changed with the arrival of the Lambda; thereafter the Lancia name was to be linked with technical innovation. With its unitary construction body, independent front suspension and V4 engine, the Lambda overflowed with new ideas, although the cars were not made in sufficient quantities for Lancia to take advantage of these design initiatives.

The effects of the world Depression were to have a devastating effect on the Italian motor industry. In 1931, Fiat produced only 16,419 cars and Alfa Romeo's plight grew so dire that there was talk of closing it down completely. The firm had been living on borrowed time – and borrowed money – since 1928 and, as it concentrated on the production of exquisite, but expensive, low-production sports cars, was especially vulnerable. The costly racing programme was suspended at the beginning of 1933 and, although it was reactivated in August, by October the wheels were set in motion for Alfa Romeo's closure. At this point Benito Mussolini, the Italian dictator, in response to lobbying by the Milan authorities and, anxious to counter Fiat's growing power, reprieved the firm. Therefore the Istituto per la Ricostruzione Industriale (IRI) was founded to rescue not only Alfa Romeo, but also the Ansaldo and Ilva companies. Thus Italy's most famous racing make was saved.

Ironically, it was a period when Alfa Romeo's racing fortunes were riding high. For 1932, Vittorio Jano produced the superlative Tipo B monoposto (single seater) – universally known as the P3 – which, until the arrival of the 750 kg formula in 1934, was rarely defeated in competition. Thereafter Alfa Romeo's racing fortunes declined in the face of Mercedes-Benz

ABOVE *Fiat's immortal 500 of 1936, which gave many Italians the chance to own a car for the first time and was a true large car in miniature. Powered by a diminutive forward-mounted 569 cc four-cylinder engine, the 500 was built until 1948 and lasted, in 500C guise, until 1955.*

and Auto Union opposition from Germany. Sadly, the firm's mainstream passenger car production was negligible and only 918 cars were built between 1936 and 1938.

When Mussolini came to power in 1922, one of his first actions was to initiate the construction of purpose-built motor roads, or *autostrade*. This not only encouraged the design of short-stroke engines, ideal for cruising at high speed for long periods, but also stimulated aerodynamic research which was increasingly reflected in Italian car styling from the mid-1930s onwards. One such vehicle was Fiat's 500, introduced in 1936; its diminutive 569 cc four-cylinder engine was the smallest of its type in the world. Here was a car which was much more within the reach of Italian customers, and it soon became affectionately known as the Topolino (Mickey Mouse).

The 1930s also witnessed the flowering of the Italian *carrozzerie* (coachbuilders). Again these firms were mostly concentrated on Turin and Milan, the former city playing host to Stabilimenti Farina (1896), Bertone (1912), Ghia (1915) and Pinin Farina (1930). Milan housed rather fewer, although two were to gain worldwide renown: Zagato, established in 1919, and in 1926, Felice Bianchi Anderloni created Carrozzeria Touring, perhaps the greatest of them all.

In 1940 Italy was once more at war, this time as an ally of Nazi Germany. Although the Italians signed a peace treaty with America and Britain in 1943, German troops continued to fight on in the peninsula, so hostilities did not cease there until 1945. The factories of Fiat, Alfa Romeo and Lancia all suffered from Allied bombing.

However, Fiat was back in production again in 1945. In 1946 Vittorio Valletta succeeded Giovanni Agnelli, who had died the previous year. He was to steer Fiat's fortunes through 20 years of outstanding growth. During the 1950s and 1960s many Italians began to enjoy the delights of car ownership and Fiat registered its first million-car year in 1965.

In 1947 a new make had arrived on the Italian scene which has since become one of the world's great marques. Enzo Ferrari, responsible for Alfa Romeo's racing programme from 1929 until 1938, decided to enter the Grand Prix arena from a small factory at Maranello, near Modena. His first 1.5-litre supercharged V12 racing car appeared in 1947 and, to finance his single-seaters, Ferrari simultaneously introduced a range of road and sports racers. To begin with, Ferrari's racers had to defer to the superiority of the Tipo 158 Alfetta, but in 1950 Ferrari commissioned young Aurelio Lampredi to design a 4.5-litre unsupercharged engine. Thereafter, the days of the supercharged power unit, popularized by Fiat back in 1924, were numbered. Ferrari was on his way and has been a force in Formula 1 racing ever since. In 1949 the firm won its first Le Mans 24-hour race and went on to become a formidable, and successful presence in sports car racing.

However, racing is an expensive business and, by the 1960s, Ferrari was starting to feel the pinch. Ford wanted to buy the firm in 1963, but negotiations fell through and eventually it was Fiat that, in 1969, took a 50 per cent interest in a business which had become a national institution. This left Enzo Ferrari to look after the motor racing side which was, after all, his first love, while Fiat assumed responsibility for refining and improving the Ferrari road cars.

Like Ferrari, Maserati decided to produce road cars, from 1947, to defray its racing costs. The firm had been bought by the Orsi engineering concern in 1937 and, two years later, had moved from Bologna to Modena. After the war, Maserati played second fiddle on the Grand Prix circuits to Alfa Romeo and Ferrari until the arrival, in 1954, of the fabled 250F model. But

LEFT *Ferrari, Italy's new racing marque, put up an impressive performance almost from its inception. This is the highly successful 2-litre 500F2, designed by Aurelio Lampredi, which won an impressive 30 out of 33 championship races in 1952/3.*

Maserati was forced to withdraw from Formula 1 because of financial problems, which were exacerbated by a costly sports racing programme. Road car production was stepped up from 1958, although sports racing cars, for private owners, continued to be made into the 1960s.

Another company that succumbed to the lure of the race track, but with disastrous consequences, was Lancia. In the 1930s, the firm had maintained its high technological profile: in 1937 the Aprilia arrived. With its aerodynamic bodywork and all-independent suspension, it was a fast model which set new standards of roadholding. Later came yet another technological milestone in the shape of the 1950 Aurelia, the first series-production car in the world to feature a V6 engine, and boasting trailing arm rear suspension, which was yet another innovation. As if this was not enough, a sports Gran Turismo B20 coupé version, by Pinin Farina, offering the comfort of a saloon with the performance of a sports car, followed in 1951. This effectively gave birth to the GT concept which soon outstripped the traditional open two-seater in popularity all over the globe.

The B20 was also an impressive testament to the skills of the Pinin Farina styling house, and a reflection of the growing international stature of the Italian *carrozzerie*. In 1960, Pinin Farina officially adopted his nickname – Pininfarina – as his surname and as the title of his company.

Lancia, in the meantime, had embarked on a costly Formula 1 programme in 1954 which culminated, in the following year, in the firm being taken over by cement manufacturer Carlo Pesenti. Lancia wilted in the 1960s, despite a new range of front-wheel-drive cars, due to vigorous competition from a revitalized Alfa Romeo and the powerful Fiat presence. Consequently, in 1969, Lancia too became part of Fiat which was headed, from 1966, by Gianni Agnelli, Giovanni's grandson.

Yet another new Italian make arrived in 1964 to challenge Ferrari's road cars. Tractor manufacturer Ferruccio Lamborghini's 350 GT offered, like Ferrari, a V12 engine, although Lamborghini's car had twin overhead camshafts per cylinder bank, and all-independent suspension – neither was available on the contemporary cars from Maranello. Then, in 1966, Lamborghini really threw down the gauntlet with the sensational Bertone-bodied Miura, the world's first mid-engined production car.

The 1973 Arab-Israeli war triggered a sharp rise in oil prices, and the consequent economic depression cast a shadow across the Italian motor industry. Maserati was bought by Citroën in 1968 and, when that company was in turn taken over by Peugeot, Maserati was left, in 1975, to sink or swim. However, salvation was at hand in the shape of the Italian government and Alessandro de Tomaso. Lamborghini became exclusively Swiss-owned in 1972, after its founder bowed out. But the arctic economic climate wrought havoc with the firm and the government was forced to step in in 1978. A suitable buyer was found in the shape of the French/Swiss Mimran group, which became Lamborghini's proprietor in 1981, though it sold out to Chrysler in 1987. The current Countach, successor to the Miura, with its stunning Bertone-styled coachwork and V12 performance, perhaps epitomises the concept of the Italian 'supercar'. In 1987, Fiat took over Alfa Romeo, a move which gave it effective control of the entire Italian motor industry.

Today, Fiat's Uno is a European best-seller; Maserati, profitable probably for the first time in its history, offers impressive performance with executive luxury; and Giorgetto Giugiaro's Ital Design styling house, founded only in 1968, is a reminder of the vitality of that sector of the industry. Italy, as ever, is setting the pace.

ABOVE *Maserati's current flagship is the Quattroporte, introduced in 1979. This Ital Design-styled luxury saloon is powered by a 4.9-litre four-overhead-camshaft V8. Automatic transmission is a standard fitment and top speed is around 225 km/h (140 mph).*

RIGHT *Lamborghini's incredible Miura, introduced in 1966, was the world's first series-production mid-engined car, conceived by Giampaolo Dallara with sensational bodywork by Bertone's Marcello Gandini. It remained in production until 1973.*

Alfa Romeo

Alfa Romeo, Italy's oldest sporting marque, has been
building cars since 1910. The Milan company gained a
great racing and sporting reputation in the inter-war
years but was nationalized in the depression of 1933. Post-war,
Alfa Romeo joined the mass-production league and rapidly
expanded, although until recently its status was in question as
profitability continued to elude the firm and eventually, in
1987, Fiat took the company over.

Although 1910 was the year when cars first appeared bearing
the ALFA name, the marque's origins really go back to 1906. It
was in this year that the Società Italiana Automobili Darracq
(SIAD) started assembling cars in the Portello district of Milan,
having already been established briefly in Naples. However the
venture, which involved producing and selling French Darracq
cars in Italy, proved short-lived as the little single- and two-
cylinder models were totally unsuitable for the country's poor,
sometimes twisting and mountainous roads. What was clearly
needed was a car designed with Italian requirements in mind.
Consequently, in 1909, Ugo Stella, formerly managing director
of the SIAD concern, hired Giuseppe Merosi to undertake the
task. He had worked for Fiat and was, from 1906 to 1909, chief
designer of Bianchi, which was one of Milan's significant car
makers. With a view to distancing himself from the unhappy
SIAD associations, Stella re-formed the firm which became, on
24 June 1910, Anonima Lombarda Fabbrica Automobili and
marketed its cars under the ALFA acronym. For its badge, the
firm chose the arms of the city of Milan with its distinctive red
cross on one side and the serpent emblem of the Visconti family,
who became Dukes of Milan in medieval times, on the other.

LEFT *This magnificent 8C 2.6-litre Alfa Romeo two-seater is a
reminder that the Milanese firm was producing some of the
finest sports cars in the world in the early 1930s. A Touring-
bodied 1932 car, it was campaigned in Britain in pre-war days by
G. Bagratouni. Provided by J. C. Bamford Excavators Ltd.*

ALFA 24 HP
1910–14

ENGINE	
No. of cylinders 4	
Bore/stroke mm 100 × 130	
Displacement cc 4084	
Valve operation Overhead pushrod	
Compression ratio 4.15:1	
Induction Single downdraught carburettor	
BHP 45 at 2400 rpm	
Transmission Four-speed	

CHASSIS	
Frame Channel section	
Wheelbase mm 3200	
Track – front mm 1450	
Track – rear mm 1450	
Suspension – front Semi-elliptic leaf	
Suspension – rear Semi-elliptic leaf	

PERFORMANCE	
Maximum speed 105 km/h (65 mph)	

Merosi wasted little time and the first Alfa appeared in 1910, a sturdy 24 hp 4.1-litre car with a side-valve four-cylinder engine, which was later known as the 20/30 hp, and evolved, in 1914, into the 15/20 hp. There was also, in 1910, an aero-engine variant marking the firm's entry into the aviation field, an activity which would become progressively more important in the inter-war and World War 2 years.

A smaller 2.4-litre 12 hp car on similar lines was introduced simultaneously, evolving into a 15 hp in 1912 and a 15/20 hp two years later. In 1913 the firm introduced its first six-cylinder model, the 6.1-litre 40/60 hp, with overhead valves. Its appearance as a sporting model helped create the image with which Alfa has come to be identified. Two special 24 hp cars had participated in the gruelling Sicilian Targa Florio race in 1911, although they did not complete the course. However, the 40/60 hp did somewhat better in the 1914 Coppa Florio, also held that year in Sicily, when examples were placed in third and fourth positions.

In 1914 the firm grew ever more ambitious and produced an advanced 16-valve twin-overhead-camshaft four-cylinder 4.5-litre racing car in the manner of the 1910 Grand Prix Peugeots. But it never ran in international events and details of its sophisticated specifications remained unknown, outside Italy, until the 1960s!

ABOVE *The first Alfa was this 24 hp model, introduced in 1910. Under the bonnet was a fixed-head four-cylinder engine. It was available in open* *(Torpedo) and saloon (Limousine) form and was a reliable alternative to the underpowered Darracqs that the firm had previously produced.*

From 20 cars turned out during 1910, production had expanded to 80 the following year, to 150 in 1912, to more than 200 in 1913, to 272 in 1914 and to 205 in the first six months of 1915 alone. But the last figure is the most significant in only covering half a year. On 22 May 1915 Italy joined the Allies, and the fighting. Not surprisingly, production came to a halt and the company turned to other activities more relevant to the country's fight for survival against the onslaught of the Austro-Hungarian forces in the mountains to the north.

Merosi himself lost no time in adapting the 15/20 hp engine to work in a new role as a generator for the Italian army. But the old financial problems were now recurring from another direction. The last of the Darracq family to hold shares in the company, Alexandre's nephew Albert, had sold his holding to the Banca di Sconto. The bank was now worried that motor manufacturers – any motor manufacturers – were not the best of commercial bets in the middle of a world war, and so began to look for a potential investor as a way of spreading the risk.

Alfa Romeo

RIGHT *Nicola Romeo (1876–1938), the industrialist whose name was immortalized in Alfa Romeo cars. A native of Sant'Antimo in the province of Naples, Romeo worked abroad, in Belgium, France, Britain and Germany, before opening a firm in Milan in 1912 to manufacture air compressors. He took over Alfa in 1916.*

BELOW *A racing version of the 40–60 hp Alfa, introduced in 1913. Capable of 125 km/h (77 mph), it was powered by a four-cylinder 6082 cc engine with pushrod-operated overhead valves.*

Fortunately for the bank, and for Alfa, they found the very man in the industrialist and mining engineer Nicola Romeo, who was so busy making pumps and compressors for the army that he was actually looking for new investments and, even more important for his overstretched business, new factory space. By the beginning of 1916 his turnover had expanded 24 times, and he was more than glad to buy some of the bank's Alfa shares and take over as managing director in return for the extra production capacity. Within two years, the Alfa works was helping to turn out tractors, aircraft engines and railway equipment as well as generators, and Romeo had bought out the other major shareholders to take over the company completely.

Just about the only thing the Alfa works did not make was cars. Romeo himself, although an enterprising engineer and successful businessman, was no car enthusiast, and parts for the last 105 cars had been stored away with no plans at all for turning them into complete vehicles. Yet history was to change that, as suddenly and dramatically as in 1914.

When the war came to an end in November 1918, Alfa technically did not exist at all. After Romeo's takeover the

company had been renamed the Società Anonima Italiana Ing. Nicola Romeo, and Giuseppe Merosi had been given the job of running another of the industrialist's plants in the south. But the return of peace meant the collapse of the market for army equipment, and while there was enough demand from the mining industry to keep the company afloat, it now had too much factory space that had stopped earning income. Nicola Romeo had become a prisoner of his own success. What use could he find for the workers and the plant now so suddenly made redundant?

Whatever his personal feelings, Romeo was far too seasoned an entrepreneur to overlook a real opportunity, and he knew full well that the car market was bound to recover in time, although the need was for very different designs from the slow, solid, heavy and expensive pre-war models. The first priority, however, was to turn out any cars at all; and the parts for the 105 production cars stored since the outbreak of war were to be priceless assets in winning a head start over the opposition.

Events moved quickly after that. Merosi came back from the south to pick up the production threads again. The cars were assembled and left the factory – 10 15/20 hps, 95 20/30 hps – to find ready buyers waiting for them, but they had one important difference from their pre-war stablemates. Nicola Romeo had changed the name of the company, but in this specialized market he knew full well the value of reputation and continuity. Calling them Romeos would mean little outside the mining industry; calling them Alfas would hide the name of the new group of which the firm was now part. So a compromise was found, and a new name added to the company badge. Alfa, first renamed Romeo, had now become Alfa Romeo. The coming years were to make that new name far better known than the company's previous titles.

New post-war models

Merosi's first attempt at the post-war generation of production cars was a failure. Although the updated 20/30 hps were selling well enough, the old 40/60 seemed to need a replacement at the larger end of the market, so in 1921 the firm produced the G1 with a 6.3-litre six-cylinder engine. It only lasted a year and a mere 52 were built.

The G1's 1922 replacement was rather more successful. This was the RL and it was hoped that the 2916 cc pushrod overhead-valve six-cylinder engine could do double duty as a Grand Prix unit; but then the formula was changed to 2 litres in 1922.

All the same, from a beginning like this the new RL could only get better. It was at least reliable, and its smaller capacity meant that the customers could have mediocre performance at a lower cost in fuel and taxes, so it began to sell. But the RL's real significance was in the family that it fathered. Although the Grand Prix hopes of the design had been blighted, there were still prospects in the sports car arena, and Merosi was developing an RL Sport version, with wider 76 mm (rather than 75 mm) cylinder bores, a capacity of 2994 cc, larger valves, stronger connecting rods, higher compression ratio and power increased to 72 bhp, an improvement of more than 20 per cent.

Alfa's sales prospects were to be transformed in the same way. The new cars, the RLN (for RL Normale) and the RLS (RL Sport), had appeared in the closing weeks of 1921, and at the end of the year three examples of each car had been built. But by the end of 1922 more than 800 RLs had been turned out, which

BELOW *A splendid Alfa Romeo RL Super Sport of 1925 with a 2994 cc pushrod six-cylinder engine. Its top speed is 130 km/h (80 mph).*

mean that the company's Portello works had produced almost as many cars in twelve months as it had in the five years leading up to the wartime shut-down.

There was more to come: the pointed radiator which distinguished the Sport version from the standard RL was inherited by its successor, the RL Super Sport (or RLSS) of 1925. This had a still more powerful 86 bhp version of the 3-litre six, and with a closer-ratio gearbox even the production model was good for more than 130 km/h (80 mph).

By this time, however, two things had happened. The sporting programme had boomed, with competition versions of the RL taking over from their essentially pre-war-based predecessors. The first RL to be entered in Alfa's traditional proving ground for its competition cars, the Targa Florio, failed even to finish. But fortunately the Alfa team went on to use the design as a basis for a more specialized version altogether. They shortened the chassis frame by 305 mm (12 in) and covered it with a tiny and carefully streamlined racing body, with frontal area cut to the minimum and panelling shaped around the two bucket seats, the fuel tanks and the spare wheels. The engine was given a higher compression ratio and lightened valve gear to boost the power to 88 bhp, and three works cars were produced to this specification; two more were built with special engines of 78 mm cylinder bore and a capacity of 3154 cc, which increased the power still further to 95 bhp. Lightened bodies, better streamlining and close-ratio gearboxes helped produce top speeds of 145 (90) and 158 km/h (98 mph) for the two versions of the RLTF (RL Targa Florio), which was the official designation for the works cars.

The result was that one of the machines, driven by Ugo Sivocci, won the 1923 race, with Ascari second and Count Masetti fourth. The cars went on to win other sports car races.

By this time, however, the Grand Prix programme had been revived all over again, and Merosi was able to start from the much-needed clean sheet of paper to produce a result that would be truly competitive. The car was originally designated the GPR (for Grand Prix Romeo) but has been known ever since as the Alfa Romeo P1. It had a twin-overhead-camshaft 2-litre six-cylinder engine.

In the event, however, the car's future was all too soon its past. Although it was capable of more than 177 km/h (110 mph), and the company felt confident enough to enter all three of the cars it had built for the 1923 Italian Grand Prix, tragedy was waiting at the trackside. Ugo Sivocci was testing the first of the

cars on the Monza circuit when he slid off the track on the Curva Vialone and was killed in the ensuing crash. Alfa withdrew the other two cars as a mark of respect, the GP was won by Fiat, and the two surviving P1s never ran again.

By 1925, and the appearance of the RLSS as the last link in the RL chain, it was clear that the buyers, too, needed something new to keep them happy. Although the cars had done well, backed up by an equivalent range of four-cylinder models, designated RM, which sold in much smaller numbers, the figures were now beginning to fall off quite alarmingly. Again, and happily for Alfa's fortunes, the answer was very close to being ready – and the amazing truth is that the new production car, which was to become one of the most famous and most desirable of all the Alfas, was to owe its origins to the design that would bring the company the much-sought-after and most elusive Grand Prix success after so much waiting and so much effort.

The man responsible for these two versions of the same basic design was a new addition to the Alfa Romeo ranks. Indeed, at the time when Merosi's P1 was taking shape, he was working for the Fiat team that led the Grand Prix world as far as Italy was concerned, and won the race for which the P1s had been entered. His name was Vittorio Jano.

The negotiations were long and delicate, involving Alfa racing driver Enzo Ferrari, who had joined the firm in 1920, as a go-between, but finally resulted in Jano taking over in the Alfa workshops, where from the beginning his priceless experience galvanized the process of racing development, inspiring the Alfa Romeo team with a new sense of urgency and commitment.

The P2's power unit, for example, owed a great deal to the Fiat 805 racing engine on which Jano had been working at Turin. It was a straight-eight with hemispherical combustion

LEFT *The first successful Grand Prix Alfa Romeo, the P2 of 1924. Note the four-leaf clover symbol on the bonnet; it first appeared on the car that won the 1923 Targa Florio and was thereafter adopted by the firm as its racing symbol.*

BELOW *Vittorio Jano's magnificent supercharged 1987 cc twin-overhead-camshaft engine.*

chambers, two rows of inclined valves set in the roof of the combustion chambers and operated by two overhead camshafts. Most significantly it was a supercharged car, Alfa Romeo's first.

This was Alfa's most formidable GP challenge yet, and with a single carburettor the first car was turning out 134 bhp on test, with more to come. On 9 June 1924, Ascari took the new car out on the Circuit of Cremona, where it won convincingly. By early August a team of four was entered for the Grand Prix of Europe, to be run at Lyons in France against the fierce opposition of four

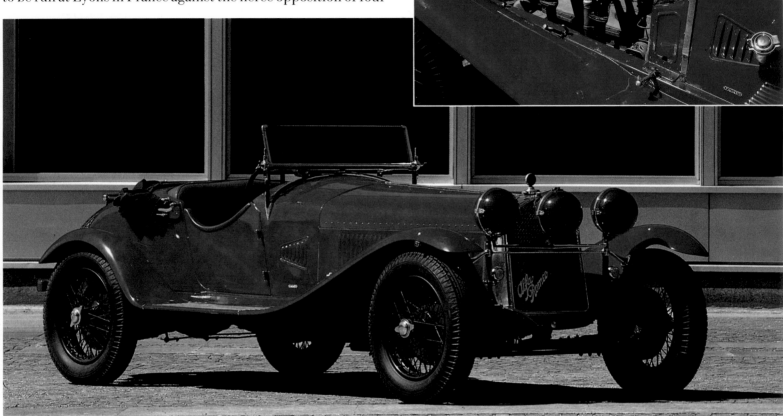

professional and highly competitive teams: Fiat, Delage, Bugatti and Sunbeam. Three of the four Alfa drivers had a disappointing race, yet the final result was better than anyone could have hoped: Ferrari's car had to be scratched because he was ill; Ascari's led the race until a water leak put it out of the running with the distance three-quarters run; and Wagner's car finished fourth. But Campari won the race against the toughest opposition in Europe, and won it so convincingly that Fiat withdrew on the spot, having heard the bells toll the end of its 20-year record of victories at events all over the Continent.

This was recompense at last for the years of wasted efforts and blighted hopes: but for Alfa there was more to come. Jano developed a faster and more powerful twin-carburettor version in time for the Italian GP at Monza in October, where the chief opponents would be Mercedes – but a fatal accident caused the Mercedes team to withdraw, and the Alfa team finished first, second, third and fourth. So impressive had the cars' speed and clockwork-like reliability proved that Jano decided to subordinate everything else to contesting the 1925 championship. The works sports cars were sold off to private owners and the team concentrated on preparing for just three events: the European Grand Prix at Spa in Belgium, the French GP and the Italian GP. Once again the cars were improved by boosting the power, and by increasing the fuel tank capacity so that fewer pit stops would have to be made.

At Spa one of the P2s, driven by Count Gastone Brilli-Peri, dropped out with a broken front spring, but all the Delages followed suit with blower problems. The other two P2s of Ascari and Campari finished first and second, the only two cars to complete the fast and gruelling race. Then tragedy struck in the French GP: Ascari carried on in driving rain on worn tyres, skidded off the road and suffered a fatal crash. The team withdrew immediately, leaving Delage to take first and second places. The Italian GP saw Campari's Alfa take the lead after the third lap and hold it for 320 km (200 miles) until he had to stop at the pits – but it was Brilli-Peri in another P2 who took over to win, with Campari in second place and the third P2 coming in fifth. So in its first full season of Grand Prix racing Alfa had taken the World Championship, a magnificent achievement by any standards. As a mark of celebration, the company's badge on all its cars was circled by a laurel wreath, a feature it wore until relatively recently.

However, despite this success, what Alfa Romeo needed was a mainstream model. Jano, fortunately, had an answer. What he did was simple enough to describe, but much less so to carry through in reality. He took the world-beating P2 and made a production sports car out of it. By taking off the supercharger, and removing two of the cylinders from the engine, he produced an unblown single-overhead-camshaft six-cylinder engine with a capacity of 1.5 litres.

In 1928 the 1500 Sport appeared with the same engine, except for a return to the twin overhead camshafts and the hemispherical combustion chambers of the P2. This pushed the power up from 44 to 54 bhp, and the top speed to 125 km/h (78 mph). But the real excitement began with the 6C 1500 SS (Super Sport), which had a shorter wheelbase to reduce weight and improve handling, a neat two-seater body, a higher compression 60 bhp engine and a top speed of 130 km/h (80 mph). Keen buyers could specify a valuable optional extra: a supercharger which, despite the fact that it was less powerful than the unit fitted to the P2, still managed to boost power to 76 bhp and top speed to 140 km/h (87 mph).

In 1929 the 1500 series gave way to the immortal 1750s. Here, too, the prescription was simple enough to describe: Jano widened the cylinder bores to 65 mm and lengthened the stroke to 86 mm to increase the capacity to 1752 cc. The oddest feature of the new car, however, was that Alfa followed rigidly the progression of the earlier model: the original 1750 reverted to the single-cam version of the engine, with a 46 bhp power output which was only very slightly better than its predecessor and was, in any case, cancelled out by a corresponding increase in weight.

Fortunately for the enthusiasts, and for Alfa's growing sporting reputation, the new versions were not long in coming:

delivering 102 bhp and reaching a top speed of 171 km/h (106 mph), with handling and acceleration to match.

What all this meant in sales terms was a steady climb in the production figures. What it signified in sporting terms was a succession of wins in every kind of event: Campari and Ramponi won the 1929 Mille Miglia in a 1750 and Tazio Nuvolari, one of the greatest racing drivers of all time, beat his arch-rival Achille Varzi to do the same a year later.

From 1930 responsibility for Alfa Romeo's racing programme was vested in the Modena-based Scuderia Ferrari team, run by Alfa Romeo racing driver Enzo Ferrari. This arrangement lasted until 1938 when racing again became a works responsibility with the creation of Alfa Corse (Alfa Racing).

Meanwhile Jano and his team were working on a replacement for the successful 1500/1750 series. His answer, as always, showed the clarity and the brilliance of engineering genius. Just as the removal of two cylinders had paved the way for converting the P2 Grand Prix engine into the power unit for the six-cylinder sports cars, so the same process in reverse would produce another straight-eight. The inspiration, however, lay in the detail differences. Jano took the 1750 version of the six-cylinder engine, and instead of simply adding two cylinders on the end of the engine, he cut the engine in half, producing two four-cylinder units, which he then turned round and joined

LEFT *The first of Alfa Romeo's superb twin-overhead-camshaft sports cars, the 145 km/h (90 mph) 1750 Gran Sport, introduced in 1929 and built until 1933. This is a Zagato-bodied example, and the carrozzeria was always to be associated with this particular model.*

INSET *The magnificent and very modern-looking 1752 cc six-cylinder engine.*

RIGHT *The engine of the 8C 2600 shown on page 12. To create this straight-eight, Jano mounted two twin-overhead-camshaft four-cylinder blocks on a common crankcase with the camshafts and supercharger drive located between them in the manner of the Grand Prix Salmson of 1929 vintage.*

and in this case the larger engine of the 1750 gave ample scope for development. The Sport version was succeeded by the Super Sport and by a new variant called the Gran Sport which became the top of the range. In its production form, aided by a supercharger, the open sports version turned out 85 bhp and could top 145 km/h (90 mph). This ample power output meant that a new breed of car, and a new term to describe it, was just around the corner: a close-coupled saloon with a slightly heavier body but a still sparkling 135 km/h (84 mph) became the 1750 Gran Turismo. Then, finally, the works racing versions were

together again back-to-back. This meant that the long camshafts and crankshafts required for an eight-cylinder in-line engine were no longer necessary. The new engine had the camshaft drives and all the auxiliaries in the centre; instead of, for example, one long crankshaft working with all eight cylinders, there were now two short crankshafts with four cylinders apiece. These were joined in the centre through a set of helical gears, which also drove the dynamo, the oil and water pumps, the supercharger and the four overhead camshafts, two for each four-cylinder bank. The engine's capacity was 2336 cc.

The 2300 in competition

From the beginning, the 2300s were set for competition honours. The first works cars appeared in 1931, with uprated superchargers, larger valves and a power output of 155 bhp giving Alfa Romeo its first Le Mans victory. Although they failed to finish the Mille Miglia of that year, this was due to problems with tyres rather than with the cars. To prove the point, the team won the Targa Florio and then went on to take the 1932 Mille Miglia as well. There was even better to come: in 1931, the Grand Prix rules were changed to allow cars of any design at all, provided that they had two seats, carried no mechanics and lasted out for races of at least ten hours' duration.

It seemed as if the 2300, with its flexibility and reliability, could have been designed with these new regulations in mind. The team began the modifications that would turn the development wheel full circle, so that Jano's design had gone from a straight-eight Grand Prix car to a six-cylinder sports car, to an eight-cylinder sports car and back to an eight-cylinder Grand Prix car again. This final step in the progression was a highly tuned 2300 with higher compression, larger valves, more boost from the supercharger and streamlined racing bodywork. A fortnight after the Mille Miglia win the first two of these Grand Prix 2300s were entered in the Grand Prix of Europe, to

be run at Monza. To the delight of the development team and of the Scuderia Ferrari, the two cars finished first and second. Consequently, this version of the 2300 was always afterwards to be known as the Monza, in honour of that first-time victory.

The freedom of the racing rules, however, was to have one inevitable result: a power race began, with the teams turning to larger and larger engines in attempts to steal a march on the opposition. In time this would limit itself because of the greater weights of the larger units, and the difficulty of ensuring that the extra power could be coped with by the crude suspensions of the time. But for the time being, the Monza's 2.3 litres were not enough and for Grand Prix racing, at least, Alfa Romeo was going to have to come up with something more powerful.

The initial stopgap was based on the idea utilized in the Sedici Cilindri Maserati, evolved to meet the same need to provide ample power without the time, trouble and expense of designing and developing a new, bigger unit: the idea was to use two engines instead. In Alfa's case, Jano designed a new racing car called the Tipo A which had two 1750 engines mounted side by side, and modified to turn in opposite directions so as to cancel out the torque reactions; but handling was always a problem.

It was clearly time for a compromise: the Monza in its original version had handled well and proved supremely reliable but had lacked enough power to be competitive against bigger-engined opposition. The Tipo A had power in plenty but had handling

ABOVE *Alfa Romeo's immortal P3, introduced in 1932. The cars were run for Alfa Romeo by Scuderia Ferrari; note the stable's prancing-horse motif on the bonnet. This is Louis Chiron in the 1934 Dieppe Grand Prix. He retired with a broken shock absorber bracket after uncharacteristically hitting a bank at the Esses of St Aubyn.*

TIPO B MONOPOSTO (P3)
1932–3

ENGINE		CHASSIS	
No. of cylinders 8		Frame Box section	
Bore/stroke mm 65 × 100		Wheelbase mm 2650	
Displacement cc 2654		Track – front mm 1380	
Valve operation Twin overhead camshafts		Track – rear mm 1300	
		Suspension – front Semi-elliptic	
Compression ratio 6.5:1		Suspension – rear Semi-elliptic, 1935 reversed quarter-elliptic	
Induction 2 downdraught carburettors, 2 Roots-type superchargers		Brakes Rod drum	
BHP 215 at 5600 rpm		**PERFORMANCE**	
Transmission Four-speed		Maximum speed 232 km/h (144 mph)	

RIGHT *A P3 today, revealing its magnificent eight-cylinder engine with twin Alfa Romeo Roots-type superchargers, which ran at approximately 10 lb. In its original form the P3 was fitted with half-elliptic rear springs, but from 1935 Scuderia Ferrari replaced them with quarter-elliptics. Provided by Chris Mann and Henry Wessells III.*

problems, and also proved prone to breakdowns. What was needed was a car with the toughness and roadholding of the Monza with some of the extra power of the Tipo A. To produce it, Jano once again went back to the P2, or more exactly its latest descendant, and produced the Tipo B monoposto, universally known as the P3.

He took the Monza engine and lengthened the stroke to 100 mm, and increased the capacity to 2654 cc. He fitted larger valves, inclined at a wider angle to fit into a revised cylinder head, and he fitted a pair of blowers instead of the single supercharger used previously. The power output climbed to 215 bhp, or very little less than the 230 bhp of the unwieldy Tipo A, and, to make the best possible use of this extra power, Jano capitalized on another change in the racing rules. From 1932 onwards, the seat for the non-essential mechanic was no longer compulsory, and the car could be a true single-seater at last.

This allowed the rear end of the car to be redesigned. The body could be lighter, sleeker, narrower and more compact, but the problem was still in the irreducible height needed to mount the driver's seat above the propeller shaft linking the gearbox to the rear axle. Jano managed to effect a useful improvement by shifting the differential forward next to the gearbox, and then driving the rear wheels through a pair of propeller shafts, each one angled outwards to one of the rear wheels, to which it was connected through bevel gears.

The 1932 season saw the Alfa team's return to Grand Prix racing after an absence of seven years: the cars failed to score overall wins at Marseilles in France and at Brno, Czechoslovakia, but in every other event they entered they won, against the toughest and most formidable opposition in the world. It seemed that nothing could stop Alfa Romeo on its way to total domination of every branch of international motor sport: nothing, that is, except a major financial crash – which was exactly what happened. So short of money was the company that the racing programme was abruptly cancelled, and the works P3s were put into storage early in 1933.

At the time, it must have seemed all too likely that the Alfa Romeo story could have ended then and there. In fact, rescue came swiftly if unexpectedly from the Italian government. A body called the Istituto Ricostruzione Industriale (IRI) was charged with the responsibility of taking over failing industrial companies with the objective of keeping unemployment at bay: and for Mussolini's regime, Alfa Romeo's brilliant racing record had a priceless international prestige value. So the IRI took over Alfa's assets, paid the bills and poured in extra cash to keep the company afloat. New cars would be made, better suited to the new market's requirements but, in the meantime, the first priority was to revive the racing programme so as to realize the maximum return on the capital spent.

The lovely P3s returned to the circuits but from 1934 they

faced a formidable challenge from the German Mercedes-Benz and Auto Union racing cars which were to dominate Grand Prix racing until the outbreak of World War 2 in 1939. Although Alfa Romeo occasionally scored racing successes (Nuvolari's sensational 1935 German Grand Prix win was a case in point), the once invincible monoposto's racing days were over. An increase in engine capacity to 4064 cc with the V12 car of 1936 was similarly unsuccessful. Designated Tipo C, it boasted all-independent suspension. At the rear was a swing axle with the gearbox integral with the differential housing.

Cheaper Alfas, larger sales

On the production front, however, the rescue operation was more successful. Jano's initial design for a cheaper and simpler Alfa was a stopgap – it had to be, with time being so vital to the company's recovery. He took the 1900 version of the 1500–1750 range which had emerged as an alternative to the 2300 during 1933, and used this six-cylinder unit as the basis for a wider-bore and longer-stroke engine with a cast-iron cylinder block that had a capacity of 2309 cc, a peak power of just 68 bhp, but better torque for greater flexibility. In less than a year, it had sold in greater numbers than the 8C 2300 had done in four years.

The 6C 2300 followed Alfa tradition in other, more welcome ways. From a fairly pedestrian beginning, more sporting variants were soon to follow. First was the GT version with a shorter wheelbase, lighter bodywork, 76 bhp and 130 km/h (80 mph). The works team ran three tuned and rebodied versions in the 24-Hour sports car race at Pescara, where they took the first three places overall. Like the Monzas before them, they were named in honour of that victory, and this additional prestige helped sales of the model range as a whole.

For the time being, the company – and the Italian government – had to be content with sporting success in other areas. Jano took the chassis of the Tipo C racing car, with its light, compact construction and its independent suspension, and fitted it with a 3-litre version of the old straight-eight as used in the P3. The result, clothed in sleek, carefully streamlined bodywork, was the 8C 2900A of 1935, one of the most magnificent Alfas of all. In racing trim, this splendid car could hit a top speed of 230 km/h (143 mph). Three of the first five built were handed over to Scuderia Ferrari and entered in the 1936 Mille Miglia. They finished first, second and third; another car won the Spa 24-Hour race. Even the production six-cylinder cars took first and second place in the 1937 race, and in honour of this more spectacular success their name was changed from Pescara to Mille Miglia.

Grand Prix victories, however, were what mattered most. Next on the drawing board was a 4.5-litre version of the V12, which was fed by two superchargers and produced 430 bhp and

a top speed of 306 km/h (190 mph). But power on this scale proved too much for the rear axle on the car's first outing in the 1937 Italian Grand Prix, and Jano resigned at what he, and others, saw as a personal failure. He moved back to Turin and to Lancia. This was a loss the company could ill afford, although for some time yet it would be able to build on the foundations he had laid so securely.

As a final attempt to win the racing crown that had eluded them for so long, the Alfa engineers extended each bank of cylinders from six to a straight-eight and produced a massive V16 of just 3 litres capacity, to meet the 1938 Grand Prix requirements. With four camshafts and two crankshafts connected by intermediate gears, it was a complex piece of engineering and the car failed to live up to its promise: a second and a fourth place in the 1938 Italian GP were small consolation for all the expense and hard work.

Ironically, the most lasting effect of the new design was a small and simple derivative intended chiefly to give the loyal Italian crowds something to cheer about. As a break from the all-too-predictable German GP wins, the racing organizers promoted a hotly contested class of racing for voiturettes (small single-seaters with supercharged 1.5-litre engines) as curtain-raisers to the main events. By fitting one of the cylinder banks and a single supercharger from the V16 into a smaller version of the all-independent-suspension racing chassis, the factory produced, in 1938, the Tipo 158, a car that was known by all as the Alfetta (the 'little Alfa'), and *did* begin to win races. But the real fame of these cars lay ten years away, on the other side of a world war, when they would bring the company the victories it had sought so single-mindedly.

The last of the pre-war years saw the final flowering of the powerful, sophisticated Alfas of the 1930s in their most splendid incarnations yet. One of the half-dozen straight-eight 2900 A sports racing cars had been fitted with a roadgoing two-seater body which was imposing and elegant, on classic sports car lines. This attracted the company to the idea of a limited production run of a roadgoing version, still with the 2905 cc engine fed by twin superchargers, but detuned from the

LEFT Not only did the Alfetta dominate Voiturette racing from its 1938 arrival, but after the war it performed a similar feat in Formula 1 racing until its retirement in 1951. This example is appropriately pictured on the start line at Monza.

ALFA ROMEO TIPO 158 ALFETTA 1938–40

ENGINE	
No. of cylinders 8	
Bore/stroke mm 58 × 70	
Displacement cc 1479	
Valve operation Twin overhead camshafts	
Compression ratio 6.5:1	
Induction 1 triple-choke carburettor with Alfa Romeo Roots-type supercharger	
BHP 195 at 7200 rpm	
Transmission Four-speed	
CHASSIS	
Frame Box section	
Wheelbase mm 2500	
Track – front mm 1250	
Track – rear mm 1250	
Suspension – front Independent, trailing links and transverse leaf spring	
Suspension – rear Independent, swing axle and transverse leaf spring	
PERFORMANCE	
Maximum speed 232 km/h (144 mph)	

ABOVE An Alfa Romeo for the autostrada – a stylish, aerodynamic Pinin Farina coupé of 1936 on an Alfa Romeo 6C 2300 Pescara.

OVERLEAF The 8C 2900 Alfa Romeo was made between 1937 and 1939, although only ten were built. This is a Touring coupé of 1938.

220 bhp of the racing car to 180 bhp. This was the 2900 B which appeared in the short-wheelbase Corto version, basically similar to the 2900 A chassis but with a 50 mm (2 in) increase in wheelbase and a weight of 1150 kg (2530 lb).

By this time, even the originally austere six-cylinder models had grown more ambitious. The cylinder bores were widened from 70 mm to 72 mm, to increase the capacity to 2443 cc in 1939, and the cars were now designated as the 6C 2500 range.

With Italy's involvement, from 1940, in World War 2, Alfa Romeo concentrated mostly on the production of aero engines though output was severely affected by the Allied bombing of

the Portello factory in 1943 and 1944, the latter raid largely reducing the works to rubble. In 1947 limited car production of the pre-war 6C 2500 began again and continued until 1952.

Jano had left the company a decade before, but Alfa had been fortunate indeed to find a worthy successor in the shape of Dr Orazio Satta Puliga, generally known as Satta. His inspiration shaped the company's efforts till his death in 1973, and his memory is still revered in the company he served so well. In 1949 he was just 37 years old, and was facing a challenge that might have daunted an engineer with three times his professional experience.

Puliga's first car for Alfa Romeo was also the firm's first unitary construction model, the 1900, aimed wholeheartedly at the mass-production market. Under the bonnet was a 1884 cc four-cylinder engine with, of course, twin overhead camshafts. The 1900's first public showing was at Turin in May 1950, and the following year a version called the TI (for Turismo Internazionale, a keenly contested category in Italian racing at that time) with bigger valves, higher compression and a double-choke carburettor to boost the power to 100 bhp and the top speed from 150 km/h (93 mph) to 170 km/h (106 mph), was unveiled to an increasingly eager public.

The bodywork of the 1900TI was very similar to the ordinary saloon: the intention was to perpetuate the wolf-in-sheep's-clothing appeal of a car that looked pedestrian but delivered exhilarating performance, that was closely in tune with the spirit of the time. However, there were still buyers who wanted more sporting looks, so that two other versions of the 1900 made their appearance in 1951. By shortening the wheelbase and

cutting the weight, Alfa was able to provide the cream of Italy's independent coachbuilders with a frame on which to hang coupé or cabriolet bodywork. Thus Pinin Farina designed an open-top cabriolet with a top speed of 170 km/h (106 mph) with the TI engine, while Touring's more streamlined closed coupé could manage 182 km/h (113 mph).

These more elegant versions were but the icing on the cake; they accounted between them for about ten per cent of total sales, as they were considerably more expensive than the basic 1900 or even the standard-bodied TI. But their very existence was a reminder that Alfas were still worthy of such expensive

**ALFA ROMEO 1900
1950–3**

ENGINE	
No. of cylinders 4	
Bore/stroke mm 82 × 88	
Displacement cc 1884	
Valve operation Twin overhead camshafts	
Compression ratio 7.5:1	
Induction Single carburettor	
BHP 90 at 5200 rpm	
Transmission Four-speed manual, and two-stage propeller shaft to rear-mounted differential	
CHASSIS	
Frame Unitary	
Wheelbase mm 2630	
Track – front mm 1320	
Track – rear mm 1325	
Suspension – front Independent, coil springs and double wishbones	
Suspension – rear Live axle, coil springs, trailing arms and triangulated locating member	
Brakes Drums on all four wheels, hydraulically operated	
PERFORMANCE	
Maximum speed 150 km/h (93 mph)	

LEFT ABOVE *Touring again, this time a 1950 Villa d'Este coupé This 6C 2500 Super Sport, built until 1952, was carried over from pre-war days.*

LEFT *The Touring-bodied 1900 Sprint, introduced in 1951. It was built until 1953 when it was uprated and renamed the Super Sprint. The model lasted until 1958.*

ABOVE *A line-up of 1900s, circa 1952, delivered to the Italian Highway Police. The split windscreen and spotlamp are distinctive features.*

RIGHT *The new Alfa Romeo of the post-World War 2 era was the 1900, introduced in 1950. It was the firm's first unitary construction model, and this four-door saloon version used the basic 1.8-litre twin-overhead-camshaft engine. The straightforward in-house designed bodywork was wind-tunnel tested.*

cosmetic treatment, and even the thrifty buyers of the 1900 knew full well the engineering under the panelling was still the same. Then, even as 1900 production began to soar far beyond any levels attained by the most popular of its predecessors, plans were already being drawn up for its successors. For the time being, the engine size was increased to 1975 cc in 1953 and the various models, the 1900 Berlina, TI and Sprint, were given an extra 'Super' tag to denote the increase in capacity and performance.

The 1900 range lasted until 1958 but it had been joined, in 1954, by a smaller, lighter car: the Giulietta.

Alfa Romeo

A new popular car

The new car started off both shorter and narrower than the 1900: the wheelbase was trimmed by 250 mm (10 in), and the track narrowed by 37 mm (1½ in) at the front and 50 mm (2 in) at the back. But the carefully shaped body not only allowed room for four passengers (or five at a squash), it gave them better visibility through larger windows and narrower screen pillars and, so far had monocoque body-chassis design advanced in five years, it achieved both of these benefits while cutting the total weight of the car from 1100 kg (2425 lb) to 900 kg (1984 lb).

Like the 1900 before it, the Giulietta was to be not a single model, but a range of different versions based on the same mechanical design. It was also highly significant, in terms of Alfa's intended policy, that the first version to reach the public gaze was not the basic saloon, elegant and attractive though that was, but the sleeker and more sporting closed coupé called the Giulietta Sprint.

This had a slightly lighter and much shapelier body, designed by Bertone as a two-plus-two of unashamedly sporting appearance. It also had a twin-choke carburettor and higher-compression version of the engine which delivered 80 bhp and propelled the car to a top speed of 165 km/h (103 mph). Its most significant virtue, however, was its price. Not only did it sell on the home market for the equivalent of £1000, but this placed it at just over half the cost of its 1900 equivalent, the only slightly faster 1900 Super Sprint. The saloon was cheaper still at just under £800, but its performance was less exciting.

The Giulietta Sprint appeared late in 1954, the saloon in the following spring. In the summer of 1955 came the third model in the range, which marked a further nod to well-established Alfa traditions: the open two-seat Giulietta Spider, with an elegant Pinin Farina body, and modern refinements like wind-up windows and an easy-to-fold hood. The Spider shared the higher-performance version of the 1290 cc engine used by the coupé, and it was slightly lighter still, so that improved performance was another of its attractions.

If the 1900 broke new ground in terms of production figures for Alfa, the Giulietta took the theme much further. More than 16,000 Giulietta saloons were made in less than three years, and even the more specialized sporting versions sold almost as well. By 1961, more than 14,000 Spiders alone had been sold, which would have seemed inconceivable by pre-war standards for a sporting two-seater.

However, this was eclipsed by the sales of the most successful Giulietta version of all, which was to set the pattern for each subsequent model range. This appeared three years after the original introduction, and was arrived at by the fairly logical step of putting the higher-performance engine of the Sprint and Spider into the saloon body, to provide sporting performance with passenger room and a lower price tag. The result was the Giulietta TI, which sold for just £85 more than the standard saloon and had a top speed of 150 km/h (93 mph). The combination proved irresistible, and although the model appeared so late in the story, by the time it was replaced in 1965 more TIs had been made and sold than all the other Giulietta models put together.

The Giulietta range suffered from only one real problem. In moving further down the market to increase production above the level of the 1900's, Alfa had left a gap in the large-car sector which might otherwise have been filled by the six-cylinder version of the 1900 – this had instead given birth to a short-lived 3000 CM racing car of 1952/3. There had been a stopgap in the form of a series of larger-bodied cars which used the 1975 cc 1900 Super power unit, but had been called, rather confusingly, the 2000 range since the introduction of the Giulietta. Not until

LEFT AND RIGHT *The Alfa Romeo sporting theme continued with the Giulietta Sprint of 1954, and this lovely Bertone-styled coupé remained in production until 1962. The twin-overhead-camshaft four-cylinder engine was capable of about 165 km/h (103 mph). Unlike the 1900, the Giulietta boasted a light-alloy block, the earlier model having used a cast-iron one. The engine, with its 8.5:1 compression ratio, developed 80 bhp. A twin-choke Weber carburettor completed the robust sporting specification. The saloon version of the Giulietta did not appear until 1955 and, like the coupé, endured until 1962.*

1962 did Alfa produce big six-cylinder cars, the 2600s, which used the body designs of the square-cut 2000 saloon, the open two-seat Pininfarina Spider and the Bertone Sprint Coupé (the last two bearing an amazing family resemblance to their smaller Giulietta equivalents), but fitted with an 83 mm bore, 79.6 mm stroke, 2584 cc version of the classic twin-cam engine delivering 145 bhp. The Sprint was an especially handsome car, but for some reason these admittedly costly models never achieved real success in sales terms, although they remain popular with collectors.

Another small-volume car appeared during the late 1950s – this time based on the Giulietta which has been even more popular with Alfa enthusiasts ever since. This was the beautiful Bertone-bodied Giulietta Sprint Speciale, or SS, with a shorter

wheelbase than the standard Giulietta Sprint and a more powerful 100 bhp version of the engine, which gave it a top speed of 200 km/h (125 mph): in other words, it was fast as well as beautiful, to the extent that many owners were able to use the car in racing to some effect.

The Giulietta was replaced, in 1962, by the similarly named Giulia. The engine was still the twin-overhead-camshaft four that had been used in the 1900 and the Giulietta. This time, however, the bores were set at 78 mm and the stroke at 82 mm, which produced a capacity of 1570 cc: the Giulietta's 1290 cc had been well placed for racing versions to be competitive in the 1300 cc racing classes, and similarly the Giulia fitted equally well into the 1600 category.

Two of the models would have the new engine, and the five-

30

speed gearbox, in the same bodies as used for the Giulietta. These were the Spider and Sprint, although here too changes were on the way eventually. But the Giulia saloon was completely redesigned, and once again a sporting version was first to appear, in June 1962, as the Giulia TI. In its original form, the Giulia TI delivered 92 bhp and was capable of 165 km/h (103 mph), with the Sprint and Spider another 7 km/h (4½ mph) above this figure. In 1963, a modified Sprint with more room for rear passengers, called the Giulia Sprint GT, appeared. A year later a Giulietta-engined version of this model,

FAR LEFT, LEFT AND ABOVE *The lovely Giulietta Sprint Speciale was built in small numbers between 1957 and 1962, boasting a 100 bhp version of the 1290 cc twin-cam four. The model's top speed was an impressive 200 km/h (125 mph). Provided by Lincoln Small.*

now called simply the 1300 Sprint, added to the options open to sporting-minded buyers.

For racing there was the Giulia GTA, introduced in 1965 and based on the GT Sprint. The A stood for *allegerita*, or 'lightened', thanks to a programme of weight reduction that included the replacement of steel body panelling with identically shaped components in aluminium. Various tuned versions of the Giulia engine were offered but the team's own cars had a twin-plug version of the engine, with 10.5:1 compression ratio, which delivered 170 bhp at 7500 rpm and helped produce a top speed of 219 km/h (136 mph). Later, other variants were added, including the GTA-SA supercharged model, and the GTA Junior which used a wider-bore, shorter-stroke version of the Giulietta engine (78 × 67.5 mm instead of 74 × 75 mm, but with the same capacity of 1290 cc), delivering 165 bhp with fuel injection and the twin-plug head.

The GTAs were phenomenally successful within their chosen field: they won their classes in almost all the big races, which brought them three European Touring Car Championships in a row in the years 1966–8. In 1970, Alfa Romeo's Autodelta racing division applied the same treatment to the 1750 GTV, but, to make it more competitive in the 2-litre class, the engine was bored out to 1985 cc, producing the 1750 GTAm, and it won

another European Touring Car Championship for Alfa Romeo in its first racing season.

So the story went on: in the summer of 1964, the Giulia saloon had been fitted with a more powerful version of the Giulietta TI engine to produce the Giulia 1300 Berlina, with a top speed of 160 km/h (100 mph). As the Giulia saloon range now had a TI and a TI Super, the third variation, added in 1965, had a medium-tune, 98–102 bhp version of the engine, with a more sporting trim (wooden dash, circular instruments, improved seats and wood-rim steering wheel) and, logically but confusingly, it became the Giulia Super.

Then in 1966, the 82 bhp, 160 km/h (100 mph) Giulia 1300 TI appeared, together with the redesigned Spider (later to be called the Duetto) which shared its 109 bhp engine with the higher-performance version of the Sprint, now renamed the Sprint GT Veloce, or GTV for short. In the autumn a smaller-engined version of the GTV appeared as the GT 1300 Junior, followed

BELOW LEFT *The Giulia Super of 1962 was a boxy four-door saloon, powered by a 1570 cc four-cylinder twin-overhead-camshaft engine.*

BELOW *The Giulia Sprint GT. Again a Bertone offering, it perpetuated the theme of the Giulietta Sprint and was good for 172 km/h (106 mph).*

two years later by the Spider 1300, which had the same Pinin Farina bodywork as its 1600 stablemate.

The Giulias as such lasted until 1972, although their replacements made their appearance early in 1968. In most respects, these were simply larger-engined replacements; however, the styling of the Berlina was tidied up by Bertone and the entire range (now that the engine capacity was increased to 1779 cc) was given the nostalgic title of the '1750'. The Berlina now had a top speed of better than 180 km/h (112 mph), and the more sporting variants could manage 190 km/h (120 mph). Four years later, with the dropping of the 'Giulia' name (the model survived, as did the Giulietta, with a numerical identification – in this case as the various 1600 models), the 1750s were

string to the team's bow in the shape of the Tipo 158 voiturette racer to compete under a 1.5-litre capacity limit. It used half the GP engine, a supercharged twin-cam straight-eight of 1479 cc, producing a creditable 195 to 225 bhp in a car that weighed 620 kg (1367 lb), substantially less than the GP car. In this hotly contested class of racing, Alfa won a succession of victories in the last two seasons before the war: but the greatest days of the Alfettas, the 'little Alfas', still lay ahead.

Once motor racing restarted after World War 2, two major changes had occurred. The German teams had vanished, for the time being, and the regulations had changed to an option of 4.5-litre engines without superchargers, or 1.5 litres with superchargers, a formula that could have been designed with the

themselves replaced by the 2000 series. These had a wider-bore version of the engine delivering 132 bhp in all three models: top speed of the saloon was 190 km/h (120 mph), and that of the coupé and spider just 5 km/h (3 mph) more.

These were the final flowerings of the Giulia range – the 2000 Spider is still in the current line-up – but by this time they had been joined by another strain of production Alfas. Their name, and some of their basic engineering, is of a different derivation altogether: from pre-war Alfas rather than post-war designs, and from Grand Prix single-seaters rather than production saloons.

A famous name revived

One of the few breaks in the gloom of Alfa's racing history in the last pre-war years had been provided by a car that was itself an offshoot of one of the promising, but ultimately disappointing, designs developed to challenge the German domination of Grand Prix events. In 1938 the old free-formula regulations, which had allowed the development of ever bigger and more powerful engines, had been replaced by a 3-litre capacity limit, which should in theory have allowed all the Grand Prix contenders a fresh start under this new set of rules.

In fact, the Germans proved to be better prepared than anyone, perhaps because of the enormous sums available from their government to finance radical new developments to suit the changing formula. Alfa for its part had developed a 3-litre V16, the Tipo 316. But, as we have seen, there was another

ABOVE *Tipo 158 Alfa Romeos took the first three places at the 1948 French Grand Prix at Rheims. Jean-Pierre Wimille won the event while Alberto* *Ascari (whose father had driven for Alfa Romeo in 1920–5), shown above, was placed third at an average speed of 163.1 km/h (101.4 mph).*

Alfettas in mind. It was just as well: with all the problems of restarting production and developing new cars, designing and building a new Grand Prix racer would have been quite out of the question.

Even so, there were problems: the pre-war Alfettas had given their transmissions a hard time, and since then the switch to higher-pressure supercharging and other improvements had boosted the power to 275 bhp. In their first appearance after the war, a race at St-Cloud, just outside Paris, two Alfettas broke down with transmission trouble – and these were the original, less powerful models. But although the problem took time to cure completely, Alfa managed to field stronger and stronger teams to win the other three races in which they were entered during that 1946 season. In 1947, they did even better: every race they entered was won convincingly by drivers of the calibre of Achille Varzi, Count Carlo Felice Trossi, Jean-Pierre Wimille and Consalvo Sanesi, against very spirited opposition from Maserati in particular.

By 1948, still higher blower pressures had pushed the power to 310 bhp, at the expense of correspondingly higher stresses. Again the Alfettas triumphed, with wins in all the events they

Alfa Romeo Spiders by
Pininfarina. RIGHT *The 1600
version called Duetto, after Alfa
Romeo had held a competition
for suggestions. Provided by
Barry Coupe.* BELOW *Still based
on the Duetto, but with capacity
increased to 1962 cc for export,
although 1600 was perpetuated
for the home market. The latest
version has spoilers and a new
hardtop.*

ALFA ROMEO 1600 SPIDER (DUETTO)
1966–7

ENGINE

No. of cylinders	4
Bore/stroke mm	78 × 82
Displacement cc	1570
Valve operation	Twin overhead camshafts
Compression ratio	9:1
Induction	2 horizontal twin-choke carburettors
BHP	109 at 6000 rpm
Transmission	Five-speed

CHASSIS

Frame	Unitary
Wheelbase mm	2250
Track – front mm	1310
Track – rear mm	1270
Suspension – front	Independent, coil spring, double wishbone
Suspension – rear	Live axle, with coil springs, trailing arms and triangular locating members

PERFORMANCE

Maximum speed	185 km/h (115 mph)

entered; one significant factor, however, was the appearance of the first Ferraris, produced by Alfa's former racing manager, as a new, and ultimately much more formidable challenge.

In 1949, faced with a shortage of drivers and the need for more development on the cars, Alfa withdrew from Grand Prix racing. The company returned in 1950 to win again, in every race in which it entered cars. But the Ferrari challenge was growing: after following Alfa down the 1.5-litre supercharged route, Ferrari had now opted for a much more successful unblown 4.5-litre engine. However, his cars were plagued with handling problems from their swing-axle suspensions and until a new design, based on the same de Dion axle used on the Alfettas, was ready, the cars were unable to make full use of their performance.

In 1951 Ferrari represented a much more formidable threat: by this time, the Alfettas, redesignated the Tipo 159, were delivering 425 bhp at 9300 rpm, at the expense of a range of only

ALFA ROMEO 33/2 SPORT PROTOTYPE (DAYTONA)
1967–9

ENGINE		CHASSIS	
No. of cylinders V8		Frame Light alloy large diameter tubes	
Bore/stroke mm 78 × 52		Wheelbase mm 2250	
Displacement cc 1995		Track – front mm 1336	
Valve operation Twin overhead camshafts per cylinder bank		Track – rear mm 1445	
Compression ratio 11:1		Suspension – front Independent, coil springs and transverse bars	
Induction Fuel injection		Suspension – rear Independent, coil springs and transverse bars	
BHP 270 at 9600 rpm		**PERFORMANCE**	
Transmission Six-speed		Maximum speed 298 km/h (186 mph)	

LEFT AND ABOVE *The sports racing 298 km/h (186 mph) 33/2* *(Daytona) was produced between 1967 and 1969.*

Like its distinguished Tipo 159 predecessor, the new Alfetta had a de Dion rear axle with integral gearbox. These changes were incorporated initially in a new body shape, with the 1.8-litre version of the twin-cam four inherited from the 1750 models. This was an entirely new Alfa saloon, which made its first appearance in May 1972: and in view of its pedigree, what better name for it than the Alfetta?

At first, the Alfetta co-existed with the 1750 and 2000 models, until new variants extended the single model into a range in its own right. Although it would eventually play its part in the company's motor-sport endeavours, for the moment those efforts were being made in other areas.

Sports racing success

By now, however, Autodelta and Alfa Romeo had become involved in a much bigger racing programme altogether with the T33 sports prototype, which had been introduced in 1967. This had no links with any production Alfa at all, although the new V8 engine that powered the car had similarities with a design produced some years before. In 1968 the cars took first and second places in their class at the Daytona 24 Hours and consequently this version was named the Daytona in honour of that victory. They went on to win the first three places in their class at Le Mans in the same season, and were replaced the following year (1969) by the 33/3, which used a box-section chassis welded up from steel sheet, reinforced with titanium in place of the tubular H-shaped original, and which was powered by a 3-litre version of the V8 engine with four valves per cylinder and delivering 400 bhp. It had open glass-fibre bodywork on top. But, to begin with, the new cars proved dauntingly unreliable: only after patient development work did they succeed in winning second place in the 1972 Manufacturers' World Championship series. Gaining that eagerly sought-after championship victory was to take a further three years, and yet another version of the car, the 33TT12, which not only reverted to tubular spaceframe construction (the 'TT' stood for *telaio tubolare*, 'tubular frame'), but also used a 3-litre flat-12 engine with twin overhead camshafts for each bank of cylinders, four valves and an output of 500 bhp. The 1975 victory was not the end of the 33 story, for two years later a sports version, the 33SC12, won the 1977 Sports Car Championship.

a mile and a half on each gallon, which was a real handicap on the longer-distance races. They won, narrowly, in the Swiss, Belgian and French GPs, chased home by the Ferraris in each case; but it was the opposition that triumphed in the British and German GPs and, worst of all, in the Italian GP at Monza. Only by a resounding win in the Spanish GP (where the Ferraris fitted larger tyres in an attempt to cut pit-stops and this stratagem misfired) was Alfa able to win its fourth season's racing in five years, and cars already more than 13 years old were wheeled away into honoured retirement.

As an achievement, it was magnificent, and in one short period it made up for much of the pre-war frustration and disappointment. Ever since then the name Alfetta has had special significance for Alfa Romeo and the marque's most loyal followers, and it was hardly surprising when, more than 20 years later, such a hallowed name reappeared in a very different guise on a new range of production cars.

As we have seen, the 33 project was unusual in that it owed virtually nothing to any production Alfa: in fact, in a reversal of the usual progression, a production version of the racing car was made in small numbers during much of the 1970s. This owed its origins to the 1967 Montreal Expo, for which Bertone had produced an elegant coupé design based on Alfa Romeo components. Two years later, Alfa turned out a production version of the car, which had a roadgoing variant of the 90-degree V8 used in the 33, but with a capacity of 2593 cc and delivering 200 bhp. Unlike the mid-engined racer, the Montreal (as the new car was called) had the engine mounted at the front, driving the rear wheels through a five-speed gearbox. The unit was fitted with electronic ignition and fuel injection, and the car's top speed was more than 220 km/h (137 mph). Although it sold for twice the price of a 2000 GTV, and at first it was available to special order only, it proved immensely popular. Between 1970 and 1977, almost four thousand were sold: in terms of the strictly limited production run, it was one of the most successful of all the larger post-war Alfas.

The 1970s and 80s also saw Alfa's continuing involvement with Grand Prix racing. This began as far back as 1970, when the McLaren team elected to use the Alfa Romeo 3-litre V8 as developed for the 33 racing programme. However, the engine's lack of power, compared with its GP opponents, brought the collaboration to an end in 1971, the year in which the March team chose to use an Alfa unit. The Alfa-engined car only appeared in two events: on one occasion it crashed and, on the other, the engine blew itself up.

More promising altogether was the Alfa Romeo flat-12, which was to give the 33s their 1975 World Championship. In 1975, the company signed an agreement to supply engines to the Brabham team for the BT45 Formula 1 car. These 3-litre engines were worked on by Autodelta to reduce the weight as much as possible (the extra weight and lack of low-speed torque had plagued the V8 in its Grand Prix form), and to raise the power to more than 520 bhp; but ultimately the whole exercise proved to be as frustrating as chasing the German cars had been during the 1930s.

In the end, the company took the only logical step remaining to it: Alfa re-entered Grand Prix racing in 1979 with a car of its own, for the first time since 1951. There was a great deal of lost ground to be made up; and there was now no question of diverting company brainpower, as in the old days, to make good this deficiency. In other words, although the Alfa GP car carried the Alfa name, the size of the team, and its resources, were really ascribable to Autodelta rather than the parent company. The Formula 1 car has so far not been all that successful, although it did achieve a creditable third place in the Italian Grand Prix at Monza in 1984. Unfortunately no world championship points were scored in 1985 and the firm withdrew from Formula 1.

Enter the Alfasud

By 1975, when the 33 had won the championship, the pattern of the Alfa range of the mid-1980s had largely been set. The biggest change occurred in 1972 with the introduction of an Alfa based on a completely different philosophy, one that owed more to government intervention than marketing possibilities. This was the Alfasud ('Alfa South'), which was produced by a new design team working under Rudolf Hruska, and was to be built in a new factory on the site of one of Alfa's wartime aero-engine plants in the south of Italy, at Pomigliano d'Arco near

LEFT Alfa Romeo re-entered Formula 1 in 1970 and withdrew in 1985. This is Patrese in the 1984 British GP.

ABOVE RIGHT The Alfasud, introduced in 1972, was Alfa Romeo's first front-wheel-drive car and employed a 1186 cc flat-four engine. This is the larger capacity 1.5TI of 1982. Provided by Vernon Thompson.

RIGHT The Montreal of 1970–7, so-called because the Bertone-bodied prototype was exhibited at the Montreal Expo. The engine is a 2593 cc V8 with twin overhead camshafts per cylinder bank. Provided by The Patrick Collection.

Naples, in an area of high unemployment. (Hruska was an Austrian engineer who had worked on the original Volkswagen project with Professor Ferdinand Porsche, and had been involved with the Cisitalia racing car scheme before joining Alfa in 1952.) The Alfasud itself was intended to broaden the range and to enter a new and important segment of the market; and in due course it would replace some of the smaller models. However, the new Alfasud really owed little to the earlier Giuliettas and Giulias in its basic engineering layout.

It was a completely new design and Hruska's VW and Porsche credentials were echoed in the Alfasud's flat-four 1186 cc engine, though water-cooled and, appropriately, with overhead camshafts on each cylinder bank. The car was Alfa Romeo's first front-wheel-drive model. Suspension featured front MacPherson struts, while the dead rear axle had coil springs and trailing arms.

The original Alfasud, despite its simple design philosophy, had instant appeal among customers who hitherto could not have afforded an Alfa Romeo – at least not a new one. But following the typical progression from pedestrian (or relatively pedestrian) newcomer to more sporting derivatives, which had continued throughout the company's history, a high-performance version was brought out just over a year after production began. In the autumn of 1973 the Alfasud TI made its appearance, with compression raised from 8.8:1 to 9:1, and power up to 68 bhp which, with a five-speed gearbox and a neat, two-door body lighter than its predecessor by a useful 20 kg (44 lb), produced a genuine 160 km/h (100 mph) top speed. This was even better news for the enthusiasts, and a year later the original version was available with a five-speed gearbox as an option – the Alfasud 5m.

But, as the popularity of the car increased, and other options with larger engines were added to the range, it became all too clear that Alfa was having problems in turning out enough cars to meet the demand. Nevertheless, the range was augmented in 1976, with the addition of a completely new model to the line-up, in the form of the Alfasud Sprint. This had a lower and sleeker body, with a larger version of the flat-four engine. It had the same 80 mm bore as the original, but the stroke was lengthened from 59 mm to 64 mm, enlarging the capacity from 1186 to 1286 cc, and increasing the power to 87 bhp. The top speed was now 165 km/h (103 mph), and even this was improved on in 1979 by the Sprint Veloces. The name Alfasud no longer appeared on these variants, in preparation for phasing out the Alfasud saloons altogether. The idea that the Alfasud operation should have a separate identity was now less essential for political reasons, and Alfa itself felt happier to emphasize the unity between the company's different operations by bringing them together under the Alfa Romeo designation.

The Sprint Veloces offered two more versions of the flat-four engine. The 1.3 had a longer-stroke 67.2 mm, 1350 cc unit delivering 86 hp (DIN) and giving a top speed of more than 170 km/h (106 mph); the 1.5 had a wider-bore 84 × 67.2 mm, 1490 cc, 95 hp version with maximum speed in excess of 175 km/h (109 mph). Most powerful of all was to be the 105 hp version of the larger engine which powered the 1983 Sprint 1.5 Quadrifoglio Verde (Green Cloverleaf) to produce a top speed of 180 km/h (112 mph). This engine was also used in the Green Cloverleaf variant of the Alfasud TI saloon.

Recent production Alfas

From this point on, the Alfa story becomes more complex still, with more models, more engines and more permutations of the two. In 1973, the original Alfetta saloon had been joined by the Alfetta GT, a Giugiaro-styled coupé, which used the 1.8-litre version of the twin-cam engine as employed in the 1750 models. Later, both the saloon and the coupé also emerged with 1.6- and 2-litre engines, inherited from the Giulias and the 2000 models respectively. The saloons were outwardly identical, apart from details like headlamps, and of course embellishments identifying them as the Alfetta 1.8 and the Alfetta 2000. In the case of the coupés, the two versions were named the GT 1.6 and the GTV 2000 respectively. Both had the elegant but unfamiliar (in terms of earlier GTV shapes) Giugiaro design, built around the Alfetta package with torsion-bar front suspension, de Dion axle at the rear, front engine and clutch, gearbox and differential at the rear of the car, and disc brakes all round. These were introduced in the mid-1970s, and in the mid-1980s the GTV still formed part of the current range.

LEFT *The Alfasud was discontinued in 1983, although the 1.5-litre Sprint Green Cloverleaf perpetuated its mechanics.*

ABOVE *The Giulietta, introduced in 1980.*

OVERLEAF *The GTV, powered by a fuel-injected V6 engine.*

ALFA ROMEO GIULIETTA 2.0
1980–5

ENGINE		CHASSIS	
No. of cylinders 4		Frame Unitary	
Bore/stroke mm 84 × 88		Wheelbase mm 2510	
Displacement cc 1962		Track – front mm 1360	
Valve operation Twin overhead camshafts		Track – rear mm 1350	
Compression ratio 9:1		Suspension – front Independent, double wishbones and torsion bar	
Induction 2 horizontal twin-choke carburettors		Suspension – rear Independent, de Dion tube, coil springs and Watts linkage	
BHP 130 at 5400 rpm			
Clutch Single dry plate, hydraulically operated		Brakes Servo assisted discs, operated by twin-hydraulic circuits	
Transmission Rear-mounted five-speed gearbox		**PERFORMANCE**	
		Maximum speed 185 km/h (115 mph)	

If the Alfettas, like the 1750s, owed their names to other cars in the company's past, the next group of models derived their names from a more recent precursor still: the Giulietta. In this case, the new Giulietta was also based on the Alfetta mechanicals and the same chassis, although with a body much more square cut, and slightly shorter, lower and wider, in a wedge-shaped configuration ending in a high boot. The original models appeared with a choice of two engines: the 1570 cc as used in the Giulia range, and a new, smaller version of the twin-cam four-cylinder unit with a bore of 80 mm and a stroke of 67.5 mm, producing a capacity of 1357 cc and a power output of 95 bhp. With this engine, the Giulietta had a top speed of 165 km/h (103 mph); with the large unit it was capable of 175 km/h (109 mph). Later the Giulietta became available with the 1.8-litre engine originally developed for the 1750 range, and eventually with the 2-litre 1962 cc unit as developed for the 2000 models, and used subsequently for the Alfetta 2000 and the 2000 GTV. In this form, the Giulietta 2.0 has a maximum speed of 185 km/h (115 mph).

This far, the recent development story of production Alfas tended to centre on new body shapes which used existing engines. In 1980, however, a modified Alfetta saloon bodyshell was fitted with a totally new, 88 × 63 mm, 2492 cc, 160 bhp V6 power unit and introduced as the flagship of the range: the Alfa 6. This was the first six-cylinder Alfa for more than a decade,

and the company hopes it will win the popularity that has seemed to elude large and luxurious Alfas. Certainly, the shape of the car seems familiar enough, and the smoothness and willingness of the engine have given the 6 a high reputation, even among those enthusiasts accustomed to the apparently immortal four-cylinder unit.

The Alfa 6 is outshone, however, by its fuel-injected stablemate, the GTV6, which uses the same engine in the GTV body, a formula that produces a top speed of 205 km/h (127 mph) – although the saloon can manage a creditable 197 km/h (122 mph) in its own right. These are the present-day equivalents of the 2600 saloons and coupés of the 1960s, Alfas that can provide the verve and performance enthusiasts expect in larger and more luxurious packages than the bulk of the range – but only time will tell whether these versions will sell in large enough quantities to be commercially viable.

Latest Alfa developments

ABOVE *An Alfa Romeo for the 1980s, the 33 Gold Cloverleaf* *used the Alfasud's front-wheel-drive flat-four engine.*

The new generation of Alfa Romeos is destined to take the company, and its customers, forward into the 1990s. Just as British Leyland went into partnership with the Japanese company Honda to produce cars like the Triumph Acclaim and, later, the Rover 213, Alfa Romeo entered into a similar arrangement with Nissan to produce an Italian-Japanese hybrid called the Arna, to make use of Alfa's spare engine manufacturing capacity. The reasoning was this: the Alfasud project was showing its age, with falling sales resulting from increased competition in this market segment. This meant spare production capacity, and a large workforce with too few cars to make. One solution was the new model designed as an Alfasud replacement, the Alfa 33, which used the chassis and mechanicals of the latest versions of that range. It featured a new body with a strong family resemblance to the Giulietta, and a completely new production line with a high proportion of robot assembly sections, together with new painting and finishing systems. A neat four-door saloon, it became available with a choice of 1.3- or 1.5-litre four-cylinder engines. With power at around 80 to 85 bhp, both versions were capable of over 160 km/h (100 mph), with 0–60 mph figures of 11 seconds.

The 33 on its own could not, however, keep the whole production capacity occupied; yet developing and producing the components for the more up-market versions of the 33 that were on the way (the Gold Cloverleaf and Green Cloverleaf variants which were to use the more powerful 1.5-litre flat-four engines) meant more expense and smaller volumes. So the solution adopted was to let the 33 find its own production level, and to use the spare capacity for the Arna. Alfa produced the mechanical parts for this car, which were then assembled into a body designed and developed in Japan but actually manufactured in Italy. This meant low costs and high volume, and a car that was produced under the Alfa name as the Arna in Italy, but would be called the Nissan Cherry Europe in some other countries.

The result, from Alfa's point of view, has been very successful. The Arna was carefully and effectively distanced from Alfa's own models at first, but the company is now making it more of an Alfa, to tie it in more closely with the rest of the range. The 33 is proving to be extremely attractive to Alfa

buyers as a worthy successor to the deservedly popular Alfasud, and the Naples operation in the south has been turned from a damaging loss into a successful and profitable project.

And what of the future? Alfa's productivity has been increased by more than 35 per cent overall, and the future promises to be an interesting one. First on the list of 1985 introductions was the Alfa 90, a sports saloon with the Alfetta chassis, the V6 engine and a new Bertone body design – leaner and more compact than the Alfa 6 and aimed at competitors like the Mercedes-Benz 190. The Alfa 90 represented the upper end of the market, with the 33 at the lower end, and a series of sporty new models progressively making their appearance in between.

Next to appear in 1985 was the 75, so named to commemorate Alfa Romeo's 75th anniversary. Engine options for this rear-drive saloon include 1.6-, 1.8- or 2-litre twin-overhead-camshaft four-cylinder units or a fuel-injected 2.5 V6 one. Front suspension is by torsion bars while a close-ratio five-speed gearbox is integral with the differential unit. A de Dion axle also features. In 1987, Fiat took over the still troubled company, and Alfa Romeo's future as a marque looks settled. An exciting project, due to appear in late 1987, is Tipo 164, a prestigious model developed jointly with Lancia, Fiat and Saab and using common chassis, gearbox and suspension components. It will be a car to look forward to.

With ideas like these on the way, improvements in quality and productivity, new models and new designs, it seems that Alfa's future may prove to be as successful, and as fascinating, as its past. For that to be the case, the company has a great deal to live up to – but it also has a great deal to inspire it.

LEFT *A sign of the times: the Italian/Japanese Arna. The engine is the Alfasud unit, available in 1186 and 1350 cc forms, plus its five-speed gearbox and rack-and-pinion steering. Nissan sells it as the Cherry Europe.*

BELOW *The Alfa Romeo 75, introduced in 1985 to celebrate the firm's 75th anniversary. A successor to the Giulietta, it can be specified with a 1570 cc twin-overhead-camshaft four-cylinder engine at one extreme, and a 2492 cc V6 at the other.*

Ferrari

Ferrari

No marque more symbolizes the vitality, self-assurance and flair of post-war Italy than that of Ferrari, produced at Maranello, near Modena, since 1947. In Grand Prix and sports car racing Ferrari has been supreme, while the firm's current road cars possess an elegance, style and performance that is second to none.

Enzo Ferrari was born on 18 February 1898 on the outskirts of Modena, a town about 257 km (160 miles) south-east of Milan. However, as heavy snow had fallen, Enzo's birth could not be registered for a further two days, so in Italian law 20 February is his official birthday! Ferrari senior owned a workshop adjoining the family house making gangways and sheds for the State Railways.

During Enzo's formative years, his father would accompany him to local motor racing circuits. Like all youths, he had heroes; his were Vincenzo Lancia and Felice Nazzaro. Enzo determined to become a racing driver but his ambitions were cut short by Italy's involvement in World War 1 and at the end of hostilities, during which he seems to have spent most of his time shoeing mules, he returned to the world of cars.

Ferrari's father and elder brother had died in 1916 and he found himself alone in the world. A letter of introduction to Fiat did not produce a job, but young Enzo obtained employment driving war-surplus Lancia light trucks the 132 km (82 miles) from Turin to Milan for rebodying and sale in the car-hungry post-war market. He was soon on the move, however, when through contacts in Milan he joined the C.M.N. car company in the Pontedera district. Run by his friend Ugo Sivocci, the firm even dabbled in racing, and Ferrari drove a C.M.N. in the 1919 Targa Florio race when he was placed ninth.

LEFT *The Daytona, the last great front-engined Ferrari. Announced at the 1968 Paris Motor Show, this magnificent two-seater was one of the most expensive, and fastest, road cars of its day, with the factory claiming a top speed of 280 km/h (174 mph). With a Pininfarina-styled body, all-independent suspension, and a 4390 cc V12 engine, the Daytona was built between 1968 and 1973. Provided by The Patrick Collection.*

Then, in 1920, Ferrari made an important move to Alfa Romeo and drove for the Milan company until the end of 1931. The end of his racing career coincided, in 1932, with the birth of his only child, a son named Alfredo after Enzo's dead father and brother, although the boy soon became known as Alfredino and, finally, Dino.

By this time Ferrari had made a momentous step. On 1 December 1929, the 31-year-old Enzo had established his own racing team, Scuderia Ferrari, in his home town of Modena. This meant that Ferrari himself was responsible for running Alfa Romeo's racing department, leaving the firm to get on with the day-to-day business of designing and building road and racing cars.

In 1932 came Alfa Romeo's fabled Tipo B monoposto (single-seater), universally known as the P3. Under Ferrari's management the P3s swept practically all before them but, at the beginning of 1933, Alfa Romeo announced that, in view of its precarious finances, it was going to withdraw from racing. Without the P3, Ferrari was forced to fall back on the older two-seater Monza cars although, in an effort to make them more competitive, capacity was increased from 2.3 to 2.6 litres.

Until this time Scuderia Ferrari cars had carried Alfa Romeo's familiar *quadrifoglia*, or four-leaf clover, motif. These 1933 Monzas, however, were the first cars to bear Ferrari's now familiar prancing horse badge which was also to be applied, post-war, to Ferrari cars. The symbol was suggested to Ferrari after he had won the 1923 Savio circuit race. He made the acquaintance of the parents of Count Franceso Baracca, a young air ace who had died while serving in the same World War I air squadron as Enzo's brother Alfredo, who died while working as ground staff. Ferrari therefore adopted the squadron's black prancing horse insignia, placing it on a field of gold — the colour of the town of Modena.

Back on the circuit, the P3's absence was short-lived for, no doubt goaded by the success of the 2.9-litre monoposto

Maseratis, Alfa Romeo let the single-seater run again at Pescara in August 1933 when it took the chequered flag. Yet, from the following year, Alfa Romeo was being continually and successfully challenged by the German Mercedes-Benz and Auto Union makes and, despite Scuderia's decision to bore out the P3's engine from 2.9 to 3.1 litres and add Dubonnet independent front suspension in 1935, the once victorious monoposto was becoming increasingly uncompetitive. In the same year Ferrari produced the fearsome Bimotore single-seater with an engine behind as well as in front of the driver.

In view of Germany's domination in Grand Prix racing, Ferrari decided to emulate Maserati and enter the smaller capacity voiturette class. The outcome was the 1938 Tipo 158 Alfetta, designed by Alfa Romeo's Gioachino Colombo. Also

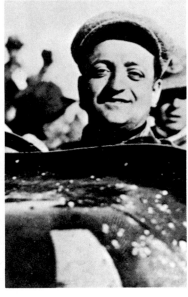

ABOVE *Enzo Ferrari at the wheel of an Alfa Romeo at the start of the 1923 Targa Florio. He failed to finish.*

RIGHT *Enzo in Scuderia Ferrari days, with Achille Varzi in a P3 Alfa Romeo.*

Ferrari

in 1938, Alfa Romeo decided that an all-out assault on the German opposition would only be possible if the racing department was, once again, within the factory precincts. So, after a nine-year existence, Scuderia Ferrari was disbanded and replaced by Alfa Corse, a corporate subsidiary at Milan. Ferrari was invited to continue administering the racing team, but he soon clashed with Alfa's managing director Ugo Gobbato and his Spanish engineer Wilfredo Ricart. So, in November 1938, Ferrari left Milan and returned to Modena. There he established Auto-Avio Costruzioni to undertake sub-contract engineering work.

Under the terms of the separation from Alfa Romeo, Ferrari was banned from building or racing any cars bearing his own name for a period of four years. While keeping strictly to the letter of these terms he did, however, construct two sports racing cars for the 1940 Mille Miglia and named them Vettura 815 (the 8 standing for the number of cylinders and 15 for the engine capacity, i.e. 1.5 litres). They were built from Fiat parts though both suffered from engine trouble and failed to complete the course.

LEFT *Laura Ferrari with Dino in 1954, two years before his death. His name would live on in Ferrari's V6-engined racing and road cars.*

BELOW *Scuderia Ferrari was responsible for the incredible Bimotore Alfa Romeo of 1935, which used two 1934 3165 cc eight-cylinder Tipo B engines.*

During World War 2 Ferrari's firm produced copies of German hydraulically operated grinding machinery. But, during hostilities, the law of industrial decentralization forced Ferrari to move premises. As it happened he owned some land in the small town of Maranello, some 16 km (10 miles) south of Modena, and there he established a new factory. During his spell at Modena he had employed about 40 people but, later on, in these new premises, his workforce increased to around 160.

Car production begins

Although the new Ferrari factory at Maranello had been bombed during World War 2 Enzo was prepared, when hostilities ceased, to re-enter motor racing. He had sufficient finance available and the nucleus of a team including the great automobile technician, Luigi Bazzi, whom Ferrari had wooed to Alfa Romeo from Fiat in 1923.

Ferrari had long admired 12-cylinder engines and decided to build such cars; and, having worked with Gioachino Colombo on the two Alfa Bimotores of 1935 and the Alfetta in 1937, he offered him the position of designer in 1946. The same year Ferrari announced that he would embark on a programme of Grand Prix, sports, and road cars, all with a V12 unit. This made a good deal of sense for it meant that with only minor modifications and some detuning, the Grand Prix engine could be used for three types of car.

At this point it should perhaps be mentioned that Ferrari has used some three systems of designations for his cars, which need to be understood. However, he also appears to have proceeded by whimsy now and again, which can cause confusion in the minds of many people even though such designations might have appeared logical to the factory. The early racing cars and the current production models were designated by taking the capacity of one cylinder in cubic centimetres and multiplying it by the number of cylinders to give the total displacement, thus the 1.5-litre V12 Formula 1 was designated 125 F1.

A second method was used from 1957 whereby the total capacity and number of cylinders are indicated, for example the 246 F1 was a 2.4-litre V6, the 158 F1 a 1.5-litre V8, and the 312 series of F1 cars were 3-litre flat-12s. As already stated there are some inconsistencies, for the first flat-12 built in 1964/5 should by right be called a 1512 F1 (1.5-litre flat-12), whereas it was designated 512 F1; this might give the impression that the 512 M and S cars were similar, but these in fact were the 5-litre V12 sports-racing machines used in the CanAm races and also for the sports-car championship series.

The third system was primarily for factory use and gave project numbers to engines based on the order of appearance of what were intended as racing cars: an example was project 116, which was the 2.5-litre in-line-2 and designated 252 F1. The odd ones were the Squalo and Supersqualo of the 1953–5 season and here speculation suggests that the 553 Squalo indicated a 1953 modification of the 500 series, and the 555 Supersqualo the final development of the engine in 1955. The Lancia-Ferrari 801 (a development of the original Lancia D50) might suggest that it was an eight-cylinder F1 car – which of course it was – but the designation is not at all clear and has no place in the ordered nomenclature of car production.

To return to the V12 project, the first post-war formula, which came into force in 1947, was for 1½-litre supercharged and 4½-litre unsupercharged cars. Ferrari thus built his supercharged racers for this formula while Alfa Romeo was to dominate its early years by fielding its Ferrari-initiated pre-war Tipo 158 Alfetta which now enjoyed its finest hour.

Ferrari intended to start with the Grand Prix car, but the sports version was the first to take its place on a grid at a minor event at Piacenza in May 1947. The Grand Prix cars appeared at the Valentino Park event in September 1948 with Giuseppe Farina, Raymond Sommer, and 'Bira' as drivers. Sommer was placed third, Farina drove into a straw bale, and 'Bira' retired with transmission trouble.

The car was designated Tipo 125 and had 12 cylinders in 60-degree V-formation, and bore and stroke of 55×52.5 mm giving a displacement of 1496.7 cc. The crankcase and cylinder blocks were of aluminium alloy with detachable heads. A single overhead camshaft per bank of cylinders was chain driven from the front operating one intake and one exhaust valve per

cylinder. A single 40 DO3C carburettor placed in the 'V' of the engine fed the fuel, and a single-stage Roots-type supercharger ran at 1.22 times the crankshaft speed. Twin magnetos driven from the rear of the camshaft sparked a single 14 mm plug per cylinder. The compression ratio was 6.5:1 and the power output was 225 bhp at 7000 rpm. A five-speed 'crash' gearbox was in unit with the engine and single clutch plate, drive was via an open propshaft to a fixed final drive, and the halfshafts were exposed. The chassis was a tubular frame and the main members were oval in section. The front suspension had unequal-length wishbones, a transverse leaf spring and at the rear swing axle halfshafts, single radius arms and torsion bars, which were discarded for a transverse leaf spring in 1949.

Apart from its appearance at Valentino Park, the Tipo 125 was entered for three other events in 1948; at a minor race at Garda, Farina drove it to first place, but at Monza and Barcelona the transmission failed.

For the 1949 Monza GP a revised car appeared, still designated 125 F1; the capacity remained as before, but with twin overhead camshafts per bank of cylinders and twin-stage supercharging, it had an increased output of 290 bhp at 7500 rpm. To counteract the earlier car's instability the wheelbase was increased to 2380 mm (7 ft 10 in) and the track was widened but handling, although improved, was still far from satisfactory. However, thanks to the absence from racing of the Alfa Romeo team, the 125 F1 was dominant and had a successful season.

During the early post-war period there were two other formulae available for racing-car constructors, namely Formule Libre and Formula 2, and for such events the early basic design of the 125 came in useful. In 1949 the 166 Formule Libre car made its début using the basic short-chassis 125 parts, but with

a bore and stroke of 60 × 58.8 mm displacing 1995 cc. For the 1950 season the car used the long-wheelbase chassis. The 166 F2 had a good and successful run, winning 13 out of 15 Formula 2 races during 1950.

By 1950 Colombo had departed and Lampredi had taken over to design and develop a larger-capacity non-supercharged V12, and to begin preparation of a 2.5-litre four-cylinder unit for F1 racing in 1954.

Ferrari was aware that Alfa Romeo was updating its cars for a return to the circuits in Tipo 159 guise in 1951 and it was one of his ambitions to defeat them, believing that he alone was able to achieve this distinction. He felt, no doubt, that the 125 design had reached the peak of its performance and little was to be gained in trying to extract any further power.

The first of the larger-capacity cars was the 1950 275 F1 3.3-litre 60-degree V12 which was used as a test bed for what followed. This was the 340 F1 with an increase in capacity to 4.1 litres, and then came the 375 F1 with a bore and stroke of 80 × 74.5 mm displacing 4493.7 cc. The chassis and suspension, except for minor modifications, followed the original Colombo-designed cars, but with a de Dion tube as standard practice and a longer wheelbase. The 275 F1 had twin magnetos driven from the rear of the camshaft and a single sparkplug, as did the early 375, but this was changed in 1951 to a single magneto driven from the front and two plugs per cylinder. The final output was 380 bhp at 7500 rpm – although the 375 Formule Libre car was boosted to 390 bhp.

The 1951 season was reasonably successful for the 375 F1, which won three championship rounds against the highly competitive Alfa Romeos. A crucial victory came at that year's British Grand Prix, when the unblown Ferrari came in ahead of the supercharged Alfa Romeo, so spelling death to the supercharged racing engine. But Ferrari came unstuck in the final round, the Spanish GP at Pedralbes, where incorrect tyre selection lost the company the race and also the manufacturers' championship. The Alfa Romeo concern having accomplished what it had set out to prove – that its cars were still the best – pulled out and put the dust sheets over the machines.

LEFT *Ferrari sports cars made their racing début at Piacenza in May 1947. Franco Cortese retired on the penultimate lap.*

BELOW *A 1951 Tipo 125 F1 Ferrari, privately owned and campaigned by Peter Whitehead and entered, with some success, by the works.*

Four instead of twelve

During 1950 Ferrari could see that the immediate future of motor racing would tend to lie with 2-litre unblown Formula 2 cars. Although he had V12s of this capacity in both blown and unblown form, they were being harassed on the circuits by four-cylinder cars that were less thirsty and therefore were not being delayed so long by pit stops for fuel.

Consequently, in 1951 Lampredi was given the job of producing 2- and 2.5-litre four-cylinder cars for the 1952–3 seasons. The 2-litre cars were intended for Formula 2 and the 2.5-litre engines were built in readiness for 1954, when new Formula 1 regulations were to come into force.

One of the main reasons for abandoning the V12 unblown cars in favour of an in-line four-cylinder engine for Formula 2 racing was the fact that such a power plant would give more torque out of corners, and Ferrari anticipated around 100 bhp per litre from the new unit.

The bore and stroke of the 2-litre engine was 'oversquare' (i.e. the bore was larger than the stroke) at 90 × 78 mm, and the 2.5-litre had a 94 × 90 mm bore and stroke. Ferrari decided to use the larger capacity unit as a test bed for the 2-litre chassis.

The 2.5-litre car, known as the 625, and built to the 1954 Formula 1 regulations, made its first appearance at the 1951 GP at Bari, where it was driven by Piero Taruffi into a respectable third place. Although this car was used in practice later that year before the Italian GP at Monza, it was a non-starter there, being returned to the factory before the race. Before the 1951 season ended two cars, using the 2-litre unit and designated 500 F2, were raced at the Modena GP by Luigi Villoresi and Alberto

ABOVE *This is believed to be the 500 F2 in which Ascari won the 1953 British Grand Prix. The model won no less than 30 out* *of 33 championship races in two years. Provided by the Donington Collection.*

Ascari. Both cars proved superior to the V12 loaned to Froilan Gonzalez and, although Villoresi did not finish the race, this debut augured well for the 1952 season when Formula 2 racing was to supplant Formula 1. (As Alfa Romeo had pulled out of racing after beating the Ferraris at the Spanish GP, the Modena concern was left with no opposition in the 'premier division', hence the temporary abandonment of Formula 1.)

The years 1952 and 1953 were certainly Ferrari's for the 500 F2 was one of the most successful Grand Prix cars ever raced, winning 14 world championship events in a row during that period. The remarkably successful works cars were beaten only three times in 33 races, at Rheims in 1952 by Gordini (Jean Behra) and at Syracuse and Monza in 1953 by Maserati (Baron Emanuel de Graffenried and Juan Manuel Fangio), Ascari, Scuderia Ferrari's number one driver, took the driver's world championship in both years. Ferrari won the manufacturers' title over the same period.

The success of these two years should have continued in 1954, for the 625 F1 had proved its reliability and the works drivers liked its handling characteristics. However, the highly organized and financed Mercedes-Benz team had re-entered the fray with some exciting cars which were to prove both fast and reliable while the Maseratis were also quick but unreliable. In fact 1954 was to be another year of experimentation and it demonstrated once more the ability of the leading designers and

Ferrari

By Lancia out of Ferrari

Scuderia Ferrari was at a low ebb in 1954 after the two preceding spectacular seasons with the 500 F2 cars. The 625 F1, although reliable, lacked power and the Squalo and Supersqualo were hardly successes.

Alberto Ascari and Luigi Villoresi left the Scuderia at the start of the 1954 season, moving to Lancia where a 2480 cc V8-engined car was being developed for Grand Prix racing. But it was dogged by mechanical and financial problems and, on 26 July 1955, the cars were handed over to Ferrari. In addition, Fiat agreed to make Ferrari an annual payment of 50 million lire (£28,571) for five years to make sure that Italian red was still seen on the Grand Prix circuits.

There was little time for any modifications when Scuderia

TOP *Maurice Trintignant wins the 1954 Monaco Grand Prix for Ferrari at an average speed of 105.91 km/h (65.63 mph).*

ABOVE *Peter Collins in a Lancia-Ferrari in the 1956 Monaco Grand Prix. On lap 54 he handed over to Fangio.*

engineers to produce, almost overnight, a new engine – or even a chassis.

To overcome the lack of power, the factory retained the lower half of the engine but used the reworked head of the 553 F1 Squalo (this type had made its début in the spring of 1954). This did not prove wholly satisfactory. As an alternative the new engine was used in the 625 F1 chassis until the more potent version of this unit, the 555 F1 Supersqualo, giving 250 bhp at 7500 rpm, was installed. The overall performance, however, was not enhanced: there was no doubt that the engine required more modification and testing. A further development of the 625 F1 chassis came in 1955 when the 750 Formule Libre engine made its debut with a bore of 100 mm and stroke of 90 mm for a displacement of 2999.6 cc. This unit, with an output of 290 bhp at 7500 rpm, was to power the sports racing 750 Monza (Ferrari's policy was to switch engines between sports and GP cars).

Ferrari took over, but Ferrari substituted Englebert tyres for the Pirellis, renamed the cars Lancia-Ferrari D50s, and added his prancing horse insignia.

During the winter of 1955–6 the factory installed a larger fuel tank in the tail to improve handling. The exhaust pipes were realigned so that they exited through the rear lower end of the pannier tanks. At the front an anti-roll bar was added, and at the rear the leaf spring was placed above the gearbox. Telescopic shock absorbers were replaced with vane-type Houdailles and to give greater strength upper frame tubes were added to the chassis. It was not long before the pannier tanks were fused into the bodywork to give a smoother line.

By mid-1956 the D50's bore had been enlarged from 74 mm to 76 mm and the stroke was reduced from 72 mm to 68.5 mm, giving a displacement of 2487 cc. For the French GP Castellotti's car had a fresh and pleasing look. A full-width nose with faired moulded section ahead of the front wheels was fitted together with moulded mudguard sections over the rear wheels with scoops to assist cooling of the tyres. Unfortunately the new additions did not help for, in side winds, the car became unstable and the sections were therefore removed.

For the Scuderia 1956 was a good year. It won five of the seven championship rounds, with Juan-Manuel Fangio taking the drivers' championship from Stirling Moss (Maserati) by three points (30 to 27).

By the spring of the following year, the Lancia-Ferrari 801 appeared with the slightly increased output of 275 bhp at 8200 rpm. The bore and stroke had been altered to 80 mm × 62 mm giving a capacity of 2494.8 cc. However, the 1957 season was not a good one for Ferrari. The 801 won minor races only although it was placed on a number of occasions. During the season the front-engined V6 Dinos were being developed and were challenging the Cooper Climax cars in Formula 2 events.

Attention must now be turned to these front-engined Dino V6, F2 and F1 cars. This name was given to all V6s in memory of Enzo's son Alfredo, who was known as Dino and who had died on 30 June 1956, of muscular dystrophy, aged only 24.

The first car in the series was the 156 F2 designed by Vittorio Jano and it followed, in many respects, his original Lancia D50 layout. Apart from the F2 car of 1957 there were seven variants of the 246 F1 and two 256 F1s in the series between 1957 and 1960, with capacities from 1860 cc to 2474.6 cc and bhp ratings from 215 at 8500 rpm to 295 at 8500 rpm. The earliest car (1957) had a bore and stroke of 78.6 × 64.5 mm and over the three-year period this increased to 86 × 71 mm.

The F2 chassis was a multi-tubular spaceframe with large-diameter main longitudinal members: the power units of the F1 cars used this frame up to early 1958 and again in 1960. Between mid-1958 and late 1959, although the spaceframe was used, it had smaller-diameter longitudinal members.

The front-engined Dinos had a chequered racing history, doing well on some occasions but being outclassed on others. However, the F1 and F2 cars could be considered successful since Mike Hawthorn took the 1958 world drivers' championship by one point from Moss, although the British-built Vanwalls gave the Dinos a tough season, finally taking the manufacturers' award. Sadly, this season was marred by the death of Peter Collins; he crashed at the German GP and the works lost a fine sporting driver.

'Small is beautiful' could certainly be said of the 1958 front-engined Dinos. Aesthetically they could not be faulted with smooth lines, and even the central bonnet fairing (at times a plastic hood), to accommodate the carburettors, appeared purposeful. The tail design of these handsome cars was just right and bore more than a passing resemblance to the rear end of the Lancia D50s.

The following year, 1959, was an indifferent one for the Dinos which, apart from suspension and other modifications, included new bodywork by Medardo Fantuzzi. This was longer and wider with the exhausts carried low, not so handsome as the earlier cars but more purposeful and aggressive-looking. No world championships were gained in the season but the British driver, Tony Brooks, came third in the driver's championship, winning the French and German GPs.

In 1960 Phil Hill won the European Grand Prix at Monza in a 246 Dino. It was the last Formula 1 victory by a front-engined car and represented the end of an era as the rear engined revolution, initiated by Cooper in 1958, swept the field.

The sports cars

As has been seen, Enzo Ferrari's first production models under his own name were the V12 Tipo 125 cars. Three were built but initially only one retained the 1500 cc engine; the others were first bored out to 1902 cc and called Tipo 159, but in 1948 all three were enlarged to 1995 cc and designated Tipo 166.

They had somewhat crude but adequate bodywork, two seats, cycle-type wings and headlamps. However, the wings and lamps were removable so that the machines could be used for formula racing as well as participating in sports-car events. They were fast, reliable and well able to outclass machines of far greater capacities. It is not surprising, therefore, that they had many successes, including long-distance races. It was not long before an all-enveloping body, by Carrozzeria Touring, clothed the chassis, giving a most pleasing appearance, and one early car fitted with a coupé top and driven by Clemente Biondetti won the 1948 Mille Miglia. In honour of this victory all 166 models thereafter had the suffix MM after the numbers. Then, in 1949, came Ferrari's first Le Mans victory.

BELOW *The Tipo 166 V12 Ferrari engine. It was given this name because each cylinder had a capacity of 166 cc.*

BOTTOM *Alberto Ascari in a Tipo 166 MM Ferrari which won the 1950 Production Car Race at Silverstone.*

ABOVE *Juan Fangio's first drive in a racing Ferrari was in June 1949 at the Grand Prix of the Autodrome at Monza. At the wheel of this 2-litre unsupercharged 166 F2, bought for him by the Argentine government, he beat the works Ferraris and won at 160.04 km/h (99.45 mph).*

LEFT *A magnificent line up of Lancia-Ferrari D50s at the 1956 British GP at Silverstone, also won by Fangio.*

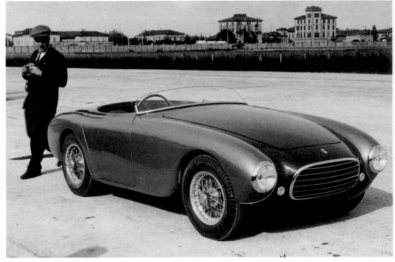

It is important to remember that the original chassis, engine, and design of many parts formed the basis for most models, with modifications, until the mid-1960s. There were a number of variants based on the 166, such as the 212 produced as the Export or Sport with a short wheelbase, and the Inter with a longer wheelbase – this was basically a road version although used in competition. There was also the 195, built with berlinetta and spider coachwork, and it was not always easy to differentiate between the 166, 212, and 195.

Ferrari's first big sports car was announced in the summer of 1950 and the same year the model 340 America appeared at the Paris Salon. The Lampredi-designed long-block engine of 4101.6 cc (bore and stroke 80 × 68 mm) powered the car, which had an output of 220 bhp at 6000 rpm and a claimed top speed of 220 km/h (137 mph). There were two other versions, the 340 MM and 340 Mexico. Although this Tipo had a number of successes in Europe, including the long-distance Mille Miglia, it was intended for the United States market and was campaigned successfully in a variety of events by American drivers.

During 1952 and 1953 Ferrari sports cars were dominant and the factory competed with five different-capacity cars – the 2-litre 166 MM, the 2.3-litre 195 S, the 2.7-litre 225 S, the 3-litre 250 Sport, and the 4.1-litre 340 MM and Mexico. The 250 Sport or MM was insufficiently developed, although it had shown promise, but Ferrari had by then turned his attention to the 4.5-litre 375.

The 1953 Le Mans event proved the first outing for a 375 MM berlinetta but, after setting a new lap record, it retired with clutch trouble; two 340 MM berlinettas were also entered and these cars, after the race, were brought up to the 375 specification so that the three cars and a Vignale-bodied 375 MM spider formed the Ferrari team for the remainder of the year. For 1954 the factory relied on the new 375 Plus which was modified and had more power than the 375 MM. The 84 mm bore was retained but it had a 74.5 mm stroke displacing 4954.3 cc, and with three twin-choke 46 DCF3 Weber carburettors it had a bhp rating of 344 at 6500 rpm.

It had been Ferrari practice from the early days to switch engines from Grand Prix to sports cars and the habit persisted with the in-line fours. There were a number of obvious

advantages to the system, not least that of being able to produce sports cars for customers. The first four-cylinder engine for sports-car racing was the 2.5-litre Lampredi Grand Prix unit, which was installed in either a 166 or 250 MM chassis. Together with a 3-litre four, the car was first seen at Monza in 1953.

During the winter of 1953–4 work went ahead on a new four-cylinder car based on the Tipo 555. This was the 750 Monza and followed the normal Lampredi practice. At the Tourist Trophy in September 1955 a larger-capacity Monza appeared that had a bore and stroke of 102 × 105 mm for a displacement of 3431 cc. It will be noted that the stroke was greater than the bore (the first time for a Ferrari type). This was designated the 860 Monza and had limited successes.

With possible customers in mind, Ferrari introduced the 500 Mondial using the 1952–3 F2 unit. In many respects the chassis followed the usual practice, as did the suspension. The model had strong opposition from the sports Maserati and to increase the power the cylinder head of the 553 F2 was substituted, and with the larger 45 DCO/A3 carburettors it developed 170 bhp at 7000 rpm. A few other modifications were carried out but these made little difference in practice, so Ferrari turned his attention to a new 2-litre four-cylinder engine conceived by Vittorio Jano and other members of the design team (Lampredi departed in

LEFT *The 212, built between 1951 and 1953. Touring's magnificent Barchetta open two-seater body has no bumpers to sully the lovely lines. Provided by John Briggs and Don Nelson.*

BELOW LEFT *A 1951 Ferrari 212 with a two-colour Vignale body. The plated beading marked the division between the colours. The engine is a 2562 cc V12 with a five-speed gearbox.*

TIPO 375 MM
1954

ENGINE	
No. of cylinders V12	
Bore/stroke mm 84 × 68	
Displacement cc 4522	
Valve operation Single overhead camshaft per cylinder bank	
Compression ratio 9:1	
Induction Triple Weber downdraught carburettors	
BHP 340 at 7000 rpm	
Transmission Four-speed	

CHASSIS	
Frame Welded tubular	
Wheelbase mm 2600	
Track – front mm 1325	
Track – rear mm 1320	
Suspension – front Unequal length wishbones, transverse leaf, anti-roll bar	
Suspension – rear Half-elliptic springs, parallel trailing arms	

PERFORMANCE	
Maximum speed 257 km/h (160 mph)	

1955 and went to Fiat). The unit was to power the 500 Testa Rossa which, making a first showing at the 1000 km Supercortemaggiore race at Monza on 24 June 1956, finished first, second, and fourth. The car appeared next at Le Mans, using the 625 F1 engine and designated 625 LM. It finished third overall.

A new 500 TRC was announced by Ferrari at his annual press day late in 1956. The car was for customers and not works use. The engine had the same dimensions as the Mondial, bore and stroke 90 × 78 mm, and used a head similar to the early 500 F2. A number of modifications were carried out including a strengthened crankshaft and rods, and the transmission was now engine-mounted with a live rear axle. Suspension was independent as usual but with coils all round. This was the last four-cylinder model, except for the delightful small ASA, nicknamed the Ferrarina. Conceived in 1957, the first model used to accompany the racing team all over Europe in the late 1950s and early 1960s. The design was finally sold off to the de Nora chemical company.

ABOVE *The 195S Ferrari of 1949. The V12 engine had a capacity of 2341 cc, the result of the bore being enlarged from 60 to 65 mm, producing 195 cc per cylinder – hence the model's title. This is a Touring-bodied example. Provided by Peter Agg, Trojan Ltd.*

BELOW *The 375 MM of 1953 was a magnificent vehicle but a real handful to drive. It was conceived for long distance races such as Le Mans and the Carrera Panamericana events. Provided by R. Cederlund.*

JLS 513

TIPO 250 TESTA ROSA
1958

RIGHT *The Testa Rossa (red head) engine with its distinctive red camshaft boxes. The model was Ferrari's front-line sports racer from 1957 until 1961.*

BELOW *Created for the 1958 World Sports Car Championship, the 250 Testa Rossa used a chassis derived from the four-cylinder 500 TR which also carried the Testa Rossa name. It had the distinction of being the first sports racing Ferrari to be fitted with an all-synchromesh four-speed gearbox; previously a 'crash' box had been employed. The 3-litre V12 was developed from the 250 GT unit. The Testa Rossa was largely responsible for Ferrari winning the World Sports Car Championship in 1958 and 1960.*

ENGINE	
No. of cylinders V12	
Bore/stroke mm 73 × 58	
Displacement cc 2953	
Valve operation Single overhead camshaft per cylinder bank	
Compression ratio 9.8:1	
Induction Six Weber 38 DCN twin-choke carburettors	
BHP 300 at 7200 rpm	
Transmission Four-speed, all synchromesh	

CHASSIS	
Frame Welded tubular steel	
Wheelbase mm 2350	
Track – front mm 1308	
Track – rear mm 1300	
Suspension – front Independent, unequal wishbone, coil springs	
Suspension – rear Live axle, semi-elliptic springs, parallel trailing arms	
Brakes Hydraulic, aluminium drums, iron liners	

PERFORMANCE	
Maximum speed 209 km/h (130 mph)	

GT supremacy

Starting with the 1956 season the Fédération Internationale de l'Automobile established specific classes for gran turismo cars and Ferrari, having built and raced berlinettas since 1950, was in a strong position to meet any new regulations. He had unveiled two different body styles on the new 3-litre 250 GT at the 1955 Paris and Turin shows respectively. These Pinin Farina designs were 'translated' into coachwork for the cars to be built by Scaglietti and raced, not only by the factory, but also

by customers in 1956 and for many years afterwards, showing a complete supremacy over all other GT cars. Although built initially for competition, these were also road cars, even though the coachwork was light and fragile.

The factory designated all the series under a single nomenclature, 250 GT, but there were in reality three variants: the Tour de France or long-wheelbase cars, the SWB or short wheelbase, and the GTO.

The GTO was the final development of the 250 GT competition berlinetta. The suffix 'O' denoted its homologation (*omologato*) within the framework of the regulations concerning the minimum numbers built by the factory; there had in fact been a dispute between Ferrari and the race authorities on the subject. While all cars in the 250 GT series (competition and road) can be identified as such, there were, as indicated, some modifications from year to year but all were smooth in line with a purposeful look that clearly implied a race-bred design. The GTO, however, is the car that has caught the imagination of the Ferrari enthusiast, with its aerodynamic lines and, in its final production form, an upswept spoiler effect blending in with the tail. The first GTO was shown to the press in February 1962, although development work had been started towards the end of 1960, and the last three cars of the series, using the 4-litre unit as installed in the 1960 400 Superamerica road cars, appeared in 1964. The demise of the series in serious racing was not the end

of the factory's highly successful competitive run, for other cars were in the pipeline and were destined to keep the Ferrari name in the motor sport headlines.

It has already been seen that Ferrari was late in accepting the idea of a mid- or rear-engined car and the first of these was the V6 246 F1, driven by Richie Ginther at the Monaco GP in 1960, while the 250 GT series had front-mounted units. In 1961 some organizers of long-distance races felt it necessary to continue with prototype cars and in November 1962 Ferrari unveiled his V12 3-litre mid-engined GT car, the 250 P. This was a highly successful competition car, even though only in limited production and therefore lasting for a short period. It was the forerunner of the 250 LM berlinetta, which the FIA considered to be a prototype, whereas the factory felt it was a production GT. Perhaps only 40 were built, one car having a 3-litre unit (acceptable as a contender for the 1962 championship for GT cars as the upper capacity limit was 3 litres), the remainder having 3.3-litre engines and considered by many as 275 LMs.

Two other cars of the period, raced at Le Mans and elsewhere, were the 330 LMB and the front-engined TR/LM Spider, which was not a particularly good-looking car and had a twin-nostril front end.

The first Ferraris to bear the name Testa Rossa (derived from a special red finish on the camshaft covers) were the 500 TR with a 2-litre four-cylinder engine and the 500 TRCs built for

ABOVE *A 250 GT of 1959. This short-wheelbase example is powered by a Colombo-designed V12 2953 engine. Introduced at the 1959 Paris Motor Show, the model remained in production until 1962. Provided by Vic Norman.*

OVERLEAF *An illustrious model with an appropriate number plate: the 250 GTO of 1962–4 is one of the most desirable and sought-after Ferraris.*

customer use and also competition in 1956 and 1957. For 1957 Ferrari had to prepare cars for the 1958 World Sports Car Championship confined to an upper limit of 3 litres and, as the 250 GT 3-litre units were well in contention in competition, this engine was chosen for further development and used in the 250 TRs. The 250 Testa Rossa had an illustrious career, winning a great variety of races and carrying off the championship spoils in 1958, 1960 and 1961. A normal-bodied sports car of the period, it resembled the factory Tipo 315 Sport (3.7-litre) and 335 Sport (4-litre), derived from the 290 S (3.4-litre) with a single overhead camshaft per bank of cylinders.

At a press conference in early 1961 Enzo Ferrari showed the 246 SP with a 2.4-litre 60-degree V6 double overhead camshaft

engine; the original design of this unit went back to 1956. With a bore and stroke of 85 × 71 mm it displaced 2417 cc and had a compression ratio of 9.8:1. There were three double-choke 42 DCN Weber carburettors located in the 'V' of the engine and the power output at 8000 rpm was 270 bhp. The type's racing baptism was in the United States at the 1961 Sebring 12-hour race, in the hands of Wolfgang von Trips, where its phenomenal speed took it to first place before the steering arm broke.

Two of the cars contested the Targa Florio in Sicily, without doubt the toughest race in the calendar, but the Phil Hill/Richie Ginther car was eliminated early on, and von Trips with Olivier Gendebien had a race-long struggle against the 2-litre Porsche of Stirling Moss and Jo Bonnier. The lap record fell with almost monotonous regularity, and on the last lap the Porsche, with a slender lead, succumbed to transmission failure to let von Trips take the chequered flag.

Championship wins

Rain getting into the 'works' via the louvres caused a minor setback to the two cars at the Nürburgring 1000 km race, although von Trips managed third place. A further miscalculation occurred during the Le Mans 24-hour race when von Trips ran out of fuel at Mulsanne when lying second after 16 hours of racing. However, the back-up team of Testa Rossas made it a one-two result with a 250 GT claiming third place.

The 246 SP cars proved that when Enzo Ferrari was convinced of the correctness of any decision, however late, he had the ability to make up time on the other constructors, for with the help of these rear-engined sports cars the factory won the manufacturers' championship in 1961 and 1962. For all that, Ferrari was still behind in his thinking when it came to chassis design and was outdated by the British constructors.

To strengthen his hand for 1962 Ferrari produced four more cars, two V6s of 2 and 2.8 litres and two V8s of 2.4 litres, all with single overhead camshafts per bank of cylinders. The 2- and 2.8-litre cars were respectively the 196 SP and 286 SP.

The 1962 Targa Florio saw the 196 SP in contention in the 2-litre class with Lorenzo Bandini and Giancarlo Baghetti as drivers and a new 268 SP with a 2.6-litre V8 unit driven by Phil Hill. A third entry from Maranello was a 246 SP driven by Willy Mairesse and Gendebien. Although Baghetti spun on the third lap and damaged his car, his co-driver Bandini brought the 196 SP home in second place overall and first in the 2-litre class, while the 246 SP was first overall.

At the Nürburgring 1000 km race the 196 SP with Bandini at

ABOVE *The 196 SP Dino of 1962, one of the Ferrari prototype racing and sports cars. It is powered by a rear-mounted 1983 cc V6 engine. Provided by John Godfrey.*

BELOW *The starting point of the Dino road cars of 1967 was the sports racing 206 SP with a 65-degree V6 engine and three valves per cylinder. Provided by D. Mason-Styrron.*

the wheel was lying fourth when, during a routine pit stop, oil was found seeping from a cracked sump plate and this caused its retirement. The car also raced at the Nassau Speed Week driven by Bob Fulp, but failed to finish.

For the second year running a 196 SP was entered for the Targa Florio. With Mairesse at the wheel it spun, damaging the rear cover. However, despite this Mairesse only lost to Bonnier's Porsche by a mere 11 seconds.

The 196 SP ended its career contesting the various European hill climbs with considerable success. In 1962, for example, Ludovico Scarfiotti won at Fornova-Monte Cassio, Mont Ventoux, Monte Bondone, Freiburg Schauinsland and Ollon Villars, and Ferrari took the European Mountain Championship, beating Porsche by 11 points.

The term SP has never been explained by the factory but is generally accepted as meaning Sports Prototype, as the numerically small and somewhat exclusive series, which included V6 cars, had a short life of some two years or so. However, its importance cannot be too strongly emphasized for from this prototype series came an upsurge in Ferrari fortunes and probably some of the finest racing ever seen, with such unforgettable cars as the 250 P, 250 LM, the early Ps, and finally the fabulous 330 P4s.

A new spider in the P series had been developed for 1965 with a wind tunnel-tested sleek body giving a low nose profile, and with diplane spoilers attached to either side to keep the front end from lifting at high speed. There were other important improvements to the body which had not, for once, been designed by the coachbuilder Pininfarina who had had a hand in all the previous sports-racing spiders. In addition to the new P2 cars there was to be a proliferation of other prototypes for the season, which must have kept the factory very much on its toes. After a poor start in America the P2 and other cars began to find their form at the Monza 1000 km race, but in general the factory P2s were not a success and the 1966 season was beset by a variety of problems such as the lack of preparation of the cars due to industrial unrest in Italy. A further blow was the resignation of John Surtees from the team after an argument with team manager Dragoni during practice for the Le Mans race.

In 1964 and 1965 the might of the Ford empire pitted itself against the other contenders for the prototype crown but on each occasion was overcome. However, with Ferrari having problems in 1966, the door was wide open and, although Porsche took the honours, the 7-litre Fords were still a potential threat to the ordered pattern of the past.

Enzo Ferrari was nevertheless a determined man and he set about preparing for what was likely to prove a titanic struggle in 1967. Although the factory had always been adept at producing new cars and engines for a particular race or series of races, it was always slow to introduce new concepts from outside sources even though these might have been proved. The P4, to be introduced for 1967, was entirely new and the chassis did not conform to the accepted monocoque or stretch-skin construction, but relied on its torsional strength from a variety, indeed multitude, of tubes to support the many other vital accessories. It was not, however, a spaceframe in accepted terms. Franco Rocchi designed the new engine, a mid-engine V12 with twin overhead camshafts per bank of cylinders and three valves per cylinder (2 inlet/1 exhaust); displacement was 3967 cc and bhp 450 at 11,000 rpm. It was a handsome, smooth-lined car giving an impression of enormous potential and power which, indeed, it had. Only three cars were built, for the fourth car used during the season was a P3 with the P4 power plant. Although the Fords won at Le Mans the P4s took the prototype title by 2 points from Porsche and by 12 from Ford.

The P4 was the end of a long era for the Ferrari sports racing

machines, for the cars from the factory that followed in its wheel tracks conformed to the practices of its rivals.

The ruling body of automobile sport decreed that the 1968 manufacturers' championship would be contested by cars with a 3-litre limit, which certainly did not suit Ferrari: he did not have a suitable car and it was the first time since 1953, when the sports-car championship was instituted, that he was not a contestant. This is not to say that Ferraris did not compete, as a number of privateers contested races, nor was the racing department dormant. Apart from running the Formula 1 cars, it produced a 6-litre car for the last event of the CanAm sports car series in Canada and the USA (although token assistance was given in subsequent years, Ferrari's interest was not really serious here). At the end of the year Ferrari showed his 3-litre prototype for the 1969 championship, the 312 P with a 2990 cc V12 unit with 48 valves, Lucas injection and an output of 420 bhp at 9800 rpm. The body was a scaled-down version of the CanAm car and one of the most beautiful sports-racing Ferraris ever, but it was a failure on the track. The same could be said of the 512 M, which was campaigned on both sides of the Atlantic in 1970/1.

ABOVE AND RIGHT *The 512 M (for Modificata) of 1970 was campaigned by Ferrari in CanAm and other prototype races in 1970 and 1971. Its aerodynamic bodywork was much crisper than its 512 predecessor's. The 5-litre cars also ran in the European sports car racing championship but proved to be no match for the ultra-reliable Porsches. However, the 512 M was never seriously developed and its full potential went unrecognized. Provided by Robert Horne.*

Ferrari now turned his attention to his new project for 1971, the flat-12-engined 312 PB to be used in the manufacturers' championship: the unit was derived from the Grand Prix cars. In fact it could be described as a Formula 1 car with full-width two-seat bodywork that was a small and simple spider design.

Two cars were available for 1971 and one was sent for the opening championship round to Buenos Aires with Ignazio Giunti and Arturo Merzario as drivers, but when lying second Giunti, unable to take avoiding action, ran into a Matra being pushed along the track. The Ferrari burst into flames, becoming a total wreck, and the driver died of head injuries and burns. The season was one of unfortunate incidents for the remaining car with Jacky Ickx as number one driver and his co-pilot either Clay Regazzoni or Mario Andretti. It had shown its potential by being placed on the front row of the grid for most of the events entered and leading at some stage in its races before retiring, crashing or 'running out of road'.

An all-out effort was planned for 1972 and six cars were built. The idea was to have three cars always race-prepared while three would be at the works to receive any necessary attention before their next outing. The experience gained during 1971 meant that a variety of modifications needed to be carried out during the winter. The result was that the 1972 cars were more than a match for the opposition and carried off the honours without having to contest the 24-hour race at Le Mans, as Ferrari decided that the 312 PB was incapable of lasting the distance.

The 1973 season was hard fought against the fast and much-improved V12 Matras and the 2.7-litre Porsche Carreras which had entered the fray. Ferrari lost to the Matras by 124 to 115 points and decided to abandon sports-car racing and concentrate on Formula 1 for the future: a wise decision as it proved.

The road cars

With the early production machines there are no really clear-cut dividing lines between the Grand Prix, sports, and gran turismo or berlinetta cars, as all or most were used in competition either by the factory or later by customers, and none could be said to be out-and-out road cars, although a number could be used for fast touring. Perhaps the 342 America 2 + 2 Ghia coachwork coupé could be considered as the first attempt by Ferrari to introduce a roadgoing automobile. The first of the series (apart from the one displayed at the Brussels show in early 1951) was exhibited at Turin in the spring of that year and was a development of the 340 with the same displacement of 4101 cc but with a new chassis and a synchromesh four-speed-and-reverse gearbox, although some featured a five-speed non-synchromesh box. Few were built and they were similar in appearance to the 250 Europa and the later 375 Americas. The chassis, it is interesting to note, was the basis for all the larger Ferraris that came after.

At the 1953 Paris Salon the 250 Europa was introduced and from this period on Ferrari devoted more production time to GT roadgoing cars as these were the forerunners of the 250 series. The Europa had a 2800 mm (9 ft 2 in) wheelbase chassis

RIGHT *The 1971 312 PB had a Forghieri-designed 2991 cc flat-12 (hence 'B' for Boxer) rear-mounted engine with twin overhead camshafts per cylinder bank. Developed from the 312 PV12, it was built for the* *Manufacturer's Championship series, winning the title in 1972. This example is shown in the 1971 BOAC 1000 at Brands Hatch. Driven by Ickx and Regazzoni, it came second to a T33 Alfa Romeo.*

LEFT *Sergio Farina, son of Pinin Farina, hands over the keys of his personal Ferrari 250 GT 2+2 to Harry Mundy, technical editor of* Autocar *magazine, at the firm's modern factory at Turin in mid-1961. This car was capable of over 217 km/h (135 mph).*

BELOW *The Ferrari 250 GT/L, introduced at the 1962 Paris Show, was informally known as the Lusso, for luxury. It had Pininfarina bodywork and was built by Scaglietti. The engine was the Colombo-designed 2953 cc V12 with single overhead camshafts per cylinder bank, developing 250 bhp at 7000 rpm. At this time Ferrari was still using a live rear axle with half-elliptic springs. Provided by Malcolm Clarke.*

similar to the 250 MM and also used by the 375 America. There was also the 250 Europa GT which had a shorter wheelbase – 2600 mm (8 ft 6 in) – but though both were powered by 3-litre units, the Europa used the Lampredi long-block design engine and the Europa GT the Colombo short-block type. Production of both continued until early 1956, at the latest, with a total number of both types around the mid-50 mark.

March 1956 brought the first appearance, at the Geneva show, of the 250 GT coupé and a subsequent production run of the type until 1960 with nearly 500 cars built. Two versions were on display, one designed and built by Pinin Farina and a cabriolet designed and built by Boano. Although it had been intended to market both, the Boano or 'low-roof' cabriolet had a small run of not more than 80 cars. Some of the coupés were designed by Ellena with a 'high roof' but the number produced was minimal. In 1958 Pinin Farina designed a new lighter-weight cabriolet for the American market, built by Scaglietti.

All the 250 GT cars had the 2953 cc V12 engine with a single overhead camshaft per bank of cylinders with bore and stroke of 73 × 58.8 mm, and the early cars had an output of 240 bhp at 7000 rpm and employed three Weber twin-choke carburettors. Some engines had two distributors, others a single unit, and as time progressed the drum brakes were replaced with discs.

Up to the end of 1959 Ferrari had given little thought to the family car, but in 1960 he decided to build the 250 GT 2+2 (or the 250 GTE as it is also called), the first of the cars being seen at the 1960 Le Mans 24-hour race where it was in use as the course car. True, the cars had two seats at the rear, but in practice they could not accommodate two adults. In fact, only young children could sit in any comfort there, for all that the extra space behind the two front seats did was to give a larger area for carrying more luggage for protracted holidays. There was an extended production run of the cars for some 900 were built, which proves that Ferrari knew his market.

LEFT *The 1956 Ferrari Superfast 410. After the Superamerica 410 had been introduced at the 1956 Brussels Motor Show, this car followed at that year's Paris Show where it was displayed on the Pinin Farina stand on a new shorter chassis. A 4962 cc V12 engine was fitted. The Superamerica family lasted until 1959. No two were alike and most were bodied by Pininfarina, although a few were the work of Ghia and Boano. Provided by Peter Agg/Trojan Ltd.*

The normal coupés were dropped from the Ferrari catalogue with the introduction of the 250 GT 2 + 2, but a new berlinetta took their place with a short wheelbase, steel body and more luxurious interior trim, giving greater comfort. The styling was a mixture of the SWB berlinettas and the GTOs and was named the 250 GT Lusso (Lusso meaning luxury) berlinetta or, for short, 250 GTL. The coachwork designed by Pininfarina and built by Scaglietti was aesthetically right with a beautiful line, and it might be said to be the first 'civilized' GT car from the factory, with an interior noise level that did not shatter the eardrums. It could be described as a classic design.

Apart from the closed GT cars, Ferrari also produced the 250 GT spider California in 1958, initially with the short-wheelbase chassis while later models had the longer 2600 mm (8 ft 6 in) chassis.

At the time of the introduction of the long-wheelbase California in Paris in 1961, Ferrari also had a new 2 + 2 on show, and on the Pininfarina stand a one-off Superfast II, an aerodynamic coupé built on the older 4.9-litre 410 Superamerica chassis exhibited at Brussels in 1956. It had a

small elliptical grille and the headlamps were retractable; this car was the prototype, if such it can be called, of the 400 Superamericas, which had a short life up to about 1964.

Towards the end of 1963 the factory produced the first version of the 330 GT 2+2, a car different in many of its concepts from the earlier GT models. Powered by a V12 4-litre unit based on the original Colombo design, it had an output of 300 bhp at 6600 rpm and used a chassis similar in layout to the 250 GT with coil springs and tubular shock absorbers at the front, solid rear axle with semi-elliptic springs and telescopic shock absorbers with concentric coil springs and equipped with four-wheel hydraulic disc brakes.

A replacement for the 410 Superamerica made its debut on the Pininfarina stand at the Geneva show in spring 1964; the car was obviously derived from the 410 SA but had a far neater, sleeker line. This was the 500 Superfast with a 4.9-litre V12 unit similar in a number of points to the 330 GT, but the cylinder had pressed-in liners and the head was detachable. There were three Weber 38 DCN carburettors and, with an 8.8:1 compression ratio, the engine developed 400 bhp at 6500 rpm. This was a luxury limousine which was faster than other vehicles in its class. Production was limited, the factory turning out one car per month.

Later in 1964 Ferrari brought out two new cars, the 275 GTB and 275 GT spider, on similar chassis, and for the first time a GT had independent rear suspension. Once again the original Colombo-designed V12 unit was in evidence and it displaced 3.3 litres (bore and stroke of 77 × 58.8 mm). The berlinetta's bhp was 280 at 7500 rpm, the spider's 260 at 7000 rpm, and both had an all-synchromesh five-speed gearbox mounted at the rear in transaxle form. A new rear suspension developed from racing experience with the 250 LM had parallel 'A' arms with coil springs and a concentric shock absorber, the lower arm being attached to the brake and hub assembly. In shape it owed its lines to the 1964 GTO and 250 LM with a long sloping bonnet,

and the headlamps were faired into the wings with plastic covers. A wraparound windscreen, set at a rakish angle, added to the aerodynamic shape and the small rear spoiler provided a touch that denoted its breeding. The usual Borrani wire wheels were discarded for handsome cast-alloy replacements. As an option the factory offered six twin-choke Weber carburettors and a 9.5:1 compression ratio, which increased the bhp to 300. The spider was a more 'refined' car, a luxury convertible.

Over the next year or so, various modifications were carried out, and in 1966 a new double-overhead-camshaft version of the 3.3-litre engine was installed in the berlinetta chassis and dry-sump lubrication adopted. At the same time the chassis was realigned to overcome problems that had arisen due to misalignment between the engine and transaxle.

The fabled Daytona

Ferrari was still determined to keep the luxury car image alive and introduced in spring 1965 the 4-litre 330 GTC, which was not only superior in finish to his other models but also offered greater interior space and a more powerful engine. In looks it possessed the front aspect of the 500 Superfast and the rear deck of the 330 GT, and earned the appellation of being the finest all-round roadgoing Ferrari ever built.

As was expected, in 1968 the United States' regulations on safety and exhaust-emission requirements caused the manufacturers of high-performance cars a number of problems, and especially in Europe where no such legislation was necessary. Maranello fell into line with the 365 GT 2+2, a luxury 4.4-litre car with a five-speed transmission in unit with the engine, and independent rear suspension. It was equipped with power steering and air conditioning as standard. Its coachwork followed that of the previous high-class cars turned out by the works, elegant without being in any way outstanding or exciting. It is almost certain that one of the 365 GT 2+2s sold

ABOVE *With the demise of the 365 GTC in 1970, Ferrari was in need of a two-seater luxury model. The result was the 365 GTC/4, introduced at the 1971 Geneva Show. Provided by Lincoln Small.*

LEFT *The 365 GTB/4, introduced in 1968, is a legendary model, also known as the Daytona. A convertible version of this Pininfarina coupé appeared in 1969, designated GTS, although this example has been subsequently converted to a spider. Provided by Peter Thorpe.*

LEFT *The Superamerica theme was perpetuated in the Ferrari 500 Superfast of 1964. The 4962 cc V12 engine was unique to the model. Only 36 had been built by the time that production was discontinued in 1966. Provided by Ken Bradshaw.*

RIGHT *What the other drivers usually saw: the rear view of a Daytona, with the superlative lines of the Pininfarina-styled body shown to great effect.*

on the American market was equipped by its buyer with automatic transmission, using the GM turbo hydraulic system, making it possibly the first Ferrari ever to be thus treated. It was not, however, until the 400 GT that a Ferrari left the factory gates with the choice of either automatic or manual transmission as standard equipment.

While the 365 GTB/4 was not a catalogue-listed type in 1967, development work for a series run was in progress and testing went ahead during the winter months. Even before it was marketed excitement was mounting regarding its specification and possible general appearance, for it was already being named the Daytona, a name that has stayed with the type ever since. Perhaps some of the many other types manufactured by the factory deserve greater recognition than they received, but the laudatory acclaim heaped on the Daytona was fully justified. There is no doubt that it was, and still is, the ultimate in gran turismo cars, even if the engine was front-mounted when current practice is to have a mid-engined car. It is a car with a

TIPO 246 FI
1958

ENGINE	CHASSIS
No. of cylinders 6	Frame Multi tubular space frame
Bore/stroke mm 85 × 71	Wheelbase mm 2160
Displacement cc 2417	Track – front mm 1240
Valve operation Twin overhead camshafts	Track – rear mm 1240
Compression ratio 9.8:1	Suspension – front Independent, unequal wishbone, coil springs, anti-roll bar
Induction Three Weber 42DCN twin-choke carburettors	Suspension – rear de Dion, transverse leaf spring, parallel radius arm
BHP 275 at 8300 rpm	Brakes Hydraulic, with cast-iron turbo-finned drums
Transmission Four-speed rear mounted	**PERFORMANCE**
	Maximum speed 273 km/h (170 mph)

LEFT *Mike Hawthorn at the wheel of a 246 F1, driving to fifth place in the Dutch Grand Prix at Zandvoort in 1958; the year in which he became World Champion.*

RIGHT *Phil Hill in a rear-engined 156 F1 Ferrari, at the 1961 Dutch Grand Prix. He was placed second, behind von Trips in a similar car who led the race from start to finish.*

will always be remembered as the fastest and probably the best GT car ever built.

By January 1969 the 330 GTC and GTS had been revitalized and, with a single-overhead-camshaft engine with a capacity of 4390 cc, were renamed the 365 GTC and GTS. However, they were phased out at the end of 1970. The following spring, at the Geneva show, Ferrari had on its stand the 365 GTC/4 with a four-overhead-camshaft engine and a new setting for the six Weber 38 DCOE sidedraft carburettors outside the engine 'V'. Although the bonnet line was low, the front end was squared off and the four headlamps were of the 'pop-up' type. The line from the base of the windscreen to the tail was still flowing but cut off more sharply giving the rear end a sawn-off appearance. This virtually ended the long and exciting run of the V12, except for the current 412 GT front-engined limousine.

Rear-engined racers

For Ferrari, 1960 was a year of transition as he had now taken up the idea of rear-mounted engines and both these and front-engined Dinos were entered in races. The rear-engined cars used both 2.5- and 1.5-litre units: the regulations were to change for 1961, allowing a maximum displacement of 1500 cc which was to remain in force until the end of 1965.

The first prototype rear-engined car was seen at Monaco in 1960, a 2.4-litre V6 using many of the 246 F1 parts and going under the same name. However, the dry multi-plate clutch was mounted at the rear of the five-speed gearbox, this being placed behind the engine and in unit with the final drive, and the brakes were mounted inboard. It was not a success and retired with final-drive trouble.

During July 1960 a much-revised 1957 1.5-litre V6 Dino 156 F2 appeared at the Solitude Ring in West Germany. The engine was rear-mounted with a bore and stroke of 73 × 59.1 mm and an output of 180 bhp. The car not only set a new lap record but won by a small margin of three seconds from a Porsche.

Ferrari was ready for the new formula in 1961 with two versions of the V6 Dino: the 65-degree unit and a redesigned 120-degree 156 F1 engine and new chassis. With the bore remaining at 73 mm the stroke was shortened to 58.8 mm giving a displacement of 1476.6 cc. Fuel was fed via two Weber 40 1F3C three-choke carburettors and output was 190 bhp at 9500 rpm. Both the 65- and 120-degree-engined cars had revised front ends with two intake nostrils.

The season of 1961 was a highly successful one for Ferrari, with Phil Hill winning the world driver's championship and the works taking the manufacturers' title. Hill, driving the 156 F1, won the Belgian and Italian Grands Prix and was runner-up in the British.

Little was accomplished over the winter months since a wholesale walkout by the key staff took place and the racing department had to be built up anew. The cars of 1962 lost the familiar twin-nostril front but this omission was virtually the only feature to differentiate the cars of 1962 from the winners of the previous year. However, they were also slower and their handling left much to be desired: all in all a miserable year.

charisma, bearing the hallmark of a man who has never accepted second best, and it stands as a monument to a living legend in the automobile world.

The V12 was a 4.4-litre engine with four overhead camshafts and produced 352 bhp at 7500 rpm. Six 40 DCN 20 Weber carburettors fed the fuel, the compression ratio was 9.3:1, and with a 3.3:1 final drive the maximum speed was 280 km/h (174 mph). Styling was superb and the design team at Pininfarina had without doubt produced a masterpiece. The low bonnet line had a full-width plastic cover with the lamps set behind, including the indicators, which gave a smooth line from the 'sharp end' to the door panels and pillars, and this line was continued through the rake of the windscreen. The bodies were made by Scaglietti who, for once, did not deviate from the original drawings.

In the autumn of 1969 a spider version was seen at the Frankfurt show, but in the main these cars were built to customer order. Of late a number of Daytona owners have taken their cars to professional coachbuilders to have them converted to the spider design.

Although the Daytona was not built as a competition car, a number of owners and racing équipes have had their cars reworked by the factory so that they could be used in long-distance races such as the Daytona and Le Mans events. Some successes have been achieved with these machines, but the type

New cars, a reorganized racing set-up and a new number one works driver – John Surtees – heralded 1963. The Dino 156 F1 still used the tubular spaceframe but the suspension was altered with the coil springs and shock absorbers mounted lower and at a greater angle. At the rear the 'A' arms were reversed and lowered with single upper links and longer radius rods. The 1.5-litre engine was now Bosch fuel-injected and produced 200 bhp at 10,200 rpm. The car showed some form in the early events of the season and won at the Nürburgring.

For the Monza race it had been hoped to use the new Aero V8 car but, as the engine was not ready, the Dino 156 F1 unit was installed. Unfortunately, Surtees had to retire with a broken valve and damaged piston.

The Aero V8 (with chassis based on an aircraft design) was soon on the scene. Ferrari had his first monocoque chassis tested at the Modena circuit in the summer of 1963. It housed a rear-mounted 90-degree V8 unit that was designed to be a part of the chassis. With a bore and stroke of 64×57.8 mm it displaced 1487.5 cc and the output was 205 bhp at 10,500 rpm; fuel injection was used. A great deal of attention was paid to the streamlining at the front, and to this end the springs were set inboard and the steering linkage lined up with the upper wishbones. The aluminium seat was part of the fuel tank, with the remainder of the fuel housed in side tanks ahead of the driver. This Aero chassis was used with the V6 engine during 1963 while the V8, designated 158 F1, was being further developed for the following year. For 1964 the bore was enlarged to 67 mm and the stroke reduced to 52.8 mm. Four coils in the 'V' fed twin ignition, and the injection pump was belt driven.

The works took the manufacturers' title in 1964 using the new chassis with both V6 and V8 engines, and John Surtees the drivers' world championship: Surtees' second place in the Mexican GP secured the title by a single point, with Graham Hill finishing second in the race for the title.

In 1964 the first of the 180-degree flat-12 cars appeared, the 512 F1 with a displacement of 1489.6 cc (bore and stroke 56×50.4 mm) and Lucas fuel injection. Four coils and distributors sparked a single plug per cylinder (the 1965 car had two plugs per cylinder) and the output was 220 bhp at 11,500 rpm (increased by 5 bhp for the 1965 car). The engine used the 158 F1 monocoque chassis and similar suspension, and although driven by Bandini in practice for the Italian GP at Monza it was not considered fully tested and so did not race. Its racing début came at the United States GP at Watkins Glen in the same year, driven by Bandini, but it was retired. The Ferrari team at Watkins Glen and also at Mexico City for the Mexican GP, ran under the North American Racing Team banner as Enzo was, at the time, in dispute with the Italian racing authorities. Also he not only had the 512 F1 but also other team cars (John Surtees' 158 F1 and, in addition, the 156 F1 for Pedro Rodriguez at Mexico City) repainted in the United States international racing colours of blue and white.

Although the 512 F1 was reliable and finished in most races it contested, it could not be said to have distinguished itself during the two seasons of its career.

The Fédération Internationale de l'Automobile (FIA) introduced the 3-litre unsupercharged and 1.5-litre supercharged capacities for Formula 1 from 1966. Few constructors had a machine ready but Ferrari managed to field one car for Surtees for the first European event at Syracuse which he won from Bandini using a Dino V6.

Ferrari reverted to the well-tried 60-degree V12 unit, but mounted at the rear for the new formula, and left the design to Ing. Franco Rocchi. The main features were Lucas high-pressure fuel injection between the cylinder banks, two spark-plugs per cylinder ignited by four coils and twin distributors, and two valves per cylinder. The chassis was still monocoque with the body/chassis of riveted aluminium sheets formed round steel tubes, and the engine was used as part of the rear

chassis member. The fuel tanks were made of rubber and were located on either side of the cockpit.

During the years 1966 to 1969, as development of the unit progressed, a number of modifications were carried out. The 24-valve engine by the end of 1966 had 36 valves (2 intake/1 exhaust) and from late 1967 until the end of the series (designated 312 F1) 48 valves (2 intake/2 exhaust). Other changes concerned sizes of wheels, and the Dunlop tyres were replaced by Firestones from 1967. From an initial bhp of 360 at 10,000 rpm, the final unit produced 436 bhp at 11,000 rpm. The wing or rear aerofoil pioneered by Richie Ginther in 1961, which improved the stability of the 246 SP, was used on the early 1968 car mounted on struts; this innovation in a variety of forms has been part of all today's racing cars.

The 312 F1 had a far from outstanding race history. During the first two years it proved reasonably reliable, but during 1968 and 1969 there were too many retirements (although for trivial reasons). It appeared that the day of the V12 as a competitive racing unit was nearly over, and that both Chris Amon and Jacky Ickx, as drivers were unfortunate in being 'in' at the tail end, although Amon came close to winning at least three GPs.

Not one to be discouraged when fortunes were at a low ebb, Ferrari started on a comeback in 1970 with the boxer flat-12, which owed much to the knowledge gained from the 512 F1 and the 212 E sports car, campaigned by Peter Schetty in 1969, which had wiped the board clean in the European Hill Climb Championship. The start to the season was encouraging but no more, although fortunes picked up with the German GP at Hockenheim where Ickx was placed second. From the last five Grands Prix of the season the 312B F1 gained four firsts, and on three occasions a one/two with Swiss driver Regazzoni following the team leader home.

There was early encouragement in 1971 up to the time of the Dutch GP, with five first places including the Brands Hatch Race of Champions. However, the remainder of the season brought too many retirements, caused on some occasions by engine failure. Both the 312 B and B2 cars were used and it was the latter that was producing the major problems. The following year only the B2 was raced and once more it was an 'also-ran', even though many of the problems of the previous season had been ironed out and it did prove reasonably reliable, retiring less frequently. The 1973 season was the same mixture as before: the B3 car, driven by Ickx, appeared at the Spanish GP at Montjuich Park, Barcelona, on 29 April but it finished in only 12th place, and it failed to provide Maranello with any successes thereafter.

By late 1974 the new T series boxer (T standing for *transversale*, describing the transverse gearbox) was shown to the press and in its first season (1975) lived up to expectations by giving Niki Lauda the drivers' world championship and Ferrari the manufacturers' award.

In 1976 Lauda continued his successful run, winning the Brazilian, South African, Belgian and Monaco Grands Prix. However, at the German GP at the Nürburgring he was very seriously injured in a horrific accident, and it was only his remarkable will to live that pulled him through. Amazingly, he was back behind the wheel for the last three Grands Prix of the season, gaining valuable points in each, and ensuring that Ferrari won the manufacturers' award.

Driving the 312 T2, Lauda was back in action in 1977 and, although he won only three Grands Prix (the South African, German and Dutch), he had been placed so many times during the season that he secured the drivers' championship, Ferrari also taking the manufacturers' title again.

ABOVE *The 312 B was the first Ferrari Grand Prix car to be fitted with a flat-four, or 'Boxer', engine.*

LEFT *John Surtees at the wheel of the 158 F1 behind Bandini's 512 F1 flat-12 in the 1965 Monaco Grand Prix. Sadly, Surtees ran out of fuel on the penultimate lap and was placed fourth.*

RIGHT *Niki Lauda in a 312 T2 Ferrari during the 1977 Dutch Grand Prix at Zandvoort which he won at 186.88 km/h (116.12 mph).*

OVERLEAF *Gilles Villeneuve at the 1979 Monaco Grand Prix in a 312 T4. He retired on lap 54 with a broken driveshaft.*

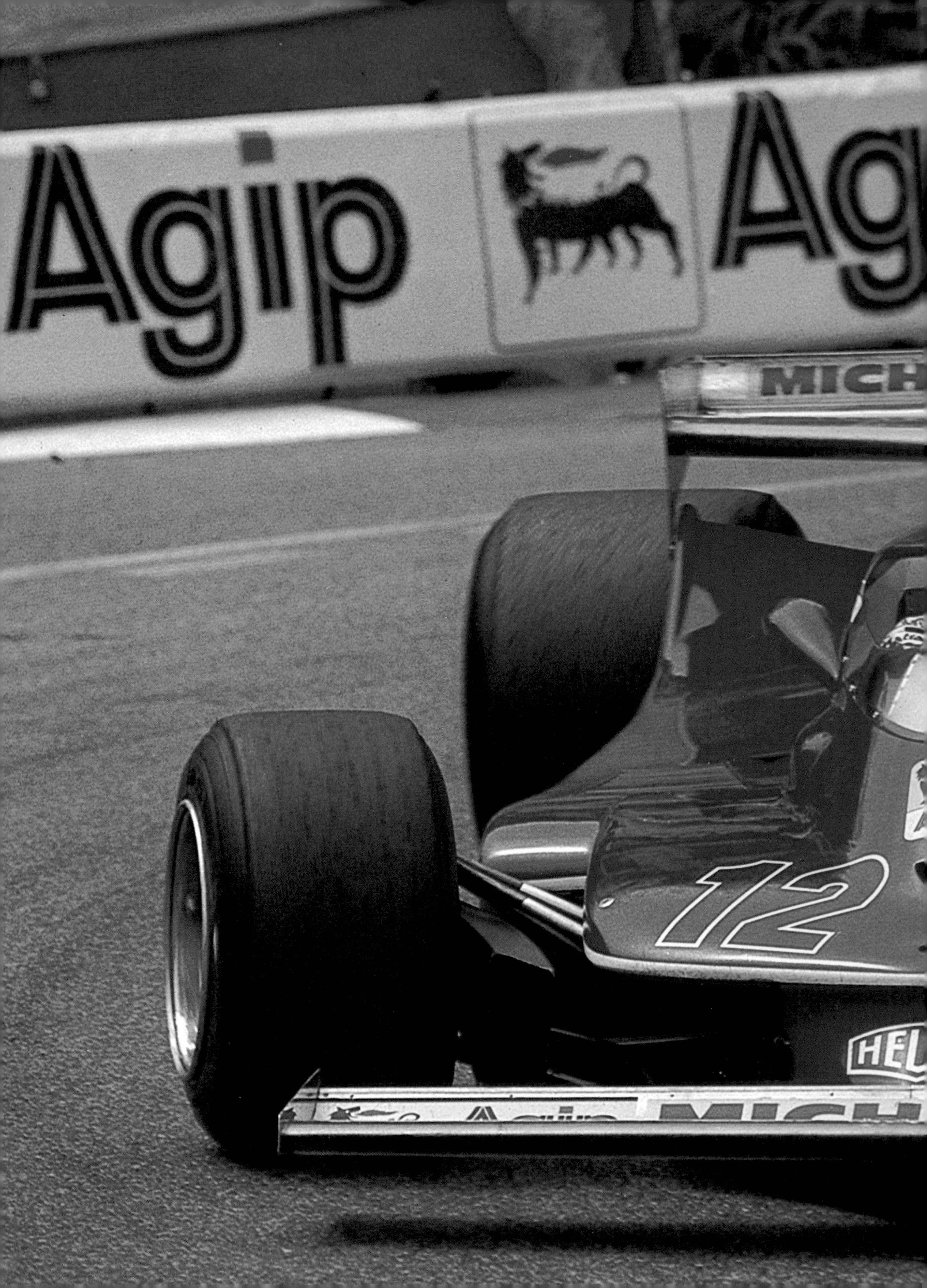
Agip
12

The 312 Ts ended in their fifth series (T5) still proving not only reliable but extremely fast, picking up their fair share of the Grand Prix spoils in the hands of the South African Jody Scheckter and the French-Canadian Gilles Villeneuve, with Scheckter securing the 1979 drivers' title at Monza. For 1980 minor modifications were made with a redesigned head to enhance airflow and ground effects, revised front and rear suspensions and brakes, with improved aerodynamics.

The 3-litre boxer-12s were replaced in 1981 by a 1500 cc V6 turbo; Renault having turned Formula 1 on its head in 1977 by introducing a 1½-litre turbocharged car, thus exploiting a hitherto ignored formula provision. The new unit was a 120-degree V6 of 1496 cc (bore and stroke 81×48.4 mm) producing 565 bhp at 11,000 rpm. The fuel system was Lucas injection and the turbo was a 2KKK. Despite its poor handling characteristics, Villeneuve managed to win that year's Monaco and Spanish GPs. A revised chassis designed by Dr Harvey Postlethwaite for the 1982 126 C2 car had improved handling as well as a weight reduction of around 60 kg (132 lb). Further modifications carried out during the winter of 1982 produced the 126 C2/B early in 1983, with the 126 C3 appearing later at the British GP and for the remainder of the season. The works took the manufacturers' title once more.

Nineteen eighty-four proved unspectacular as the cars were, in essence, no more than revised versions of the 1983 winners. Despite this, Ferrari was placed second to McLaren in the manufacturers' championship. It was much the same story in 1985, although Alboreto was pipped to the drivers' championship post by Prost of McLaren. By then the V6 of 1980/1 was running on borrowed time, a projected slant-four replacement being sidelined. For the 1986 1200 cc supercharged formula, Ferrari fielded a V6 engine again, but this has struggled to find its form.

Enter the Dino

From around the mid-1960s Ferrari's financial position gradually deteriorated as the cost and sophistication of Formula 1 cars soared, while the all-important American market demanded expensive safety regulations on road cars from 1968 onwards. But the requirements of homologation resulted in the arrival of a small Ferrari, the mid-engined V6 Dino, in 1967. This timely offering provided a welcome alternative to the thirsty V12 road cars and lasted until 1974, when the effects of the oil crisis were beginning to be felt in Italy. However, Ferrari was able to weather the worst effects of the depression as, in 1969, the Fiat empire took a 50 per cent interest in the firm.

At the Paris Salon in October 1965 Pininfarina had exhibited a road version of the Dino 206S with rear engine, designated 206 GT. Its lineage came down through the Dino 246 (1961 Grand Prix car) and the Dino 166P. The latter had a north/south engine but, when the 206 Dino appeared in 1967, it had a transversely mounted 1987 cc V6 one. It had been built for Ferrari by Fiat because, from 1967, Formula 2 participation demanded the use of a mass-produced engine – if 500 units a year could be so judged! Consequently there was a conventionally engined Fiat Dino of 1966–72 which shared the same V6 engine. On the Ferrari Dino the bodywork styling was highly

pleasing, with flowing aerodynamic lines from front to tail and the engine air scoops recessed from the doors to the front part of the rear mudguards.

The Dino 246 GT followed in the spring of 1969 and was first shown at Geneva where it made an immediate impact on the press and public. With a transverse mid-engine enlarged to 2418 cc (bore and stroke 92.5 × 60 mm) the 246 GT had a power output of 195 bhp at 7600 rpm. It had twin overhead camshafts per bank of cylinders and a five-speed all-synchromesh-and-reverse gearbox. After the model ceased production in 1974 this unit continued to power the in-house Lancia Stratos which has proved so enormously successful in rallying.

The coachwork was sleek and very smooth and followed the lines of the handsome 206 GT; by 1972 a spider version was on the market (in effect only the roof panel was removable). Both cars were built by Scaglietti. The 246 GT was marketed in direct competition with the Porsche 911 S and its derivatives although, perhaps, its performance – a top speed of 235 km/h

LEFT AND BELOW Ferrari's Dino, though it was never badged as a Ferrari, appeared in 1967 and, in its original 206 GT form with a 1987 cc V6 engine, lasted until 1969. It was replaced that year by the 246 GT with an enlarged 2418 cc engine. Right-hand drive became available with this model which was 76 mm (3 in) taller than the 206. The spider version, as shown below, carried the GTS designation and was introduced at the 1972 Geneva Motor Show. The opened and closed versions both lasted until 1974. Provided by John Swift.

(146 mph) – did not quite match that of the quickest versions of the German car. Nonetheless the Dino caught the imagination of the young executive and other potential buyers who had always hankered after a Ferrari (even though the Dino was never badged as such).

To replace the Dino 246, Ferrari unveiled his next production, the Dino 308 GT4 2+2, at the 1973 Paris show. Although the styling was pleasant, the original production models did not have quite the same aesthetic appeal as their predecessor. This could be accounted for by the fact that Ferrari had the coachwork styled by Bertone, a company not noted for giving a

'roundness' to its designs although, when not attempting a compromise design, it does produce some 'no-nonsense' and pleasing styles. With the 308 GT Bertone did have the added problem of designing a 2+2 car, since this seating arrangement does not allow for a flowing line at the rear, especially when the engine is rear-mounted.

The chassis and suspension followed the well-tried pattern of the 246, which had given outstanding handling characteristics, and the only change was to increase the track to give a greater body width. Fore and aft suspension consisted of upper and lower wishbones, coil springing, telescopic dampers and anti-

RIGHT *The 308 GTB continued the mid-engined theme of the Dinos but was a larger car with a 2927 cc V8 engine. Built by Scaglietti, it appeared at the 1975 Paris Motor Show and styling was once again the work of Pininfarina. It was unusual in that it was built mostly of glass fibre, although later models were all-metal. The car was still available in 328 form in 1986.*

roll bars. The 90-degree 2927 cc V8 engine was set transversely behind the centre line and had twin overhead camshafts per bank of cylinders. To keep a low profile at the rear the five-speed all-synchromesh-and-reverse gearbox was placed at the rear of the engine and not beneath it. A helical spur-type final drive with limited-slip differential drove the rear wheels through solid shafts.

Since the early days the line of the 308 GT has been improved and now looks like the thoroughbred it is, with a maximum and genuine top speed of 246 km/h (154 mph). It is a high-performance car with superb all-round visibility. In 1976, the

RIGHT *Ferrari made a bid for the executive market in 1972 with the 365 GT4 2+2 fitted with a 4.4-litre front-mounted V12 engine. The model was modified in 1976 to produce the 400 GT, with enlarged 4823 cc engine. Although the five-speed manual gearbox was retained, a General Motors Turbo 400 three-speed automatic gearbox version, shown here, was also on offer. The car remains in production as the 412.*

LEFT *In 1976, the 512 BB replaced the 365 GT/BB, which it closely resembled. It carried over the 12-cylinder boxer engine, although the capacity was increased from 4390 to 4942 cc. Production continued until 1985. Provided by L. Page.*

number of manufacturers, although few of the cars could carry a prestige label. Ferrari reverted, once more, to the familiar V12 front-engined car that had served the factory so well over many years. Labelled the 400 GT, it may be bought with either automatic or manual transmission. The manual operation is through a five-speed synchromesh-and-reverse gearbox. The model is a full four-seater luxury car with power-assisted steering and air conditioning as standard equipment. The coachwork, styled by Pininfarina and also built by the firm, is pleasant to look at but has nothing outstanding that would make a passer-by stand and stare. It follows in the footsteps of the 365

Dino 308 GT4 changed its image: it was officially designated a Ferrari and given the famous prancing horse as its badge. The Mondial 8 replaced the 308 GT4 in 1981.

If the 308 GT4 2+2 lacked aesthetic appeal, the next offering from the factory was awaited with impatience, for the rumours and some sneak preview pictures suggested a very exciting car. As so often with new models from Maranello, the 308 GTB, as it was called, made its appearance at the Paris show, in 1975. Unlike all previous cars of the marque, it had a glass fibre body. Ferrari had, very wisely, gone back to the artistry of Pininfarina to design the body line. Pininfarina made a superb job of it, combining the best from the 246 GT and the 365 berlinetta boxer to create something new that would be very difficult for other coachwork designers to emulate. Scaglietti built the bodies and it was extremely difficult to tell whether steel or some other material had been used, so superb was the finish, although metal was re-introduced from 1977.

Ferrari — or should it be Fiat? — was quite late in entering the quality-limousine market, for it was not until the Paris show in 1976 that his first such offering was on view. There can be little doubt that the factory had been missing out on a growing trend — a top car for the top executive — and this was being met by a

GT4 2+2, which was marketed between 1972 and 1976.

The V12 unit has a bore and stroke of 81 × 78 mm giving a capacity of 4823 cc and a robust power output of 340 bhp at 6500 rpm. There are twin overhead camshafts per bank of cylinders and the electrics are fired by twin distributors. Originally six twin-choke sidedraft 38 DCOE 59/60 Weber carburettors fed the fuel, but recently fuel injection was substituted. Suspension is fully independent fore and aft.

At the same Paris show in 1976 where the 400 GT was on display, Ferrari introduced the second version of his berlinetta boxer, the 512 BB, as he phased out the earlier model which had been in production for three years. The newer type retained the horizontally opposed (boxer) 12-cylinder rear-mounted engine, but the capacity had been increased by 552 cc to 4942 cc by lengthening the stroke from 71 to 78 mm and increasing the bore from 81 to 82 mm. The usual twin overhead camshafts per bank of cylinders were in evidence and electronic ignition and a single distributor fired the plugs. The lubrication was dry sump and the fuel was at first fed via four triple-choke downdraft Weber 40 1F3C carburettors, but fuel injection was used later. Suspension was independent all round and the gearbox had five forward gears and a reverse.

The styling was quite similar to that of the 308 GTB, with sleek flowing lines, a spoiler at the sharp end, and again the hint of an uplift at the tail. The body in fact differed only in some detail from the earlier model. From whichever angle it was viewed it exuded a brutish and extremely powerful presence, but for all that had an elegance befitting a Pininfarina creation.

The Mondial 8, marketed in 1981, was the replacement for the 308 GT4 and, like its predecessor, was a 2+2, but with a more comfortable interior for four people. Its basics were similar to the 308 series, but with modifications including Marelli Digiplex ignition and Bosch K-Jetronic injection. For 1983 further modifications were carried out; the chassis was lengthened, the body widened and the height increased to give even more room. Performance was enhanced using four instead of two valves per cylinder and the figure 8 was dropped from the name. By 1983 all Ferraris were fitted with fuel injection denoted, where appropriate, with an 'i' suffix.

At the 1984 Geneva Show Ferrari revived one of its most illustrious model names of the 1960s: that of the GTO. Intended for Group B racing, it was powered by a 2885 cc V8 engine, with two IHI turbochargers and heat-exchangers, developing no less than 400 bhp and mounted longitudinally at the rear. The all independent suspension followed the usual coil spring and wishbone practice. This most exclusive of Ferrari models closely resembled that of the 308, apart from its larger air dam and rear spoiler though, in the interests of weight saving, the

ABOVE *The Mondial, which revived a 1950s' model name, appeared in 1980 and was a 2927 cc mid-engined V8. The current version has a 3185 cc V8 and is called the Mondial 3.2.*

LEFT *Enzo Ferrari (born 1898), wearing his customary dark glasses.*

RIGHT AND OVERLEAF *The works flagship is the Testarossa, the Pininfarina styling dramatically highlighting the mid-engined location. Provided by Maranello Concessionaires.*

Pininfarina bodywork was made of a plastic material. Top speed was an eyebrow-raising 305 km/h (189 mph). Over 200 – the number required for homologation purposes – were built, but GTO production ceased in 1985.

The 1984 V8 models, which had been developed from the 1980 Mondial 8 and also the 1975–7 308 GTB/GTS (all mid-engined cars), were fuel-injected and had four instead of two valves per cylinder. Other modifications to the power unit have led to an increase in performance.

Ferrari

The 400 underwent cosmetic changes in 1984 and the following year it was designated the 412 as engine capacity was upped from 4823 to 4942 cc and output to 340 bhp, an eight per cent increase in power. The works flagship, the 512 BBi, was replaced in 1985 by the Testarossa, perpetuating its flat-12 4942 cc engine and reviving a legendary Ferrari model name. Like its distinguished predecessor, it comes complete with red cam boxes. The striking bodywork, developed in Pininfarina's wind tunnel, promises stability up to 289 km/h (180 mph)

without extra aerodynamic aids. For 1986 the capacity of the V8 engine was increased from 2927 cc to 3185 cc. This means that the mid-engined V8 models – the 308 and Mondial – become the 328 and Mondial 3.2 respectively. Both models are also available in open form.

Throughout, Ferrari's record has been one of the most outstanding in the history of car production and, today, it continues to produce the world's most sensational road cars – cars that still look, and sound, totally unique.

TESTAROSSA 1985 TO DATE	
ENGINE	
No. of cylinders Flat-12	
Bore/stroke mm 82 × 78	
Displacement cc 4942	
Valve operation Twin overhead camshafts per cylinder bank operating four valves per cylinder	
Compression ratio 9.2:1	
Induction Bosch K-Jetronic	
BHP 390 at 6300 rpm	
Transmission Five-speed	
CHASSIS	
Frame Steel tubular	
Wheelbase mm 2450	
Track – front mm 1560	
Track – rear mm 1560	
Suspension – front Independent, wishbone, coil springs, anti-roll bar	
Suspension – rear Independent, wishbones, coil springs, anti-roll bar	
PERFORMANCE	
Maximum speed 290 km/h (180 mph)	

FIAT

Fiat *is* the Italian motor industry. Nowhere in the western world does one car company dominate its home market in the way that the Colossus of Turin does. However, Fiat does not just make cars. It manufactures trains, tractors and jet engines, is Italy's largest company and, as such, is a front-line European one. In 1985, Fiat's Uno became the continent's best-selling small car and profits are running at record levels.

Ever since its creation in 1899, Fiat has had a unique profile: its founding fathers were drawn from the Turin aristocracy and upper classes of liberal and socialist persuasions, and were dominated by the towering personality of Giovanni Agnelli, a former cavalry officer, who had a strong engineering bent.

The motor car was born in Germany in 1886 and was quickly taken up by the French. But Italy, like Britain, was rather slow in adopting the horseless carriage. The origins of Fiat, and of the Italian motor industry, are to be found far in the north of Italy in the city of Turin, capital of the province of Piedmont, and are rooted in the emergent bicycle industry.

It was in the 1890s that Giovanni Battista Ceirano established a small two-room workshop on the ground floor of a house at 9 Corso Vittorio Emanuele II, which was where the well-to-do Lancia family from Fobello spent their winters. Ceirano was one of four brothers. Their father was a watchmaker from Cuneo, and Giovanni initially sold imported Rudge bicycles from Britain. Later, becoming more adventurous, he started to produce his own machines, marketed under the Welleyes name – supposed to have English connotations . . .

Then, in 1898, Giovanni was joined by 'short, thin, black-bearded' Aristide Faccioli, a qualified engineer from Bologna. The newcomer had gained an engineering degree from the Turin Polytechnic, had patented a double-acting gas engine in 1883, and had made improvements to a four-stroke unit two

LEFT *The 1970 Fiat Dino spider with Pininfarina body which shared its 2.4-litre four-camshaft V6 engine with the Ferrari of the same name. Provided by Michael Morris.*

years later. He was thus well qualified to design Ceirano's Welleyes car, for that was Giovanni's objective. But first the business had to be placed on a firmer financial footing. So, on 23 October 1898, the bicycle and motor car manufacturing company – grandly titled *Ceirano & Cie, Società per la Costruzione di Campioni per la Fabbricazione di Vetture Automobili* – was registered.

At least two of Ceirano's small band of workers were delighted by this development. One was 17-year-old Vincenzo Lancia, who had joined the firm that year and whose family owned the house in which the business was located. Although he was listed as 'bookkeeper', his great preoccupation was the motor car. The other, Felice Nazzaro, was the same age as Lancia and had joined Ceirano two years previously, in 1896. The son of a coal merchant, who had come to Turin from his native village of Monteu da Po, Nazzaro had first worked for his father before joining the bicycle maker.

Although the capital required to incorporate the business – such as it was – was a mere 6000 lire (£238), Ceirano, who was encouraged in this flotation by a lawyer, Cesare Goria-Gatti, needed further financial support. This duo were joined by three further directors, of which the most significant was a 29-year-old ex-cavalry officer, Count Emanuele Cacherano di Bricherasio, a member of one of Turin's oldest and most distinguished families. He was described as 'a tall, slender figure . . . His small head on broad shoulders . . . the large aquiline nose, his fair "Kaiser-style" moustache, his natural eloquence and . . . calm speech set him apart.' But di Bricherasio was no self-seeking aristocrat. He was a passionately committed socialist and always kept an annotated copy of Karl Marx' treatise open on his desk. The Count's vision was of a large car factory, giving employment to thousands and exporting its products all over the world.

With financial backing assured, Faccioli was able to proceed with Ceirano's Welleyes car. The eventual design was built at the Turin workshops of the Martina brothers in the Via Vanchiglia. It emerged in 1899 as a 3½hp four-wheeler with a two-cylinder rear-mounted water-cooled engine and final drive, by belts, in the Benz manner. The little car successfully competed in the Turin–Pinerolo–Avigliano–Turin road race of April 1899 when it averaged a little under 32 km/h (20 mph) with Goria-Gatti at the wheel. But, as will be obvious, Ceirano's business was drastically under-capitalized, although it was soon to be transformed in a way which he could never have imagined.

Count di Bricherasio, having delighted in helping to make one of Turin's first cars a reality, was pursuing his ambition of creating a massive car factory, and he had succeeded in interesting Gustave Deslex, a Turin-based Swiss banker, in undertaking the specialist task of raising the capital.

It was in February 1899 that news of these plans reached the ears of another former cavalry officer: 32-year-old Giovanni Agnelli had aleady been thinking along similar lines, and was soon to emerge as the driving force of the Fiat company.

Enter Agnelli

Giovanni Agnelli was born on 13 August 1866, the son of Edoardo and Aniceta Frisetti Agnelli, whose family estate was at Villar Perosa, near Pinerolo, some 35 km (22 miles) south-west of Turin. After receiving a 'military education', he entered the military academy in Modena in 1884 and passed out with a commission two years later. He subsequently attended the

Cavalry School in his home town of Pinerolo and joined the Savoia cavalry regiment as a lieutenant.

By 1892, when he was 26, and stationed in Verona, he and his fellow officer and friend, Count Giulio Figarolo of Gropello, were already fascinated by motor cars, which had been in existence for just six years. They obtained articles on the subject from a certain Professor Enrico Bernardi who had established a workshop in Padua where he was to design, in 1896, the first all-Italian car. Fired by their new-found knowledge, the enterprising pair decided to generate their own electric light and obtained an old Daimler oil engine for the purpose. Unfortunately it exploded at a crucial moment, much to the dismay of all concerned! A few months after this incident, Agnelli decided to resign his commission, leave the army and return to the family estate at Villar Perosa. He had already, in 1889, married Clara Boselli, and they were to have two children; a daughter Tina and a son, named Edoardo after Giovanni's father.

For a time Giovanni remained on the family estate but he soon became frustrated with this rural existence and, in 1898, moved to Turin. There he obtained an apartment in the Corso Valentino, just across the road from the workshop of Luigi

LEFT *Giovanni Agnelli (1866–1945). He began as secretary of Fiat and was its driving force almost from the outset, running the firm until his death in 1945.*

RIGHT *Pope Pius XI inspecting the 3.7-litre side-valve six-cylinder engine of a specially equipped Fiat 525, presented to him by Fiat in 1929. Senator Giovanni Agnelli is at hand to answer any technical queries.*

Storeo, who that year had begun selling motorized tricycles. Giovanni bought one of Storeo's machines and was soon familiarizing himself with its mechanism. Agnelli even toyed with the idea of going into partnership with him and they travelled to Paris together to visit Giuseppe Prunello, who hailed from Pinerolo and was soon to market the Prunel, a de Dion-engined tricycle, in the French capital. Although these three-wheelers were eventually imported into Italy under the Phoenix name, by that time Agnelli's attention was already elsewhere.

Soon after he moved to Turin, Agnelli gravitated to the Cafe Burello, down the road from Giovanni Ceirano's bicycle business in the Corso Vittorio Emanuele II and on the corner of the Via Urbano Rattazzi. The café was a 'yellow two-storeyed house, none too clean and badly in need of decoration' and was known locally as 'La Pantalera', a dialect name for the canopy which faced the Corso to protect its customers from the summer sun and winter snows.

This unlikely setting saw two distinct groups of patrons. First there were travellers arriving and departing from Turin's Porta Nuova railway station, and then there were members of the city's aristocracy and the higher echelons of society who met to talk of horses, carriages and motor cars.

Agnelli soon asserted himself among his contemporaries at 'La Pantalera'. 'We were all young and enthusiastic, and obsessed by motor cars. Instinctively we felt that Giovanni Agnelli was our leader. He made us turn up to all his discussions, in which he gave a clear indication of the future he envisaged, and of his great ability'. The author of these words is Count Carlo Biscaretti di Ruffia, who was present for these historic gatherings and whose father, Count Roberto Biscaretti di Ruffia, was one of the original directors of the Fiat company.

Talk and argument

Another member of the Agnelli coterie was Michele Lanza, then 31, manager of a candle factory, who had designed a number of experimental cars, built, it should be noted, by the versatile Martina brothers. But he soon clashed with Agnelli. Lanza was all for proceeding cautiously, buildings cars on a progressive basis, while Agnelli was in favour of mass-producing one model and then improving on it. After this heated discussion, which ended in Giovanni stating: 'Thank God you make candles in your factory; you'd go bankrupt if you manufactured only motor cars', di Ruffia asked his friend to expound the problems involved in creating a large car factory.

Walking along the Corso under the flowering plane trees, Agnelli began to think aloud about the problems involved in such a venture. 'Whoever wants to produce motor cars today must solve the very serious problem of specialized labour', he opined. At the time there had been serious industrial disquiet in Milan about which Giovanni commented: 'I will tell you frankly that, always deprecating excesses, I am all for the workers and their claims. Industrialism has created a new exploited class . . . When I was an officer engaged in preserving law and order, during riots of workers my uniform was the object of more insults than I care to remember. Yet I am convinced that in a few years time all these demands, apparently so dangerous to society, will be obtained by peaceful means.'

Obviously Agnelli had a clear idea of the sort of business he wanted to be involved in and placed great stress on the all-important labour question. Consequently, when he heard, in February 1899, of Count di Bricherasio's plans for the creation of a large car factory in Turin, Giovanni immediately became involved in the project.

By April, sufficient progress had been made for there to be a meeting of interested parties, and this was held in the house of

Enrico Marchesi in Via Passalacqua. There it was decided to call the car company, which would require a capital of 800,000 lire (£31,460), by the somewhat cumbersome title of *La Società Italiana per la Costruzione e il Commercio dello Automobili Torino* (Italian Company for the Manufacture and Sale of Motor Cars).

Fortunately, by the time that the firm's founders gathered in Count di Bricherasio's sumptuous palace on the Via Lagrange on 1 July 1899, there had been a change of heart and the firm's name was altered to the less elaborate *Fabbrica Italiana Automobili Torino*, which could be conveniently shortened to the more memorable F.I.A.T. acronym. The name was not officially registered until 10 days later, on 11 July, although curiously the document omits *Torino* from the title! The chairman was Ludovico Scarfiotti, while di Bricherasio was vice-chairman and Giovanni Agnelli held the important post of company secretary. Di Ruffia headed a six-man board of directors, while Enrico Marchesi, a qualified engineer who had hosted the April meeting, was managing director.

It had already been decided that, rather than design the first F.I.A.T. car from scratch, the new company would purchase the patents of Giovanni Ceirano's Welleyes car and the services of his engineer Aristide Faccioli, who became the firm's technical director. In addition, Felice Nazzaro and Vincenzo Lancia would join the company: they were both to carve international reputations for themselves racing F.I.A.T. cars – Lancia, of course, would also go on to found his own car company. The 30,000 lire (£1190) which Ceirano received helped him to establish a firm to manufacture automobiles under his own name. He was assisted in this by his brother who was also, confusingly, named Giovanni!

There was a feeling that it would not be long before French imports would come flooding over the Alps, so speed was of the essence in establishing the F.I.A.T. factory. The firm wanted to build it in the Viale Stupinigi on land owned by Count Bricherasio. Unfortunately, the municipal authorities would not countenance such a choice so instead the firm bought a 12,000 sq m (129,000 sq ft) site in the Corso Dante from Count Peracca, which had housed the 1898 Turin Exhibition. The cost was 70,000 lire (£2777).

The factory was officially opened by the Duke of Genoa on 19 March 1900 in the presence of 500 guests. But production, thanks to Agnelli's urgings, was already under way with the help of Ceirano, the Martina brothers and coachbuilder Marcello Alessio. Based on the 3½ hp Welleyes, these first cars, introduced in 1899, bore a close resemblance to it though, at Agnelli's insistence, chain drive replaced the belts of the original. The demanding gradients of the nearby Alps must have soon shown up the deficiencies of that arrangement, and it is thought that only eight examples of this first car were sold.

With a view to improving performance, Faccilio was soon at work designing a more powerful derivative, which appeared in 1900. This was a 6 hp model with a 1082 cc engine which had a top speed of 45 km/h (28 mph) – a substantial improvement on the 3½ hp's 34 km/h (20 mph). The 6 hp had the distinction of being the first racing F.I.A.T. when, in April 1900, with Castore

LEFT *The first F.I.A.T. of 1899, derived from Ceirano's Welleyes car, powered by a rear-mounted water-cooled 3½ hp 679 cc two-* *cylinder engine. No less than three of the original eight built survive today.*

at the wheel, it won the Asti–Turin race. Later, in July, with Lancia and Nazzaro, the car proved victorious in the more demanding Venïce–Bassano–Trevasio event, when it averaged 59 km/h (37 mph).

For his next model, in 1901, Faccioli decided to follow in the wheeltracks of the French Panhard, so the new design boasted a two-cylinder engine of 1082 cc which was front- rather than rear-mounted. Chain drive still persisted, however. This model, which was built in 1902, was the Italian company's best-selling car and more than 80 found customers.

Faccioli departs

But Aristide Faccioli's stay at Corso Dante was destined to be short-lived. In December 1900, while Faccioli was hard at work on the 1901 models, Agnelli was away at the 1900 Paris Motor Show. He returned to Turin enthusing about the efficient and visually impressive honeycomb radiator he had seen on the new Daimler models. Pointing to the omnipresent snow-covered Alps, Agnelli insisted that Faccioli produce a car that could reach the mountain top without boiling – a continual bugbear on early cars. He therefore proposed that F.I.A.T. purchase a car from the opposition to evaluate its performance. The technical director, by contrast, favoured first-hand research, and believed that the company should conduct its own

experiments. Agnelli stuck to his guns, so Faccioli had no alternative but to tender his resignation, although this had to be confirmed by a board meeting.

During the meeting, which took place in April 1901, Faccioli pointed to the growth of the British motor industry where the emphasis was being placed firmly on quality. Agnelli countered by quoting the growth of the American industry with its emphasis on quantity claiming that, with viability ensured, quality would follow. Agnelli had his way and F.I.A.T.'s first technical director departed after 19 months in the job.

After Faccioli had left Corso Dante he designed a 16 hp four-cylinder car for Giovanni Battista Ceirano, his old employer, who was now selling cars under his own name. He then went on to produce an aero-engine for the Turin-based SPA company and, although the SPA Faccioli triplane was the first aircraft in the country to be powered by an Italian engine, the project foundered. Faccioli then became a recluse and maintained an enduring hostility towards Agnelli until his death, in 1920.

Above all, this incident reveals Agnelli's growing authority over the running of F.I.A.T's affairs, despite the fact that he was still only company secretary. His appetite for work was legendary although it was combined with a short temper; he was not a man to cross! There is little doubt, however, that he had a flair for spotting talented people. It was he who found Faccioli's successor, even though the new man had no motor industry experience: Giovanni Enrico, although a qualified engineer, had spent most of his life in the new, progressive world of electric power. He had begun his engineering career in 1884 when he opened a small business specializing in the manufacture of steam engines, but subsequently became director of Rome's electric power station. At the time that Agnelli was persuading him to come to Turin, he was in charge of the Edison power station at Paderno D'Adda.

Enrico wasted little time in designing a new model for F.I.A.T. This was the firm's first four-cylinder car of 1901, with a 3770 cc 12 hp engine. Not only was it the first F.I.A.T. to be built in respectable numbers – around 100 were produced – but it was also the first car to be exported, with early examples finding their way to France. The model initially used the traditional gilled tube radiator, although later examples were fitted with the honeycomb type following an intervention by the company secretary; once again, Agnelli got his way!

A succession of fours followed. There was a 24/32 of 1903 and a smaller 16/20 of the same year. These, significantly, had T-head engines in the Mercedes manner, and were F.I.A.T's first. With plenty of demand from the luxury overseas market, in 1904 the firm produced a massive 10-litre four, rated at 60 hp. Ninety examples of this 24,500 lire (£972) model were made.

By this time F.I.A.T. was beginning to acquire an international reputation, with its products being judged in the same company as the German Mercedes, which its cars closely resembled, and the Napier or Daimler from Britain. The 60 was replaced in 1905 by another 60 hp model and, in 1907, came the firm's first six – still a 60 but with an 11-litre engine.

F.I.A.T. was growing up. Output rose from 73 cars sold in 1901 to 134 two years later, by which time the Turin company was Italy's leading make. Nineteen hundred and three was also a significant year as the Corso Dante factory was considerably extended, and in 1905 F.I.A.T. effectively took over the Ansaldi machine tool company. The outcome was the Fiat-Ansaldi car, designed, it should be noted, not by the hard-working Enrico,

but by Cesare Como, a Turin Polytechnic graduate, who had joined F.I.A.T. in 1901 and worked under Enrico. This 3052 cc four had the distinction of having torque tube and thus shaft drive, rather than the less efficient chains. The cars were known as *Brevetti* (patent) Fiats from 1906 when Michele Ansaldi, who had initially co-sponsored the project, departed to found, with Matteo Ceirano, brother of the Giovannis, the SPA concern. They were there joined by Cesare Como. But the Brevetti was an important model; it sold 1500 examples until 1908 and marked a trend towards smaller, more popular cars.

Racing success

By this time, F.I.A.T. had a well-established racing reputation, Agnelli recognizing that this was the best form of international publicity. Racing had begun in earnest in 1903 and, after success in the British 1000 Miles Trial and failure in the Paris–Madrid road race, Cagno took the Turin make to a third place in the Circuit des Ardennes. In 1904 Vincenzo Lancia was placed eighth in the prestigious Gordon Bennett race but he was luckier with the Coppa Florio, which he won. The make made the running in the 1905 Gordon Bennett through a new 16.3-litre 100 hp car with a more efficient overhead- rather than side-valve engine. Although Lancia dropped out, Nazzaro was placed second and Cagno third: the red cars from Italy were starting to go places. However, 1906 was a less successful season, although Lancia did gain a hard-won second position in the American Vanderbilt Cup. At the end of the year he left Fiat (the initials and full stops having been dispensed with late in 1906) to found his own car company. Nevertheless he continued to race for the firm in 1907/8.

Nineteen hundred and seven was a golden racing year for Fiat for it won no less than three major events. In each instance these were personal triumphs for Nazzaro, who drove the winning cars. Fiats won the Targa Florio race for the first time, the hard-fought French Grand Prix and the German Kaiserpreis.

LEFT *A 1903 16/20 hp with 4179 cc four-cylinder side-valve engine and chain drive. One hundred were built in 1903, and in 1904 the model became the 4503 cc 16/24 hp, but the 16/20 was back again in 1905.*

RIGHT *In 1907, Fiat's golden racing year, the firm built three special cars for the German Kaiserpreis Imperial Trophy run at the Taunus circuit in June. This so-called Taunus model had a four-cylinder 8004 cc four-cylinder overhead-valve engine. The winner, shown here, was Felice Nazzaro, who averaged 84.68 km/h (52.6 mph), with Wagner and Lancia placed fifth and sixth respectively.*

However, on the corporate front, 1907 was a watershed year. Output had risen to 1365 cars, but in the following year production dropped to 1213, for this was a time of economic depression. Later, Agnelli was under something of a cloud for, along with Fiat's chairman Ludovico Scarfiotti, he was accused of manipulating corporate stock and falsifying the accounts. The charges were brought on 5 May 1909 and the trial was to involve the pair for a protracted 450 days. They were finally acquitted on 9 April 1912.

By this time Fiat had yet another technical director. Enrico had retired in 1906, worn out by his efforts, and died three years later, aged only 58. His replacement was yet another Agnelli appointee who, like his predecessor, came from outside the motor industry. He was Turin-born Guido Fornaca, who had briefly worked for the Romanian railway before becoming involved in the Savigliano hydro-electric project.

Fiat was also spreading its wings. A British subsidiary, Fiat Motors, had been opened in 1903, and was ably administered by D'Arcy Baker, a former army officer with a flair for publicity. This London company imported complete cars and also chassis from Turin, whereas the Vienna-based Austro-Fiat concern actually manufactured cars there under licence, from 1907 until 1921. It was much the same story across the Atlantic: in 1911 the Fiat Motor Company opened a factory in the Poughkeepsie district of New York to produce locally-made Fiats under licence. In addition to the Italian range there was also the Type 56, a six-cylinder model, available only on the American market. Sadly, the US venture proved short-lived, and by 1920 the Poughkeepsie factory was no more.

A trend towards medium-sized cars was descernible from 1907 with the arrival of the 4.5-litre 18/24 four-cylinder car. Rather more traditional was the 28/40 with a 7.3-litre four-cylinder engine, derived from the 1907 Targa Florio winner. No less than 953 examples of the 28/40 were produced.

In 1908 Fiat introduced its most popular, and smallest, model yet. It was also the most successful with more than 2100 produced between 1908 and 1910. Tipo 1 was a 2.2-litre Taxi which saw service not only in Italy, but also in Paris, London and, across the Atlantic, in New York. It followed the lead given by the Brevetti and was advanced in that it was the first Fiat to have its cylinders cast in one piece. Not only this, it saved Fiat from the financial doldrums of 1907/8, and its straightforward chassis and cheap, all-round half-elliptic springs were to influence Fiat design for the next decade.

At the other extreme was the extraordinary purpose-built S.B.4 car, named *Mephistopheles*, which upheld Fiat honours in a celebrated contest at Brooklands, England – the world's first motor racing circuit, opened in 1907. The following year Fiat responded to a challenge for a race around the concrete oval from Napier propagandist S.F. Edge. He fielded *Samson*, an elderly six-cylinder Napier of 1904 vintage, driven by Frank Newton, but the big 18-litre Fiat, with Nazzaro at the wheel, was triumphant after the British car broke its crankshaft. The Fiat averaged 152.48 km/h (94.75 mph) although it was electrically timed at 195.75 km/h (121.64 mph) on its best lap. (This has been a source of controversy among the motoring *cognoscenti* ever since, as the figure is thought to be excessive.)

There was no Grand Prix racing in 1909/10, and a spate of large-engined cars resulted. Fiat maintained its past record by winning the 1911 Grand Prix de France with a massive 10.5-litre four-cylinder overhead-camshaft engine under its awesome bonnet. But this was a minnow compared with the fabled S76 record car of 1911, produced in response to Germany's Blitzen-Benz. This monster had a massive 28.3-litre four-cylinder engine which was so large that the bonnet line had to be an incredible 1500 mm (5 ft) above the ground!

A popular taxi

Meanwhile, there had been significant developments as far as Fiat's road cars were concerned. This new generation of six vehicles was designated Tipos 1 to 6. The most popular was the Tipo 1, powered by a 1.8-litre four-cylinder engine and it perpetuated the small car theme established with the Taxi. Around 1000 examples were manufactured over a two-year period. Sharing a similar chassis was the Tipo 2, although it had a 2.6-litre four. This model had the distinction of being the first car to be adopted by Italian forces during the Libyan campaign of 1911/12. It was slightly less popular than its predecessor with 908 cars sold over two years.

Rather more substantial was the 4-litre Tipo 3 which endured, with minor modifications, until 1921. The 5.6-litre Tipo 4 was next in line and one was used by Italy's King Vittorio Emanuele II during the First World War. It boasted 12-volt electrics from 1915 and remained in production until 1918. Tipos 5 and 6 shared the same 9-litre four-cylinder engines, but the latter was the more luxurious of the two and, although initially chain-driven, soon changed to the more conventional torque tube transmission.

ABOVE *The Fiat Zero, made between 1912 and 1915, was the first small Fiat to be produced in large numbers. More than 2000 of this 1846 cc four-cylinder model were built. Initially it was only available with this touring bodywork. The Zero can be considered as Agnelli's response to Henry Ford's ubiquitous Model T.*

LEFT *A Fiat 2B of 1916 with 2813 cc four-cylinder side-valve engine. Over 10,000 were made between 1912 and 1920. Its top speed was 70 km/h (44 mph).*

In 1912, a year in which Agnelli travelled to America to study its motor industry at first hand, Fiat introduced the Zero which, like the Ford Model T, was available only with four-seater touring bodywork. It was also substantially cheaper than its Tipo 1 predecessor, which had cost 14,500 lire (£573) and with which it shared the same 1.8-litre engine. The Zero sold for 8000 lire (£316), and by the time it ceased production in 1915 more than 2000 had been produced. Eventually the Zero was made available to specialist coachbuilders. Locati and Toretta were responsible for a handsome two-seater, and the model was also available in landaulette form. There was also the slightly more powerful 1A derivative, available with a range of coachwork, and built over the same period.

Nineteen fourteen saw Fiat return to the Grand Prix fray. The S57/14B bore no resemblance to previous racers and had a four-cylinder 4.5-litre overhead-camshaft engine, while the front-wheel brakes were a revolutionary feature on a racing car.

Three cars entered that year's French Grand Prix, but the team was unable to repeat the success of 1907 and all failed to finish.

In August 1914 the First World War broke out, although Italy did not become involved on the Allied side until May of 1915. After 16 years of the company's existence, Agnelli could look back on an era of impressive growth for Fiat. In 1913, the last full year of peace, Fiat produced 3050 cars; more than any British firm, but lagging behind Benz and Opel in Germany and the French Peugeot, Renault and Darracq companies. However, where Fiat differed from all its contemporaries – with the exception of Daimler, which produced Mercedes cars – was in the fact that Agnelli had implemented a deliberate policy of diversification. Commercial vehicles had appeared in 1903 and marine engines two years later. Agnelli had founded the RIV company in 1906 to supply Fiat with all-important ball bearings and had established a factory in his home town of Villar Perosa. Aero-engine production began in 1908 to buttress the firm as car output slumped and, with the coming of war, this was complemented by aircraft manufacture.

During hostilities the Italian army took supplies of the Tipo 2A and 3A – derivatives of the original 1910 series – and also bought the original Tipo 4. In addition there was the Tipo 70, introduced in 1915 and produced throughout hostilities. This was a 2-litre four and was significant in that it adopted a unit construction engine and gearbox in the cheaper American manner. The dated three-quarter-elliptic rear springs, a feature

since 1908, were replaced by simpler half-elliptics. However, only small numbers of cars were manufactured and the 472 built in 1916 was the lowest output figure since 1905. Armoured cars were also produced.

Although car manufacture dwindled, lorry output soared, so that by 1917 Fiat could claim that it had produced more military vehicles than any other firm in the world. In that year no less than 17,217 commercials were built, a figure not surpassed until 1955! There was yet further diversification that year into railway rolling stock and iron and steel production.

The enormous growth of Fiat's activities during the First World War, and its future potential, meant that the firm needed a completely new factory for the post-war years. Designed by Giacomo Matté-Trucco, with input from Agnelli, Count Biscaretti and Fornaca, it was a five-storey building with raw materials entering on the ground floor and complete cars emerging to be tested on a banked circuit unexpectedly located on the roof! Work on the project began in 1916 and the factory, in the Lingotto district of Turin, was opened in May 1923. It was the largest reinforced concrete structure of its type in Italy.

With the coming of peace, Fiat considerably simplified its model line-up. The pre-war cars were phased out and the first of a new generation of more cost-conscious models made its appearance in 1919. This was the 1460 cc Tipo 501, for the pre-war success of the Zero had pointed the way to the popularity of the small-capacity four, and it had a straightforward side-valve engine, with detachable cylinder head. This new model was available with a range of bodywork and, by the time that the 501 ceased production in 1926, over 45,000 examples had been built. Two sporting variants had arrived in 1921: the S, which had a 5.5:1 rather than 4.7:1 compression ratio, and 26 instead of 23 bhp; and the somewhat rarer SS with twin overhead camshaft head.

Carlo Cavalli, who had taken over as Fiat's technical director in 1919, was responsible for the overall design of the 501. A lawyer by training, he entered the law in deference to his father's wishes, even though his first love was always engineering, and in 1905 he joined Fiat's technical office. Cavalli soon displayed his ability with his involvement in the design of the 1907 French Grand Prix winner. There were also changes higher up the Fiat management ladder when Guido Fornaca, who had been technical director up to 1916 and was then made general manager, took over, in 1920, as managing director. At this time Giovanni Agnelli was holding this position, so he moved up to the Fiat presidency.

ABOVE *Fiat's first mass-produced car was the 501 of 1919–26. The engine was a 1460 cc four-cylinder unit. This is a 1925 Taxi version.*

alas, retired. John Scales is in the foreground with Antonio Fagnano and Allessandro Cagno behind.

FAR LEFT *The special S57/14B Fiats built for the 1914 French Grand Prix were fitted with a 4492 cc four-cylinder overhead-camshaft engine. All the cars,*

LEFT *An unexpected feature of Fiat's Lingotto factory, opened in 1923, was this 1 km (1100 yd) banked test track. This structure remained in use until 1982 and is now an exhibition centre.*

Mass production begins

At the same time that the 501 made its appearance, in 1919, Fiat introduced a larger version. This was the 505 with a 2.3-litre engine, and a respectable 30,000 had been made by 1925. The top-line model was the 510 with a 3.6-litre six-cylinder engine built over the same period. There was also the 510S (S for sports) version with V-shaped radiator and four-wheel brakes. Its speed was around the 90 km/h (60 mph) mark.

Despite the war, Fiat had not ignored its racing activities. An enlarged version of the 1914 French Grand Prix racer had been developed in 4.9-litre 57A form, it having been built in 1916 for that year's Indianapolis 500 race in America, although the war prevented it from competing. Its first major success came in 1921 when Masetti took one to victory in the Targa Florio.

With the German Mercedes team temporarily banned from participation in Grand Prix events, Fiat expanded its racing department and soon had an unrivalled design team which went on to produce an engine of such stature and sophistication that it influenced racing practice for nearly 30 years. The team was

headed by Giulio Cesare Cappa who, like many of Fiat's top engineers, was a graduate of the Turin Polytechnic. Soon after obtaining his degree he became, in 1905, technical director of the Turin-based Aquila Italiana car company. There he designed four- and six-cylinder cars, with their cylinders cast in one piece instead of in the traditional batches of two or three pots. As if this was not enough, he fitted aluminium rather than cast-iron pistons – a good eight years ahead of the rest of Europe!

In 1914 Cappa joined Fiat as head of its technical office where he concentrated on aero-engine design. But, once the war was over, he turned his formidable talents to the design of Fiat racing cars. He was assisted in this work by Tranquillo Zerbi, an Italian designer who had previously taken an engineering degree at Mannheim, Germany and had joined Fiat in 1919. His speciality was the supercharging of power units. Other key members of this team were Vittorio Jano, who had come to Fiat as a draughtsman in 1911, and Luigi Bazzi, who had joined Fiat in the same year.

The first post-war Fiat racing car was the four-cylinder 801/401 with a 3-litre twin overhead camshaft engine. This was a stop-gap but, unfortunately, its 801/402 eight-cylinder replacement was not ready for the 1921 French Grand Prix because of labour troubles at the factory, of which more later. However, it appeared at the first Italian GP, held at Brescia. There it put up the fastest lap of 150.36 km/h (93 mph), although it was subsequently forced to retire.

Unluckily for Fiat, the 3-litre formula ended in 1921 before the new car could really prove its worth. With a new 2-litre formula due to begin in 1922, Cappa came up with a twin-overhead-camshaft six-cylinder engine, designated 804/404. Like its predecessors, this sophisticated unit had light, welded-on cylinder jackets which was Fiat aero-engine practice and 'borrowed' from Mercedes. The body, with its delightful pointed tail and wind-cheating undershield, was wind-tunnel tested by Rosatelli, the firm's aerodynamicist. Alas, two of the three cars entered for the 1922 French Grand Prix at Strasbourg crashed. Tragically, the rear axle housings broke, both cars losing their wheels and one driver his life, while the third car, driven by veteran Felice Nazzaro, went on to win. Happily, Fiat had better luck in the Italian Grand Prix at the new Monza

LEFT *The 1924 French Grand Prix at Lyon. Nazzaro is in a 805/405 Fiat, the world's first supercharged racing car. He retired with braking trouble and the event was won by a P2 Alfa Romeo.*

RIGHT *The first Fiat to have left-hand steering was the 520 of 1927–9. This well-appointed model had a 2244 cc six-cylinder side-valve engine.*

BELOW *The 21-litre Fiat* Mephistopheles *in which Ernest Eldridge took the world land speed record at Arpajon, France in July 1924 at 234.98 km/h (146.01 mph). The power unit is a six-cylinder Fiat A12 aero-engine.*

circuit where the red cars from Turin came in first and second, nine laps ahead of the Bugatti in third place.

The sixes had proved their worth, but Cappa produced an even more impressive design for the 1923 season. The 805/405 had an eight- rather than six-cylinder engine. But, in addition, it was fitted – the first time for any racing car – with a supercharger, the Wittig unit being intended to boost the engine's performance. Unfortunately these blowers cost Fiat the 1923 French Grand Prix at Tours when, because of inadequate filtering over the supercharger intakes, the engines ingested dust and grit to the detriment of their working parts and were forced to retire. Ironically, Henry Segrave, who took the chequered flag in a Sunbeam, was driving a 'Fiat in green paint', because Bertarione and Becchia from Fiat had been lured to the Wolverhampton company to produce a car which was to all intents and purposes a straight copy of the transitional six-cylinder design!

Fiat made no mistakes for the Italian Grand Prix when the troublesome Wittigs were replaced by Roots units. Thus-equipped the straight-eights were victorious, with Fiats taking first and second places. The 805/405 had a profound impact on the design of racing engines up until 1951, when Enzo Ferrari inspired the creation of a 4.5-litre unblown engine which beat the supercharged opposition at the 1951 British Grand Prix. In the meantime, Fiat ran its 1923 cars in the 1924 season.

Racing supremacy

Although the 2-litre formula was destined to run for a further year, in 1924 Agnelli announced that Fiat was intending to withdraw from racing and the talented design team was disbanded. Young Luigi Bazzi had already departed for Alfa Romeo, having been wooed there by a persuasive Enzo Ferrari. But the Milan company hooked an even bigger fish when Vittorio Jano (Ferrari again played the role of intermediary) left Fiat to join Alfa Romeo in the autumn of 1923. There he designed the P2 racing car which gave the firm the 1925 World Championship, and was later responsible for the immortal P3 monoposto of 1932. Cappa also left Fiat, in 1924, and became a

freelance consultant: he was to design an aero-engine for the French Lorraine company and later did work for Ansaldo, Itala, and Alfa Romeo. Only Zerbi remained with Fiat.

Although the firm withdrew from the racing circuits in 1924, a Fiat held the world land speed record. Nevertheless, it was an Englishman, rather than an Italian, who was responsible. Probably taking the elderly Fiat *Mephistopheles* that had been victorious at Brooklands in 1908, Ernest Eldridge removed its 18-litre engine, lengthened the chassis and fitted a wartime A12 six-cylinder 21-litre overhead-camshaft Fiat aero-engine. In July 1924, on a length of specially prepared public road at Arpajon, France, Eldridge succeeded in pushing the record up to 234.98 km/h (146.01 mph). It lasted until September of that year when Malcolm Campbell again raised the record.

Meanwhile, Fiat's range of road cars was continuing to evolve. There had been considerable factory unrest in 1920 when a workers' soviet took control of the Turin factory, but Agnelli and Fornaca were soon back at the helm. It was a time of depression all over Europe, so it was rather curious to find that Fiat now embarked on its one and only V12-engined car, the Super Fiat Tipo 520 of 1921 with 6.8-litre overhead-valve engine. Maybe this was Agnelli's response to the Isotta-Fraschini Tipo 8, with its pioneering straight-eight engine, or to Lancia's 50 hp V12, although the single example of the latter never got beyond the 1919 Paris Motor Show. The Fiat 520 lasted only a year and was discontinued in 1922. However, the proportions of its Rolls-Royce style radiator were adopted by Fiat, and other Italian makes, for the remainder of the decade.

The Tipo 520 also inspired the 519 of 1922, a luxury 4.7-litre car with a six-cylinder engine – effectively half the 520's V12 unit. Designed by Giulio Cappa, the 519 boasted such sophisticated features as servo-assisted hydraulic brakes; indeed, it was the first European passenger car to be so equipped. This impressive vehicle, capable of around 112 km/h (70 mph), lasted until 1927. There was also the S, for sports, version with Mercedes-like V-shaped radiator, Rudge Whitworth wheels, and 126 km/h (78 mph) top speed.

Until 1925, the 1460 cc Tipo 501 had been Fiat's lowest capacity model, but in that year it introduced the 509, a much

FIAT MEPHISTOPHELES
1923

ENGINE	
No. of cylinders	6
Bore/stroke mm	160 × 180
Displacement cc	21,706
Valve operation	Single ohc
Compression ratio	4.8:1
Induction	Four updraught carburettors
BHP	320 at 1800 rpm
Transmission	Four-speed, chain drive
CHASSIS	
Frame	Channel section
Wheelbase mm	3450'
Track – front mm	1480
Track – rear mm	1390
Suspension – front	Half-elliptic
Suspension – rear	Half-elliptic
PERFORMANCE	
Maximum speed	234 km/h (146 mph) +

smaller car with a 990 cc overhead camshaft engine. Although this was a surprisingly sophisticated layout for such a cheap car, it was immensely successful and more than 90,000 had been sold by the time that production ceased in 1929. This impressive sales figure was no doubt aided by the fact that the 509 was the first Fiat that could be bought by hire purchase through the in-house SAVA scheme. There was also the 509S, usually fitted with handsome two-seater boat-tailed coachwork. A few supercharged SM versions were available, but even rarer was the competition version, the 509 SM Sprinto Monza (Monza Special).

The long-running 501 was replaced, in 1926, by the 503, which carried over its four-cylinder engine and remained available for only two years, although some 42,000 were built. The 2.2-litre four-cylinder 505 was discontinued in 1925, and was succeeded, briefly, by the 507 which perpetuated its engine. The 507 was replaced in 1927 not by another four, but by a six of the same capacity. This was another 520, with American influences, a side-valve engine and, for the first time on a Fiat,

left-hand drive. Rather more expensive, and also a six, was the 512 of 1926/28 vintage with a 3.4-litre side-valve engine. It proved popular in England and found equally appreciative owners as far afield as Australia.

In 1927 Fiat made a brief, and final, appearance on the racing circuits with the extraordinary Tipo 806 single-seater. A 1.5-litre formula had been introduced in 1926 and Fiat responded with what was, in effect, a V12 engine which consisted of two six-cylinder units geared together. It had no less than two crankshafts and three overhead camshafts! This ingenious device developed an amazing 187 bhp but, sadly, it only ran once, in the Milan Grand Prix at Monza in September which it won at an average speed of 152 km/h (94.6 mph). Soon afterwards Fiat finally withdrew from racing.

The Italian economy took a turn for the worse in 1927. In that year Fiat built 44,404 cars and production fell steadily to a mere 16,419 in 1931, Fiat's worst peacetime figure since 1923. These were also difficult years for higher echelons of the company, for in 1927 Guido Fornaca stepped down from the managing directorship, owing to ill health, and died the following year. Then, in 1928, technical director Cavalli resigned, also suffering from health problems, and retired to his native Val Vigezzo though, fortunately, he lived on until 1947.

Fornaca's place as managing director was taken by Vittorio Valletta. An economics and commerce graduate of Turin University, he had originally intended to pursue an academic career and lectured on banking procedures. But he soon gravitated to industry when he took over the running of the

Chiribiri automobile and aircraft engine works in Turin. In 1921 he was snapped up by Agnelli to streamline the Fiat organization, although he also continued his academic work. He was made central, and general manager, then finally managing director, on Fornaca's retirement. The all-important post of technical overseer went to Tranquillo Zerbi.

More diversification

Despite the fluctuating economics of the 1920s, the decade was one of sustained expansion and diversification for Fiat. Tractor production had started in 1919, and in 1924 Fiat built its first diesel-electric train. The SPA company, which built cars and lorries, was taken over in 1926 and OM, with a similar product range, followed in 1933. In 1934 Fiat was to diversify further into electric train production, and machine-tool manufacture began the following year.

Yet the inter-war years in Italy were dominated by the figure of Benito Mussolini, whose fascist dictatorship came to power in 1922. In 1914, during a period in which he appeared a committed socialist, he received financial support from Fiat and, when he came to power, Agnelli was made a senator. But the Fiat president professed little interest in politics and spent most of his days in Turin rather than Rome. Mussolini had few illusions about the Fiat workforce. He used to say, with the short-lived workers' soviet no doubt in mind, that they were 'like figs, black on the outside but red inside'.

In 1920 Agnelli initiated a holiday camp for Fiat workers, the first of many such facilities. He was later to provide hospitals and an International Technical Institute in Turin, named after his son Edoardo. Vice-chairman of Fiat, and chairman of the board of the Fiat-owned newspaper, *La Stampa*, Edoardo died in July 1935, aged only 43. He was a passenger in a seaplane which had been taxi-ing on the water outside Genoa when it struck a log and capsized. Edoardo was struck by a propeller as he tried to get out and was killed instantly. His eldest son, Giovanni, always known as Gianni, was one day to take over the running of the Fiat empire. Edoardo's death was a great personal tragedy for Giovanni Agnelli. His only other child, Tina, had died in 1928.

Although the effect of the Depression began to be felt from 1928, the policy of refining Fiat road cars continued. In that year Fiat increased the capacity of the 520 from 2.2 to 2.5 litres, the car being available only in saloon form. There was also a fashionable Weymann fabric saloon and a stately limousine. A straight-eight Tipo 530 was mooted but never went into production because of the world Depression. In its place the company introduced the 525, built in 1928/9, and Agnelli presented one to Pope Pius XI. In the latter year an unlikely short-chassis version was produced which was, surprisingly, more popular than its grander parent.

The diminutive overhead-camshaft 509 lasted until 1929, although its 514 replacement reverted to cheaper side valves. It was a basic, no-frills model with disc wheels and gravity petrol tank. It was, perhaps, a rather anonymous car that looked more like a baby Chevrolet than a Fiat. Only 36,970 were produced by 1932, although this was through the trough of the Depression years. There were sporting variants – the 514S with 34 rather than 28 bhp and an MM (for Mille Miglia) version with 37 bhp and 106 km/h (66 mph) top speed.

At the other extreme was the 522 of 1931, a 2.5-litre successor to the six-cylinder 521 with which it shared the same engine.

LEFT *The best-selling 501 lasted until 1926, with front-wheel brakes fitted in the final year. There was also the longer wheelbase 502 which shared the same engine.*

RIGHT *The 525 appeared in the dark economic days of 1928/9, and only 511 were produced. Derived from the 512, it had a top speed of 97 km/h (60 mph).*

BELOW *The 522, with a 2516 cc six-cylinder side-valve engine, was introduced in 1931, and this is the 522S of 1932/3. Unlike the mainstream model's four-door standard saloon coachwork, the 522S had mostly coachbuilt two-door bodies.*

The model was notable for its use of synchromesh on the top two gears of the four-cog box and a free wheel was available at extra cost. Hydraulic brakes were employed, a progressive fitment for a European manufacturer, and these were to be a feature of all Fiats thereafter. The same engine was available in the more expensive 524, a model which was available only in closed form and on which disc wheels provided a discordant note of austerity. However the S version of 1932, with a short chassis and a 65 rather than a 52 bhp engine, was offered with more appropriate Rudge Whitworth wheels.

Fiat's commitment to the mass production market was further underpinned in 1932 by the arrival of the 995 cc Tipo 508. Best remembered as the Balilla, this model was the first Fiat of the inter-war years to be known by a name rather than a number. Designed under Tranquillo Zerbi's direction, it was also the first Fiat to feature a cost-conscious three-speed gearbox; hitherto the four-cog concept had been inviolate. The standard two-door saloon sold for 10,800 lire (£162) and the Balilla had a top speed of 85 km/h (53 mph). It could also be had with a more powerful engine, with 6.6:1 compression ratio and a 95 km/h (59 mph) top speed.

More memorable was the competition version, the lovely Balilla Sport with 30 bhp, rather than 20, on tap and stylish two-seater open bodywork with exquisite finned tail. The original rendering was by Ghia, Fiat buying the design rights and putting it into production with only minor modifications. There were two versions; the Coppa d'Oro (Gold Cup) with stylish front wings, and the somewhat starker Mille Miglia version with cycle ones. Even better was the second-series Balilla Sport of 1934, with a four-speed gearbox – a modification it shared with the saloon – and its own overhead-valve engine which gave a respectable 46 bhp. It could also be purchased in handsome aerodynamic saloon form.

The Balilla's Tipo 518 sister was better known as the Ardita, its mainline model being a boxy four-door saloon. It had a 1758 cc four-cylinder side-valve engine and was capable of 96 km/h (60 mph) plus. In 1934 came a six-cylinder 527 with a 2516 cc six-cylinder engine. This model was discontinued in 1936, while the more popular four-cylinder Ardita survived until 1938.

Progressive 1500

Fiat's next model, the 1500, was the first to be known only by its cubic capacity. It also featured a body that was demonstrably the product of aerodynamic research and the 1500 can rightly be regarded as the first truly modern Fiat. It bristled with features that reflected the advances made by the European motor industry: the first indication that Turin was beginning to move away from American design influences. The radiator grille of the four-door saloon was stylishly raked, while the headlamps were progressively incorporated in the front wings. The 1500 boasted a backbone chassis, so beloved in Germany, independent suspension of the Dubonnet type and a 1493 cc six-cylinder overhead-valve engine. Like the Balilla of 1932, this featured a short 75 mm stroke, making it ideal for flat-out motoring on the *autostrade*, Europe's first motor roads, that had been growing in number since 1923, when Mussolini introduced the first, between Milan and Lake Maggiore.

Although offered as a saloon, the 1500 was also available in open form and there were plenty of versions by specialist coachbuilders. Capable of around 112 km/h (70 mph), the 1500

RIGHT *Dante Giacosa, who played a leading role in the creation of the Fiat 500, and who was responsible for the overall design of Fiat cars from 1946 to 1969.*

FAR RIGHT *Fiat's 1500 of 1935 had aerodynamic bodywork, faired-in headlamps, independent front suspension (the first on a Fiat), a backbone chassis and a six-cylinder 1493 cc overhead-valve engine. It lasted until 1948.*

BELOW *The lovely 508S Balilla Sport of 1932–7. Fiat bought the original Ghia design, modified it, and this was the result — the Coppa d'Oro (Gold Cup) model. There was also a Mille Miglia version with cycle front wings.*

was sufficiently modern to survive the war and last until 1948. However, in 1940, the model's front end was revised with a new horizontal radiator and, ironically, the headlamps reverted to their more traditional positions – free standing, on either side of the radiator.

Until 1936 Fiat produced its cars to a well-established pattern. But in that year the firm introduced a completely new type of car that was peculiar to the Italian market and Fiat. The 500, lovingly nicknamed 'Topolino' or Mickey Mouse, had the distinction of being the smallest-capacity four-cylinder car in the world. With only a 2000 mm (6 ft 6¾ in) wheelbase, it was in the spirit of the British Austin Seven which had been introduced in 1922 and was then still in production. The 500 can also be regarded as an answer to the German DKW and Goliath baby cars with their two-stroke engines.

If Fiat had really wanted to be adventurous, it could have opted for front-wheel drive for this model, but Agnelli was against that layout on cost grounds. However, in 1931, design engineer Oreste Lardone came up with an experimental three-cylinder air-cooled low-cost car with backbone chassis, front-wheel drive and all-independent suspension, very much in the manner of the Czechoslovakian Tatra. A prototype was built but, unfortunately for Lardone, it caught fire when Senator Agnelli was in the passenger seat. The luckless Lardone lost his job and Fiat did not produce a front-wheel-drive car under the company name until 1969.

The Topolino's origins really go back to 1932 when 30-year-old Dante Giacosa, who had just been made a department head of Fiat's aero-engine section, was asked whether he would like to try his hand at car design. (Agnelli was a firm believer in inter-departmental competition!) Giacosa, a Turin Polytechnic graduate, had joined Fiat in 1926, via its SPA subsidiary. He

progressed from commercial vehicles to aero-engines where the technical director was Antonio Fessia, another Polytechnic graduate, who had joined Fiat in 1925. It was Fessia who asked Giacosa to undertake the all-important car project.

He and Fessia agreed on a conventional front engine/rear drive layout. But the really unusual aspect of the design was the positioning of the engine which, for space considerations, was mounted ahead of the front-wheel line with the radiator behind. Drive was by the usual propeller shaft and the rear axle was located by radius arms with quarter-elliptic springs providing the suspension medium. At the front, independent suspension, by transverse leaf spring, was employed while hydraulic brakes and 12-volt electrics also featured, which made the 500 a genuine large car in miniature. The chassis was a simple A frame, drilled for lightness.

FIAT 500	
1936–48	
ENGINE	
No. of cylinders	4
Bore/stroke mm	52 × 67
Displacement cc	569
Valve operation	Side
Compression ratio	6.5:1
Induction	Single sidedraught carburettor
BHP	13 at 4000 rpm
Transmission	Four-speed
CHASSIS	
Frame	Channel section
Wheelbase mm	2000
Track – front mm	1114
Track – rear mm	1083
Suspension – front	Independent, transverse spring and wishbones
Suspension – rear	Series 1, quarter-elliptic; Series 2, half-elliptic
PERFORMANCE	
Maximum speed	85 km/h (53 mph)

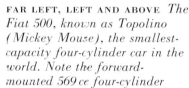

FAR LEFT, LEFT AND ABOVE *The Fiat 500, known as Topolino (Mickey Mouse), the smallest-capacity four-cylinder car in the world. Note the forward-mounted 569 cc four-cylinder side-valve engine. This is essentially a two-seater and the canvas roof was a popular feature, particularly on the home market. Bumpers were an optional extra.*

The heart of the 500 was a diminutive 569 cc four-cylinder engine, detail design being the responsibility of Virgilio Borsattino, who had previously been employed designing aero-engine carburettors for Fiat . . . and the little Topolino unit was about the same size as one of those carburettors! It was the simplest possible engine with side valves, non-adjustable tappets in the Ford manner, no water pump and a two-bearing crankshaft. Petrol supply was by gravity, so the cost of a fuel pump was avoided.

The two-door bodywork by chief engineer Schaeffer was coupé-like in appearance and could carry two adults in the front, with room for two children or luggage in the somewhat sparse rear. Most 500s were fitted with roll-back canvas roofs, ideal for Italian climes. The car was sold without bumpers, although these were available at extra cost.

Selling for a mere 8900 lire (£144) on its 1936 announcement and capable of a spirited 85 km/h (53 mph) the 500 was an instant success and is, indeed, one of the great designs of automotive history. After the first 46,000 had been built, the original quarter-elliptic rear springs were converted to full half elliptics and the chassis frame was altered accordingly. Apart from this, the car remained in substantially the same form until its production finished, in 1948. During this period more than 122,000 examples were sold.

Another model, sharing a family resemblance with the 1500 and 500, made its début in 1937. This was the 508C Balilla 1100, derived from the original 1932 model and boasting a 1089 cc engine with overhead valves and aluminium cylinder head, as pioneered on the Balilla Sport. Dubonnet independent front suspension again featured and a four-door saloon was the most popular option – a convertible was also available. The immensely successful 508C was good for 110 km/h (68 mph) and it sold an impressive 250,000 during its two-year production life, setting a new record for a Fiat model.

Aerodynamic excursion

Like practically all its predecessors, the 508C was also available as a sports model: in this guise, the 508C had the distinction of being the world's first series-production aerodynamic sports car. The version came about almost accidentally and sprang from experiments which Dante Giacosa, by now transferred to Fiat's car design department, carried out with a van version of the 500 saloon. During tests, he was surprised to find that the van was faster than the standard model. It was realized that the extra speed was due to the van's superior aerodynamics, and Giacosa immediately thought of incorporating these features into a production car.

A number of experimental models were built and tested in the Turin Polytechnic wind tunnel, established at Castle Valentino by Professor Panetti. The design was restricted by the fact that the 508C chassis had to be used, so it was not possible to get the front of the car as low as desired. The only way to increase the model's performance was to improve its aerodynamics, but on the debit side this meant a loss of interior room and rear visibility. The engine had a 7.1:1 compression ratio, instead of 6:1, and developed 42 bhp, 10 bhp more than the standard car's. The 508C MM (for Mille Miglia) was also more expensive and sold for 29,500 lire (£310), which was 10,000 lire (£105) more than the mainstream 508C. In view of the model's limited appeal, coachbuilding was sub-contracted to Savio in Turin. Top speed was 140 km/h (87 mph) – an impressive figure for a 1-litre car.

The model was clearly at home in the Mille Miglia where it dominated the 1100 cc class. Although his car was delivered only ten days before the 1938 event, Piero Taruffi drove an outstanding race, winning the class at an average speed of 111 km/h (70 mph), way ahead of all the other entrants. Incidentally, no less than 38 Fiats started in this class, and the drivers included two generations of the Mussolini family, *Il Duce*'s son Vittorio and grandson Vito. This success high-lighted the marque's sporting side for, although Fiat had finally withdrawn from Grand Prix racing in 1927, if you wanted a cheap way to go racing, you simply bought a production Fiat and tuned it!

Back in 1921 a sports version of the 501 had won the 2-litre class in the Targa Florio and a 509SM won the 1928 Monte Carlo Rally, with another in second place. By the time of the 1933 event, there was rather more competition and a Balilla managed only eighth place. Rather more successful was the 508S Balilla Sports which dominated the 1100 cc class in many events. Its best-known driver was Amédée Gordini, who took one to victory in the 1935 Bol d'Or. From 1936 Fiat dominated the 1100 class in the Mille Miglia, and the 750 cc class, introduced in 1937, was purpose-made for the Turin cars. They also won the 1500 section in that year.

It was much the same story in the 1940 event (the Mille Miglia was not held in 1939) when Fiat took its customary first places in the 750 and 1100 classes, although Lancia won the 1500 cc

BELOW *The world's first series-production aerodynamic coupé, the 508C MM of 1937/8. It was capable of 140 km/h (87 mph).*

RIGHT *Fiat's Mirafiori factory, unlike Lingotto, was a single-storey structure, opened in 1939 and extended in 1955.*

section in which Enzo Ferrari's first cars made their racing début. However, under the terms agreed when he left Alfa Romeo, Ferarri was not allowed to use his own name, so the two cars entered for the 1940 race carried the Vettura 815 title. They featured plenty of Fiat components and were built around 508C Balilla chassis frames, while the suspension, gearboxes, differentials and steering gear all emanated from Turin. The 1.5-litre straight-eight engine featured two aluminium 508C overhead-valve units, although the blocks were specially cast in Modena by Calzoni. Both cars failed to finish, but Ferrari and Fiat were destined to meet again after the war.

The last new Fiat to appear before the outbreak of the Second World War was the low-production 2800, introduced in 1938. This was a 2.8-litre car with a six-cylinder overhead-valve engine and the inevitable Dubonnet independent front suspension. Its horizontal radiator grille and separate headlamps were extended to the 1500 for 1940. Production was interrupted by the war, nevertheless a few were built for the Italian army carrying the 2800 CMC designation. Only 621 of all types were produced.

In 1939 Fiat opened its second major factory since Lingotto had started production in 1923. This earlier factory had probably been inspired by Henry Ford's four-storey Highland Park plant in Detroit, but by the time it was completed the trend was to single-storey structures. So, in 1936, when work began at Mirafiori, on the outskirts of Turin, the plant was built on just one level. Ironically it was in this area that Fiat had originally wanted to build its factory back in 1899! Designed by Vittorio Bonade-Bottino, the new plant was opened on 15 May 1939 by Mussolini. He was presented on the occasion with a 700 saloon which was to be Fiat's first unitary construction model, while the four-cylinder overhead-valve engine was to be mass-produced using a revolutionary die-casting process. Unfortu-

nately, Italy's involvement, from 1940 onwards, in World War 2, put paid to the 700 project and a lilliputian 400 model, with open two-seater bodywork, suffered a similar fate.

Fiat at war

Fiat had to switch to war production, manufacturing the Daimler-Benz inverted V12 liquid-cooled fuel-injected aero-engines under licence at Mirafiori. This unit was used to power Italy's monoplanes, although Fiat also built the reliable but archaic 'Freccia' biplane. A few cars were produced but, as in World War 1, the demand was for trucks, and these were built by the firm and its SPA and OM subsidiaries.

But, despite Fiat's industrial potential, it spent a remarkably unproductive war. During hostilities the firm did as little as possible to aid Mussolini's German allies. In September 1943, following Italy's surrender to the Allied forces, the Germans occupied Turin and remained there until April 1945. These troops used all means at their disposal to operate Fiat's factories, but were answered with strikes, sabotage and indifference. The workers had downed tools in a 'bread, peace and freedom' stoppage in March 1943, and matters rapidly deteriorated under German pressure.

The firm was supposed to produce 180 planes a month, but the first few months' total was a mere 18. Of the 1500 aero-engines scheduled, first a batch of 300, then 90 were built. Consequently, in 1944, Berlin ordered that Fiat tooling and machinery be transferred to Germany. Fiat workers responded with a general strike that soon spread across Northern Italy: Fiat stayed put. Then, early in 1945, when the company was supposed to be producing 10 trucks a day, only about half that number were built: the remainder mysteriously 'disappeared'.

In April 1945, with peace in the offing, the *Comitato di Liberazione Nazionale* (the Committee for National Liberty), a resistance organization, together with the army called a general strike. They informed Vittorio Valletta that they were taking over Fiat and he and Agnelli were stripped of power. It was like 1920 all over again. However, by this time Agnelli was an old man and he died, aged 79, on 16 December, so that he did not live to see Fiat's stupendous post-war growth.

The stalemate was soon resolved when Valletta returned to Fiat in April 1946 having, in addition, stepped into Agnelli's shoes as chairman. He had been detained by the Allied military government, accused of fascist sympathies, but this was now in the past and he got down to putting Fiat back on the road to recovery. Lingotto had been badly damaged by bombing during the war, while, fortunately, Mirafiori had suffered less and was

back in production – for trucks, at least – in June 1945.

Valletta had an unenviable task before him: Italy lay in ruins. But, Fiat's pre-war record had been an impressive one and most Italians did not own a car, so the potential market was vast. From 1946 onwards, however, that peculiarly Italian confection, the motor scooter, began to make its appearance, although Lambrettas and Vespas did not begin to make a real impact until the 1950s.

Valletta's brief was 'to regain our former ascendancy, to re-establish the prestige of Italian technology and to safeguard the jobs of our skilled workforce'. By the time he retired in 1966, he could look back on two decades of almost uninterrupted growth. Fiat had built a mere 28,360 cars in 1947, rising to more than 145,000 in 1953; the half-million mark was reached in 1960, and 1966 was the first year in which a million cars were built — a feat of great significance for both Fiat and Italy.

But, back in those early post-war years, Valletta's priority was to get production moving again and then to lay down plans for a new generation of Fiat cars. In 1946 he moved Dante Giacosa up to be head of car design, a position he held, with great distinction, until 1970.

This is an appropriate moment for mentioning a freelance project that Giacosa undertook for industrialist Piero Dusio, who had decided to establish a new make – the Cisitalia – in the post-war years. First Giacosa designed a Balilla-engined single-seater racing car with Topolino independent front suspension which proved, for a time, a popular curtain-raiser at Grand Prix events in the late 1940s. This was followed, in 1948, by a road car which was fitted with a magnificent coupé body by Pinin Farina and was universally acknowledged for its purity of line and proportion. Although Dusio made Giacosa a tempting offer to join him, the latter wisely decided to stay with Fiat: the industrialist subsequently bankrupted himself with an over-ambitious racing car project.

Once back at Fiat, Giacosa immediately turned his attention to updating the popular but ageing Topolino, which continued in production in its original form until 1948. It was replaced that year by the 500B, virtually identical to its predecessor, but with overhead rather than side valves. At the same time a Giardiniera station wagon, with a longer wheelbase, and consequently a genuine four-seater, was introduced. The 500B lasted until 1949. Minor changes were also made to the 1100, which acquired a B suffix in 1948, although these modifications were more cosmetic than mechanical and, like the 500B, the 1100 remained available until 1949. The 1500D, also with minor modifications, was produced over a similar period.

Much more significant changes followed in 1949 when the 500C appeared. This, although similar in concept to its predecessors, boasted a revised front end with a new wing line, incorporating the headlamps, while the engine was fitted with an aluminium cylinder head. The C proved even more popular than its forebears: output continued until 1955 and no less than 376,370 found owners. Changes to the 1100 and 1500, both of which acquired the E suffix, were less radical, but the pair benefited from rear-opening boots. The latter lasted only until 1950 and, by 1953, the 1100E was no more. However, in 1950 the 1100 had been offered in handsome coupé form by Pinin Farina. This was a replacement for the 1100S, introduced back in 1947, and a successor to the aerodynamic 508C MM of pre-war days. Savio was again responsible for the bodywork as a mere 401 were produced. Examples were placed second, third and fourth in the 1948 Mille Miglia, but the event was, significantly, won by a Ferrari. Italy's new post-war make had bared its teeth.

Post-war progress

Fiat's first truly post-war car did not appear until 1950. This was the 1400, a no-frills four-door saloon and the firm's first unitary construction production model. It was a completely new car with a very oversquare (82 × 66 mm) 1395 cc overhead-valve engine, four-speed gearbox and fashionable steering-column gearchange. Gone was the Dubonnet independent front suspension to be replaced by more conventional coils and wishbones, although the rear layout was unusual with coils and quarter-elliptic springs. Top speed was 120 km/h (75 mph), but the acceleration was distinctly unimpressive. A diesel-engined version was to follow in 1953, but before that, in 1952, came a 1900 derivative, with a 1901 cc version of the smaller-capacity engine, and a five-speed gearbox. A semi-automatic option was also available, the first time this was offered on a Fiat car. The power unit was shared with the Campagnola, a Jeep-like vehicle with optional four-wheel drive which Fiat had introduced in 1951. The Campagnola continued to be made in this form until 1955 and was replaced by petrol (A) and diesel (B) versions, which were manufactured until 1973.

LEFT *The 500 went to overhead valves in 1948 with the 500B, and this is its C successor, with new front end and 569 cc engine with aluminium cylinder head. This is a 1953 car. Built between 1949 and 1955, total 500C production amounted to an impressive 376,370 cars.*

RIGHT *The 1400, introduced in 1950, was Fiat's first new post-war model and boasted unitary construction and a heater as standard. It was powered by a new 1395 cc four-cylinder engine and lasted until 1954, by which time more than 77,000 examples had been built.*

LEFT *Spiritual successor to the Topolino was the Nuova (New) 500 of 1957 with its rear-mounted air-cooled 479 cc vertical two-cylinder engine and all-independent suspension. It evolved as the 500D in 1960 and the F in 1965, remaining in production in Italy until 1972.*

RIGHT *The 8V coupé of 1952–4 was a rare Fiat extravagance; only 114 were made. Powered by a unique 1996 cc V8 overhead-valve engine, it was capable of 190 km/h (118 mph). It was also the first Fiat to feature all-independent suspension which was by wishbones and coil springs. This is a Vignale-bodied version of 1954.*

The 1952 Geneva Show was the venue for Fiat's announcement of a car very much in the spirit of the 1921 Super Fiat. This was the exclusive 8V coupé, so called because Ford owned the V8 model name. It was a presitigious model, styled and built in-house by Fiat, with a 105 bhp 1996 cc overhead-valve V8 engine. Suspension was all-independent, the first such on any Fiat, and was by coil springs. A top speed of 190 km/h (118 mph) was claimed. The 8V lasted for two years and sold for £2,800,000 lire (£1600), but only 114 were built. Its engine was never used in another production Fiat because Giacosa's plans to fit it in a prestige saloon were shelved.

Fiat's 1100 of 1953, by contrast, was a car for the masses. It followed the 1400/1900 unitary construction theme and, although the 1089 cc engine had a similar capacity to its predecessor's, the unit had, in fact, been extensively reworked. It was made available in 50, rather than 36 bhp, TV (Turismo Veloce) form, and there was also a short-lived 'convertible' version, introduced in 1955.

All these models had been relatively conventional, but in 1955 Giacosa unveiled Fiat's first rear-engined car, the 600 – the apparent successor to the 500. The roots of this project were anchored in the war years when Giacosa had created three alternative designs to replace the Topolino. One had a transversely mounted 570 cc four-cylinder engine with front-wheel drive, another was rear-engined, and the third had a conventional front engine/rear drive layout.

Giacosa opted for rear drive, on cost grounds. An air-cooled flat two-cyliner engine was considered, but eventually a water-cooled four was standardized. However, as the engine was mounted lengthways, it proved impossible to fit the radiator without extending the body, so Giacosa had the idea of placing the radiator alongside the engine. The 633 cc overhead-valve unit was a model of simplicity and powered what was a genuine four-seater. Suspension was independent all round, with a transverse leaf spring at the front, and rear trailing arms and coil springs. Not only did the 600 prove immensely popular, it also handled well for a rear-engined car, and more than 950,000 examples were built over a five-year period . . . and at a price of 590,000 lire (£265) it brought the joys of car ownership to many Italians for the first time. There was also the ingenious long-wheelbase Multipla, with seating for four or five, but with coil and wishbone front suspension courtesy of the 1100.

The 500C had been discontinued in 1955 and it was assumed that the 600 had taken its place. But, in 1957, came the two-cylinder Nuova (New) 500 which clearly followed in the wheeltracks of the 600. Here again the model's origins can be found in Giacosa's wartime experiments, although in 1953 German Fiat had, in fact, proposed a rear-engined design powered by a one- or two-cylinder two-stroke engine. Giacosa was averse to two-strokes, but he did recognize the increasing threat in the bottom end of the market from the motor scooter, and even master-minded a styling exercise inspired by the lines of the Vespa!

Eventually, Giacosa decided on a vertical two-cylinder air-cooled design as being the cheapest possible power unit. Although a flat-twin engine was considered, it was discounted on cost grounds since it required twice the manifolding. The engine was designed by Giovanni Torazzi, who at the time was with Lancia but was 'poached' by Giacosa for the purpose.

Like the Topolino and 600, the new 500 could be had with an opening fabric roof, with the air of austerity underlined by the absence of hub caps. The price was 465,000 lire (£265) and top speed was claimed to be a rather breathless 85 km/h (53 mph). However the acclaim that had greeted the 600 was not so lavishly extended to its smaller brother. Improvements were therefore made to the engine which helped to push the top speed up to 90 km/h (56 mph). These improvements meant that the 500 was all set for a 16-year production run.

Six cylinders again

Fiat had fought shy of six cylinders since the demise of the 1500 in 1950, and the first new post-war sixes – the 1800 and 2100 – did not arrive until 1959. These were basically the same car with new, rather American styling, and the two alternative engines of 1795 and 2054 cc were unusual in that they featured inclined overhead valves, actuated through twin rocker shafts. Front suspension, by torsion bars, was also a first for a Fiat. Sadly, it was hardly a successful design, and only around 30,000 were produced over a three-year production run. The range was uprated in 1961, with the arrival of the 1800B with all-round disc brakes. The 2100 became the 2300, identifiable by its twin headlights, and with an enlarged 2279 cc engine, while there was also a 2300S coupé by Ghia which lasted, like the 1800B, until 1968. The 2300 saloon, however, was discontinued in 1963.

In 1961 the same styling was extended to a new 1300/1500 range. Engines were of 1295 and 1481 cc, sharing the same unusual valve gear pioneered on the six, and front disc brakes, a first on a Fiat, were a notable feature. The range lasted until 1967, by which time more than 600,000 examples had been built. There was also a station wagon version: this body variant was available in most Fiat model ranges from the 1950s.

In May 1964 Fiat unveiled a new, small model intended to slot in between the 600 and 1100. This was the 850, derived from the 600, and powered by an 843 cc version of its engine, attained by increasing the bore size from 62 to 65 mm. As with the 500, there were two versions available – the standard model producing 40 bhp and capable of 120 km/h (74 mph), and the 125 km/h (77 mph), 42 bhp Super. The 850 was somewhat roomier than its 600 parent with a 2027 mm (6 ft 7⅞ in) wheelbase rather than a 2000 mm (6 ft 6¾ in) one.

In 1965 came a sporting version, a pretty, fastback coupé, styled in-house and manufactured by Fiat, although the spider was the work of Bertone and produced by them. The coupé boasted 52 bhp while the open car was even nippier, with 54 bhp on hand. Front disc brakes were another departure from standard on a model that, on a good day, could reach as much as 135 km/h (84 mph).

The 1300/1500 range was replaced in March 1966 by a deceptively orthodox model. In fact, the 124 was a completely new car. The boxy four-door saloon, produced a zippy 140 km/h (87 mph) from its 60 bhp, 1197 cc engine. This engine was the work of Aurelio Lampredi, Ferrari's engine designer who had joined Fiat back in 1955. Disc brakes were fitted all round and suspension was by coils, the live rear axle employing trailing arms and a Panhard rod.

Later in the year, at the 1966 Turin Show, Fiat unveiled the 124 Sport Spider, styled and built by Pininfarina. Unlike the saloon car, which used a pokey pushrod engine, the Sport had a 90 bhp 1438 cc twin-overhead-camshaft unit. Such an expensive configuration was made possible by Fiat following the German Glas company in adopting a neoprene-toothed belt in place of pricey chains to drive the twin shafts. It was the first twin-cam Fiat since the short-lived 501SS of 1921 vintage.

As if all this was not enough, Fiat also introduced its Dino spider at that 1966 Turin Show. The story of its antecedents has already been recounted in the Ferrari section of this book on page 76 but, in short, it was powered by a 2-litre V6 Fiat-built Ferrari engine with twin overhead camshafts per cylinder bank,

and was a 210 km/h (130 mph) sports car with bodywork styled and built by Pininfarina. In the following year came a coupé version, by Bertone, and in 1969 the V6's capacity was increased to 2418 cc and independent rear suspension was introduced. The Dino lasted until 1972.

Meanwhile, the 124 family was continuing to grow. At the 1967 Geneva Show Fiat introduced its 124 Sport Coupé. The 1438 cc engine was the same as that used in the spider, while a five-speed gearbox was an optional extra.

Then, in May 1967, what was effectively an upmarket version of the 124 made its début: the 125. This was a cocktail of the 1300/1500 floorpan and 124 body panels, easily identifiable by its twin headlamps. Under the bonnet was a 1608 cc version of the twin-cam four that had already appeared in the sporty 124s. The 160 km/h (100 mph) 125 lasted for only a year in this form, for in 1968 it became the 125 Special with uprated 100 bhp engine and five-speed gearbox; this version survived until 1972. A 124 Special appeared at the same time, also with twin headlamps, but powered by a 1438 cc version of the pushrod four. Sadly, it enjoyed only a two-year production life.

Overseas expansion

Fiat was growing not only at home but also abroad. By the mid-1960s subsidiaries had been established as far afield as India, Brazil and Argentina. In Europe, Fiat also had a long-standing German presence, having taken over NSU's Heilbronn factory in 1932, when that firm bowed out of cars to concentrate on motor cycle production. SEAT, the firm's Spanish persona, had been established in 1953 by the Spanish government and produced Fiats under licence. In due course Fiat agreed to take the business over and, in 1979, assumed full management control, although the following year it was forced to withdraw from the scheme as part of a corporate economy drive. Since 1986 Volkswagen has had a majority holding.

But by far Fiat's most important foreign involvement came in August 1966 when the company gained a valuable contract, worth around £21 million, to establish a car factory at Stavropol (renamed Togliattigrad after the Italian Communist leader Palmiro Togliatti) in Russia to produce a more robust version of the 124 saloon. Although externally similar, the VAZ 2101 of 1969 was powered by a 1198 cc single overhead camshaft engine which replaced the usual pushrod unit. A starting handle was offered as standard! For export markets, the car was sold under the Lada name. Another involvement behind the iron curtain is in Poland, where the Balilla was produced under licence between 1932 and 1939. The Polski-Fiat name was revived in 1968 and the first model, although outwardly it looked like a 124, was mainly based on the obsolete 1300/1500 series, discontinued in 1967.

In 1966 Vittorio Valletta had, at last, stepped down from the Fiat presidency. Heaped with honours, he had been given the title of Honorary Papal Academic in 1956 by Pope Pius XII, while in 1959 the Turin Polytechnic had awarded him a degree in industrial engineering. His place as president was taken by Giovanni Agnelli's grandson, Gianni, thus perpetuating the dynasty. The new president inherited a company which was much larger than the one that Valletta had taken over in 1946 for, in addition to its burgeoning car production, Fiat had expanded into earth-moving machinery, nuclear energy and, later, gas turbine production.

LEFT *The handsome 124 Sport Coupé, introduced in 1967. This is the second series version of 1969–72 with 1438 or 1608 cc twin-overhead-camshaft engine. The larger capacity one was derived from the 125 Special unit.*

ABOVE RIGHT *The 125 of 1967/8 was a cocktail of the 1300/1500 floorpan and 124 body panels. The engine was a 1608 cc twin-overhead-camshaft unit.*

RIGHT *The Fiat-styled 850 coupé with 843 cc rear-mounted four-cylinder engine.*

OVERLEAF *A 1970 Fiat Dino spider. It was introduced in 1966, and in 1969 engine capacity was increased from 1987 cc to 2481 cc, while independent rear suspension, similar to that used in the 130 saloon, also featured. Provided by Michael Morris.*

RIGHT *The 128 of 1969 was the first front-wheel drive Fiat. Its transversely mounted 1116 cc engine featured a toothed belt to drive the single overhead camshaft. The 128 was built in these forms until 1976, then facelifted.*

BELOW RIGHT *The elegant 130 coupé, by Pininfarina, built between 1972 and 1977, far outlived its saloon parent of 1969–71. Its V6 engine had Dino origins and all-independent suspension featured. The top speed was 190 km/h (118 mph).*

Gianni Agnelli, a lawyer by training, had not been at the helm for long before a series of mergers, take-overs and investments were set in train. Fiat had already absorbed the Turin-based Autobianchi company by 1963, but an announcement made in November 1968 involved Fiat for the first time with a partner in another European country. The company's interest centred on Citroën, number two in the French market, and owned, since 1935, by the Michelin tyre company. There were, however, protests from the French government, which was reluctant to see a foreign company taking a share in what it considered to be a national institution. Finally, an uncontroversial statement was issued by the two firms declaring that they would engage in a programme of technical cooperation and research, 'in investment and production programmes and in supply and sales'. Through Pardevi, a holding company, Fiat took a 15 per cent stake in Citroën. Interestingly enough, the French company had absorbed the Italian Maserati concern in January 1968 so that it could acquire a sophisticated engine for its planned Grand Tourer, which emerged as the SM in 1970.

Fiat's next corporate involvement was announced in June 1969 when the firm revealed that it was taking a 50 per interest in Ferrari. The links between Enzo Ferrari and Fiat were long-standing indeed: in 1919 Enzo had unsuccessfully applied for a job there! His 1940 815 was largely Fiat-based and when, in 1955, Ferrari made a public appeal for funds it was Fiat who came to his rescue. Then, in the 1960s, came the joint project for Fiat to build Ferrari's V6 engine. This was at a time when Ferrari's finances were becoming increasingly precarious and Ford had been making a determined effort to buy Italy's most prestigious make. It was against this background that Agnelli and Ferrrari were able to come to an agreement, as a result of which Fiat took over responsibility for the marketing and production of the Ferrari road cars, leaving the *Commendatore* to handle the racing side of the business which was, after all, his first love. In fact, Fiat's involvement with Ferrari ensured the Maranello firm's survival for, without Fiat's protective umbrella, Ferrari would never have been able to survive the post-energy crisis storms of the 1970s.

Then, five months later, in November 1969, Fiat announced the even greater prize of taking over Lancia, which in that year had built 31,556 cars compared with Fiat's 1.2 million. Again there were long-standing connections between the two firms, for had not Vincenzo Lancia joined Fiat at its inception in 1899 and raced Fiats in the early years of the century? The Turin firm had been second only to Fiat pre-war but had slipped to a poor third place behind a revitalized Alfa Romeo in the 1950s and 60s. In marked contrast to Fiat, Lancia had always maintained a higher technological profile: in 1961 it had become the first major Italian car maker to adopt front-wheel drive, the resultant Flavia having been designed by Antonio Fessia, formerly of Fiat. All this had culminated in an accumulated 69 billion lire (£46 million) debt. Again Ford had been interested, but the Italian government was not, and Fiat paid a nominal 1 lira for Lancia *and* those debts. Fiat maintained that it would respect Lancia's independence as a car manufacturer, although there has been the inevitable cross-pollination of models in order to rationalize production facilities. Under Fiat's direction

Lancia's output has trebled, yet the marque has nevertheless managed to maintain its very distinctive persona.

The association with Citroën had a less happy conclusion. In 1973 Fiat unscrambled its involvement by pulling out of the Pardevi partnership while, in the wake of the energy crisis, Michelin finally ceded control of Citroën to Peugeot in a deal finalized in December 1974.

All this corporate activity did not interfere with the continuing evolution of the Fiat range. Until 1969 the firm had largely ignored the upper end of the market, but in that year it unveiled its 130 model, aimed straight at the executive customer. The 130 was a completely new car, with a 2.8-litre V6 engine based on the bottom end of the Dino unit: the elaborate twin-cam heads were dispensed with, along with their driving chains, and were replaced by single-cam units driven by toothed belts. Although automatic transmission was a standard fitment,

traditional front engine/rear drive formula and adopted a transverse engine/front-wheel drive layout: maybe Giovanni Agnelli's antipathy had cast a long shadow . . . The 128 replaced the 1100 range although the transverse location had already been pioneered on the in-house Autobianchi Primula of 1965. The 1116 cc engine was also notable for its use of an overhead camshaft driven by a toothed belt in the manner of the 124/125 engines. As far as suspension was concerned, front was by struts, while the time-honoured transverse spring did its faithful duty at the rear.

Rally recognition

In 1971 Fiat introduced the 1290 cc 67 bhp Rally version of the 128 and although the 150 km/h (93 mph) car lasted only until it was dropped in 1972, it did reflect Fiat's growing commitment

a five-speed gearbox was available. All-independent suspension was employed, but the 130 had a relatively brief life and was discontinued in 1971. That was, however, not the end of the model, for Pininfarina came up with a sensational coupé version and, with engine capacity upped to 3235 cc, the top speed rose to an impressive 190 km/h (118 mph). The 130 coupé was destined for a longer production life than the original model, as its timeless good looks ensured that it remained in production until 1977. It was available with three-speed automatic transmission or a five-speed all-syncromesh manual gearbox.

Nineteen sixty-nine was significant for another reason: with the announcement of the 128, Fiat at long last abandoned the

to rallying as a valuable publicity aid. A rally department had been opened in 1969, and in the following year Fiat took over the Turin-based Abarth company, which had been making Fiats go faster since 1950. Initially the firm fielded the 124 Sport in Italian events, and in 1972 the 124 Abarth Rally was introduced as an official Fiat model. This had a 128 bhp version of the versatile twin-cam four, with capacity increased to 1756 cc, and the principal design modification was the introduction of MacPherson strut independent rear suspension. In 1972 Raffaele Pinto won the European Rally Championship for Drivers in an Abarth, the same year in which in-house Lancia won the World Rally Championship for the first time.

In 1974 the 124 Abarth won the Yugoslavian, Bulgarian and Eastern Alps title, and was second in the World Championship behind Lancia which was sweeping all before it with its mid-engined Stratos: it was much the same story, and another second place, in 1975. By now the creation and preparation of the Fiat rally team was vested in Abarth and directed by Aurelio Lampredi, but the 124 was becoming outdated and in 1976 it was replaced by the 131 Abarth. In 1975, before the 131's 1995 cc single-overhead-camshaft four-cylinder engine was ready, Lampredi had fitted a 270 bhp 3.2-litre V6 unit derived from the 130 saloon. All-independent suspension featured and, to the surprise of one and all, the 131 Abarth 031 won the Tour of Italy in this form.

By 1976 the new engine was ready and, in addition to successes in Italian events, the 131 Abarth went on to win the important Finnish 1000 Lakes Rally. In 1977 Fiat drove off with the coveted World Rally Championship courtesy of the same model, with victories in the Portuguese, New Zealand and Canadian events, along with pivotal successes in the Corsican and San Remo rallies.

At the end of the year, in order to rationalize resources, the Fiat and Lancia teams were combined in a single organization, *Ente Attività Sportiva Automobilistica*, better known by its EASA initials, which were shortened to ASA in the following year. Nineteen seventy-eight proved a marvellous year for the Fiat team when the 131 won five events and again took the championship title. Fiat was once more victorious in 1980 with the proven 131 Abarth and enjoyed noteworthy success at the Monte Carlo Rally – its first victory there since 1928. An ASA-prepared car again won the 1983 championship title, although on that occasion the Lancia Rallye was victorious.

These successes on the rally field undoubtedly helped the sale of Fiat's road cars in a difficult decade. The company maintained the front-wheel-drive theme, established with the 128, when it introduced the 127 to replace the 850 range in 1971. The 903 cc pushrod engine of the 850 coupé was perpetuated

and the 127 proved a great success for Fiat, particularly when the hatchback version arrived in 1972 which was responsible for greatly popularizing the three-door small car theme which is now the norm. The 127 was destined for a ten-year production life, lasting until 1981. In 1977 the model was facelifted and a 1049 cc engine option, courtesy of Fiat's Brazil factory, was added. During its long career more than four million examples of the 127 were made.

It was back to rear drive for the 132, the 125's successor. The 1592 cc twin-cam engine was derived from the 124 and 125 Sport models but, despite its 165 km/h (103 mph) performance, the model remained in production only until 1974. Its engine, however, formed the basis of that used in the new Campagnola off-road vehicle of 1974 which is still in production.

RIGHT *The mid-engined X1/9, styled and conceived by Bertone, was powered by a version of the 128 Sport 1300 four-cylinder overhead-camshaft engine. It was made in this form until late 1978 when it was revised with an enlarged 1498 cc engine and five-speed gearbox. From 1982 Bertone took the model over, and thereafter the X1/9 was badged as such. This is the top-line VS model.*

BELOW *The 127, replacement for the 850, appeared in 1971 and perpetuated the front-wheel-drive theme, pioneered by the 128 in 1969. The 903 cc pushrod engine was derived from that of the 850 Sport.*

In the same year, the 126, successor to the 500, made its appearance. Styling showed similarities with the 127, although the rear-engined theme was maintained. However, the air-cooled vertical-twin engine was increased in capacity from 499 to 594 cc, and the gearbox now boasted synchromesh on the top three gears. From September 1980 output was concentrated on the Polski-Fiat factory in Warsaw, and the 126 is still being produced there.

A mid-engined sports car

Most of Fiat's sports cars had been created by rebodying existing models, but in 1972 Fiat introduced its X1/9 mid-engined model. The car had been conceived not by Fiat but by Bertone, who was responsible for the sleek, wedge-shaped styling. The mid-located power unit was effectively the 1290 cc single overhead camshaft of the 128 Sport of 1971/75, mounted transversely ahead of the rear axle line. The X1/9 was a coupé, although the roof panel was detachable and could be stored in the front luggage compartment. Suspension was independent all round, by struts, and this 170 km/h (106 mph) model was soon making plenty of friends on both sides of the Atlantic. For 1979 the X1/9's capacity was increased to 1489 cc. However, Fiat found that the numbers produced – 140,519 in nine years – although impressive by sports car standards, were not viable in the depressed market of the early 1980s, so Bertone took over the entire project and, from 1982, the car was badged not as a Fiat, but as a Bertone, and is still built in this form.

Although by now fully committed to front-wheel drive, Fiat continued to uphold the more traditional rear-drive approach with the 131 Mirafiori of 1975, introduced to replace the 124. Engines could be either 1300 or 1600 cc, and were unusual in that they were overhead-valve units but with belt- rather than chain-driven *side*-mounted camshafts. The 131 soldiered on until 1978.

Nineteen seventy-six saw the 128 facelifted, with a new radiator grille and rectangular headlamps. An additional 1300 engine was introduced, and this remained available until 1978; thereafter only the 1100 cc unit could be specified. The 126 also benefited from new interior trim, and in 1977 it was given a 650 cc engine. Fiat had introduced the rear-drive 1592 cc twin-cam 132 in 1972, and this was revised in 1974 as the GLS series. It was again uprated in 1977, given an additional 1995 cc engine, and remained in production until 1981.

As will have been apparent, Fiat was slowing down the rate at which it introduced new models and even relied for a time on updating existing ones for, in 1974, a halt was placed on new car development. This was as a result of the effects of the 1973 Arab-Israeli war, which sent shock waves through the industrialized world. Gianni Agnelli responded by doing just what his grandfather had done after the 1907 depression: he diversified. Fiat expanded into civil engineering equipment and telecommunications with the result that profitability was maintained, but at the expense of the car line. More than 1.5 million Fiats were built in 1973, but this dropped to 1.1 million in 1978.

Another 1978 revelation was that, while the Japanese Toyota employees produced 43 cars per worker per year and the West German Opel firm managed 29, Fiat employees could average only 11.2. This poor productivity record coincided with the growth of Red Brigade activities in Italy which made Fiat, as Italy's largest private enterprise company, a prime target for its activities. From the end of 1973, until the beginning of 1980, Fiat employees suffered 29 terrorist attacks, four people were killed, one kidnapped and 27 wounded. There was sabotage

inside the factory and, in 1979 alone, about 200,000 cars were lost through sabotage and strikes.

Consequently, in October 1979, Gianni Agnelli received a deputation of middle managers, and 61 left-wing militants were later sacked for such charges as sabotage, intimidation and vandalism. Although the union protested, and took the case to court, the company's action was upheld.

Changes were made to Fiat's corporate structure: the old pyramid system was disbanded and Fiat became a holding company with its interests grouped into 11 wholly-owned subsidiaries responsible for their own design, production and marketing facilities. But by the time that this enormous undertaking had been completed there followed the second, and more damaging 1979 oil crisis and Fiat made its third massive loss. The firm therefore announced it would be laying off 23,000 of its 136,000 car workers and those remaining would have to agree to increases in productivity.

Consequently, the *Federazione Lavoratori Metalmeccanici* (FLM) union called a strike in September 1980 that lasted for 35 days. The stalemate was broken by the so-called 'March of 40,000', a spontaneous procession through the streets of Turin by Fiat foremen and workers protesting against the stoppage. As a result the strike was broken and the management had a decisive upper hand. First it was a matter of dismissing the proposed 23,000 but, in view of falling demand, Fiat began laying off 70,000 members of its workforce for one week in every month. The combination of wage-saving and industrial peace provided Fiat with some much-needed breathing space. However, the 1980 production figure of 874,419 was the lowest since 1964.

Even more significantly, a £4 billion investment plan was under way and, already, a new Fiat, the first for four years, had made its appearance – in 1978. This was the front-wheel-drive Ritmo, with 1100, 1300 and 1500 engine options. A popular 1.7-litre diesel version followed in 1980, and the model continued to be built until 1982.

RIGHT *The front-wheel-drive Fiat Ritmo of 1978 was offered with 1116, 1301 and 1498 cc engines. It was marketed as the Strada in English-speaking countries.*

BELOW LEFT *The 131 Mirafiori appeared in 1974, and this is the new 131 Supermirafiori of 1978–81. Larger-capacity 1301 and 1585 cc engines were available.*

BELOW *Fiat is renowned for its robots, developed by its Comau division, and initially used for body production, as shown here. Robots have since been employed for engine assembly at a new factory at Termoli.*

New models and methods

The Ritmo, sold under the Strada name in English-speaking countries, was significant because it was the first Fiat to have its bodywork built by robots, which carried out the time-consuming and unpleasant spot-welding operation. Fiat had initiated automated welding back in 1961 and these Smart robots were manufactured by its own Comau subsidiary.

A major new Fiat arrived in 1980. This, the Panda, was an important development as it was the first mass-produced Fiat in which the all-important styling was entrusted to an outside consultant – in this instance the Turin-based Ital Design. Inevitably front-wheel-drive, the Panda is available with a choice of overhead-valve engines: a two-cylinder air-cooled 650 cc of 126 antecedence and only available on the Italian market, or a 900 cc water-cooled four. Front suspension is by struts, but the cost-conscious Panda has a cart-sprung rear.

The Uno, another important model, and an effective successor to the 127, appeared in 1983. The hatchback body, again by Ital Design, is available in three- and five-door forms and the

ABOVE *The top-selling Giugiaro-styled Uno of 1983, which perpetuated the 127 theme and its 903 cc engine.*

all-independent MacPherson strut suspension.

ABOVE RIGHT *The front-wheel-drive Croma of 1986, Fiat's latest bid for the executive market. Giugiaro-styled, it has*

RIGHT *The Panda of 1980 spawned a 1982 Super version, the first Fiat to feature the now-familiar five-bar logo which was subsequently extended to all Pandas.*

903 cc engine was inherited from the 127. A diesel version followed in 1983, and two years later came the result of yet another phase of Fiat's robotized production process. Previously, robots had been used only for body assembly, but in 1985 the FIRE (Fully Integrated Robotized Engine) made its appearance, this 999 cc overhead camshaft unit being fitted in the Uno 45 and 45S.

Fiat was back in the black again in 1981 and has been in profit every year since. The new models have come thick and fast: in

1983 came the Regata, a Ritmo derivative with a conventional boot. This 'notchback' can be specified with 1300, 1500 and 1600 power units. In the same year a four-wheel-drive version of the Panda made its appearance. This particular project was undertaken in conjunction with the Austrian Steyr company who have many years of experience in this field. The engine is also different from the usual Panda unit and is a 965 cc one.

Fiat achieved its greatest corporate coup in 1987 when it took over the loss-making state-owned Alfa Romeo company. It has set up a subsidiary with Lancia under which that firm will concentrate on the luxury end of the market and Alfa Romeo will maintain its traditional sporting role. De Tomaso's Innocenti and Maserati interests apart, this has given Fiat control of the entire Italian motor industry.

In 1986 Fiat again made a bid for the executive market, with the Croma, a four-door saloon which looks like a notchback but has a rear-opening tailgate. This is Fiat's contribution to the so-called Type Four project, in which the company has combined with Alfa Romeo, Saab and in-house Lancia to share component costs without jeopardizing individuality. For the front-wheel-drive Croma, Fiat's well-tried 2-litre twin-overhead-camshaft engine is mounted transversely, and there is a top-line turbocharged model.

The Croma typifies the Fiat design philosophy which reaches back nearly 90 years. It is to innovate – not agressively but with deliberation, sagacity and flair and the continuity of this philosophy has ensured the marque's survival. Giovanni Agnelli laid a sure foundation.

Lamborghini

The booming 1960s witnessed the birth of a handful of new Italian makes, and those that managed to last the decade were mostly killed off by the effects of the 1973 oil crisis. However, one car company has succeeded in weathering 24 sometimes turbulent years: Lamborghini, a marque of almost unparalleled distinction and allure.

Ferruccio Lamborghini was 47 years old when his first car appeared, in 1963. In the early 1900s, Lamborghini's father was a wealthy farmer, with an estate at Renazzo, just 32 km (20 miles) from Modena, the birthplace of Enzo Ferrari. Like many young men, Ferruccio grew up to love cars and motor cycles. Luckily his father presented him with a motor bike and he even won a race on a Norton 500 at nearby Ferrara, though Ferruccio is not particularly proud of that victory. (While he was in fifth position the leader crashed, leaving the rest of the field in disarray and allowing Lamborghini a way through.)

But young Ferruccio had seen enough of agriculture to realize that he did not wish to follow in his father's footsteps. He decided instead that he wanted to work with machinery, so he took a course in industrial technology at the Fratelli Taddia Institute near Bologna, and just graduated in time before he had to enlist in the armed forces. Italy was at war in 1940 and, once in uniform, Ferruccio was stationed on the island of Rhodes, where he had plenty of opportunities to put his mechanical abilities to good use. There he was surrounded by the internal combustion engine, be it in cars, aircraft or trucks.

The Italian garrison on Rhodes was in a difficult position because, while Italy had made peace with the Allies in September 1943, Germany certainly had not. So, although Greece fell to British troops in November 1944, Rhodes, with its

LEFT *The epitome of the Italian supercar, the over 289 km/h (180 mph) Lamborghini Countach, introduced in 1974, is still in production. It represents an outstanding combination of a mid-located longitudinally mounted V12 engine and breathtaking Bertone-styled bodywork. The engine capacity was originally 3929 cc, although this was increased to 4754 cc for the LP500S of 1982, and to 5167 cc, with four-valve cylinder heads, in 1985.*

German divisions, held out until 1 May 1945, only a week before VE Day. When the British eventually occupied the island, Ferruccio Lamborghini became a prisoner-of-war, although he was happy enough, as he was responsible for running the motor pool. By the time Ferruccio returned to Italy, in late 1946, he considered himself to be a good mechanic, thanks partly to the demands of wartime improvisation.

With the coming of peace, Ferruccio decided to build on his wartime experiences and opened a garage in Cento, near his birthplace, where he was fully occupied keeping mostly pre-war cars, lorries and tractors in running order. He married but, tragically, his wife died giving birth to their son Tonino in 1947.

Like many other Italians, Lamborghini owned a Fiat 500, but it was barely recognizable as such for he had removed the original body and replaced it with an open two-seater one of his own design. In addition the engine had been bored out to 750 cc, and Lamborghini had produced a special bronze overhead-valve cylinder head, which he called *Testa d'Oro* (gold head). Lamborghini was one of the 167 participants in the 1948 Mille Miglia with his Fiat 'special', entered in the 750 class. His co-driver was Gian Luigi Baglioni, a farmer friend of Ferruccio from Ferrara. The race went fairly well until, while Baglioni was at the wheel, they skidded off the road in the town of Fiano, near Turin, and the Fiat ploughed through the wall of a local restaurant: Lamborghini's disgruntled father had to pay for the damage. The eventual winner of that Mille Miglia was a Ferrari—Italy's new post-war make. Despite his accident, Lamborghini was approached by other Topolino owners for whom he produced a number of his *Testa d'Oro* conversions.

Lamborghini thereafter lost interest in racing, as he saw little point in pursuing something for which he had no talent. Ferruccio did have a talent for making things, however. His farming father was desperate for a tractor, so Ferruccio set to and made him one. With his knowledge of both British and Italian cars and lorries, he cobbled together a vehicle probably powered by a 60 hp six-cylinder Morris engine, with General Motors transmission and Ford differential! He christened this unlikely device *carioche*, after the Spanish word *carioca* which means a song of many parts. Such was the paucity of tractors in the immediate post-war years, that his father's neighbours were soon queuing up for similar machines. Fortunately, Lamborghini junior managed to secure a supply of war-surplus Morris engines, sent to Italy as spare parts during hostilities. One of the attractions of these tractors was that they were fitted with what Lamborghini called *La Vaporizza* (vaporizer), which enabled the tractor to be warmed up on petrol. After a few minutes the owner could switch to a cheaper, low-octane brew.

In 1949 Lamborghini decided that the demand for tractors was such that he would set up a production line and *Lamborghini Trattrici* (Lamborghini Tractors) was established on his garage site which was soon turned into a production factory. When supplies of the long-suffering Morris engine dried up in 1950/1, Ferruccio was sufficiently confident of the demand for his products to begin designing his own unit and, in 1952, came the first; a water-cooled diesel, with indirect fuel injection. Two years later, in 1954, he scored a notable first with an air-cooled direct-injection diesel, based on Deutz designs.

Lamborghini was on his way: his tractor business grew to be one of the largest in Italy, behind Fiat and Massey Ferguson. Ferruccio's strong sense of competition came to the fore at this time. By all accounts, a feature of market days in local towns was back-to-back tugs of war between Lamborghini's and rival

manufacturers' tractors. The winners, more often than not, were the redoubtable products of the Cento factory!

A multi-faceted talent

Soon, as demand increased, and output rose, 25 tractors were leaving the Cento works every day. Lamborghini was now a wealthy man and began to look around for something else to make. He was attracted by helicopters and, in 1959, two prototypes, coded L59, were flying. Unfortunately for Ferruccio, the Italian government would not sanction production, so Lamborghini had to look for an alternative product.

In 1960, as part of an Italian economic mission to America, Lamborghini conceived the idea of manufacturing oil heating systems for domestic and industrial use. When it was gently pointed out to him that this was bound to be seasonal business in view of the predictable quality of Italian summers, Ferruccio responded, 'We can make air-conditioning equipment when the machinery is idle.' And he did. A new factory was built at nearby Pieve di Cento, and *Lamborghini Bruciatori* (Lamborghini Burners) was established. The venture proved a success: the products were well built, sensibly priced and available through a nationwide dealer network.

Having now made two fortunes, Lamborghini once again turned his attention to cars, for he was determined to build his own model. As a rich industrialist he ran the best that Ferrari, Maserati, OSCA or Jaguar could offer, but he was more than aware of their shortcomings. He was later to recall that a certain, unnamed car was so hot inside that it caused his young lady companion's make-up to run. One was noisy, another was uncomfortable and yet another had poor brakes. Any Lamborghini car would have to be free of all these defects but, like a

ABOVE *Lamborghini has effectively produced two engines, both in aluminium, since car production began in 1964: the*

V12 created for the 350 GT, and the Urraco's V8 of 1971. Today they power the Countach and the Jalpa, respectively.

ABOVE LEFT *Ferruccio Lamborghini with the Miura V12 engine in which the five-speed gearbox is incorporated in the sump.*

TOP *Part of the Lamborghini factory at Sant'Agata Bolognese, located on the Via Modena that runs between Ferrara and Modena.*

to his amazement, discovered that its Borg and Beck unit was almost identical to the one he used on his tractors. Significantly, Ferrari was charging about ten times the price. . .

This anecdote rings much more true than the statement often attributed to Lamborghini – that he was anxious to 'get even' with Ferrari after being snubbed by the *Commendatore* on a visit to Maranello. Indeed, Ferruccio later confessed himself slightly apprehensive of Ferrari, as he had poached so many of his engineers and technicians!

The two did indeed meet and, in the summer of 1962, Ferrari recounted that during their talk Lamborghini (Enzo did not actually name him but described him as 'that fellow that builds tractors near Modena') had told him that he considered Ferrari produced the fastest road cars of all. He had come to this conclusion by driving all his cars at 200 km/h (125 mph), flicking the gear lever into neutral, and then counting the kilometres they covered under their own momentum before coming to a halt. The Ferrari had come off best.

Having made the decision to create the Lamborghini car, Ferruccio now needed somewhere to build it. He chose a site just north of the Milan to Bologna *autostrada* in Sant'Agata Bolognese. This small town lay on the minor road of Via Modena, which runs between Ferrara and Modena. Although the plant would not be completed until 1964 it was going to be Italy's most modern car factory. As Lamborghini was an industrialist of international repute, he discussed his idea with many of his contemporaries and was greatly influenced by German and Japanese engineers. The latter – Soichiro Honda in particular, who was a close friend – were to have a profound influence on the Lamborghini works. The result was a magnificently equipped and impeccably clean car-manufacturing plant; probably the most modern in Italy at that time.

Ferrari, it would have to have a V12 engine . . . but a better V12 than anything then emanating from Maranello.

Ferruccio also believed that he could make money out of the venture. When the clutch failed on his Ferrari it was returned to the factory for rectification, but the trouble persisted. So, in desperation, Lamborghini took the car to his tractor works and,

New recruits

Meanwhile Lamborghini proved to be the indirect beneficiary of a Ferrari management upheaval that occurred in November 1961. In that month no less than eight of the *Commendatore's* top staff left Maranello. They were headed by Girolamo Gardini, Ferrari's commercial manager and for many years considered the administrative power behind the throne. Then there was chief engineer Carlo Chiti, engineer Giotto Bizzarrini, team manager Romolo Tavoni, financial expert Ermano Della Caso, Maranello factory manager Federico Giberti (whose service went back to pre-war Scuderia Ferrari days), personnel manager Enzo Selmi, and foundry manager Giorgio Galassi.

The reasons for this mass exodus have never been fully explained. Ferrari's autocratic management methods may well have been the cause. Then again, there was talk of his wife Laura having meddled in the firm's affairs, with two managers deciding to quit as a result, and the others following. In the event, two of the eight – Della Casa and Giberti – returned. But Chiti and Tavoni set up the rival Bologna-based Automobili Turismo e Sport, where they produced the disastrous ATS Formula 1 car of 1963. In that year, Chiti left to found Autodelta in Undine which, in 1966, became part of Alfa Romeo. ATS had also produced its own mid-engined GT in 1962, but it had lasted for only two years.

From a design standpoint, Chiti was a serious loss to Ferrari, but so was 35-year-old Giotto Bizzarrini and he, like his former chief, set up in business on his own account. Bizzarrini had already had a distinguished career, working first for Alfa Romeo, then moving to Ferrari where the legendary GTO sports racer was designed under his direction. Immediately after leaving Maranello in 1962, he set up his own company, Prototipi Bizzarrini, in the west-coast town of Livorno, to carry out prototype work for other manufacturers. He had already been responsible for the A.S.A. – financed by the de Nora chemical company – with its Ferrari-derived 1100 cc single-overhead-camshaft engine, which was built in Milan from 1962 to 1966. In addition, Bizzarrini designed the Chevrolet Corvette-engined Iso Grifo of 1962. Even then, he did not rest on his laurels. After he had broken with Iso, he produced the Chrysler V8-powered GT Strada under his own name, between 1965 and 1969. He was a busy man!

Bizzarrini's role in the Lamborghini story is a crucial one, because it was he who was responsible for the V12 engine which powered Ferruccio's first car of 1963 and, in another form, the present-day Countach.

Fortunately for Lamborghini, during his time at Ferrari, Bizzarrini had designed a 60-degree 1.5-litre V12 engine which, in keeping with the Maranello Grand Prix engines, had twin overhead camshafts per cylinder bank. What Bizzarrini did was to scale up the design to 3.5 litres. He calculated that this would produce about the same power as the 4-litre single-overhead-camshaft V12 of the Ferrari road cars. Aluminium castings for the new engine were undertaken by ATS in Bologna, while Lamborghini's Cento tractor factory produced the all-important crankshafts from steel billets.

With work on the engine under way, Bizzarrini then turned his attention to the chassis for the new Lamborghini. Here he was able to give his talents free rein. Ferrari's well-known dictum was, 'I build engines and attach wheels to them', with chassis design playing second fiddle to the care lavished on the power unit. Bizzarrini would have dearly loved to have given the

GTO independent rear suspension, but the *Commendatore* was insistent that it have a conventional cart-sprung rear.

However, when Bizzarrini came to design the Lamborghini chassis, he was able to incorporate all-independent suspension, with unequal-length wishbones and coil spring damper units all round. It was Bizzarrini's fond hope that Lamborghini would make his first model a *corsaiola* (competition), rather than a Grand Touring car, so this first frame, made from 25 mm (1 in) diameter tubes and a network of smaller ones, weighed only 85 kg (188 lb).

Bizzarrini's completed engine produced an impressive 360 bhp at 8000 rpm. Lamborghini now had a crucial decision to make: was he to produce a sports racer, which would give Ferrari a run for his money on the race track, or should he build a superlative Gran Turismo car? He gave himself a week to think the matter over, and decided on the GT option. At this stage, in June 1963, Bizzarrini departed to concentrate on his Iso work, as the Grifo A3/C was to be built at his Livorno factory.

Bizzarrini was replaced by Giampaolo Dallara, who was only 24 years old but had impressive technical credentials. Dallara was a graduate of the Milan Polytechnic, where he had taken a degree in aeronautical engineering. His professor had been so struck by the young man's abilities that he made a direct approach to Ferrari and, in 1960, Dallara joined the design staff. He stayed at Ferrari until mid-1961 and then moved down the road to Modena and Maserati, where his cousin Giulio Alfieri was technical director. He remained there for two years before joining Lamborghini. Like his predecessor, Dallara hoped that he could convince his new employer to produce a sports racing

rather than a GT car, so his first assignment must have been a painful one. Lamborghini had made his decision, and asked his new recruit to detune Bizzarrini's potent power unit so that it could be used in a road car and have a running life of 70,000 km (43,498 miles) between overhauls.

Dallara's next task was to design a new chassis for the car that would be more suitable for a GT model. It was a completely different design to Bizzarrini's – heavier, and built up around two 60 mm (2.36 in) square section extrusions, with smaller diameter outriggers. Both chassis shared the same 2450 mm (8 ft) wheelbase and 1380 mm (4 ft 5 in) track. Like the earlier frame, Dallara's design was built by Neri and Bonaccini of Modena, who also produced Ferrari's frames.

Before long, Dallara acquired an assistant, Paolo Stanzani, a graduate of the nearby Bologna University, and a positive greybeard at 25! Soon a third member arrived for the

ABOVE AND LEFT *The Lamborghini marque got off to a rather hesitant start with the 350 GTV, revealed at the 1963 Turin Show, although the four-camshaft engine and all-independent suspension had the edge on Ferrari. The 3497 cc V12 was used in Giotto Bizzarrini's original lightweight chassis, but the 360 bhp output was to be tamed to 270 bhp for the production 350 GT of the following year. The GTV's hastily constructed bodywork, styled by Franco Scaglione, was an uneasy amalgam of styles, with the curvaceous frontal lines contrasting strangely with the angles of the rear. The six exhaust pipes were unique to this one car. Also note the small Lamborghini 'charging bull' badge on the right hand side of the bonnet. It was to be enlarged and mounted centrally on the 350 GT.*

Sant'Agata team. He, too, was 25 years old; a lanky, dedicated New Zealander named Bob Wallace. When he first came to Italy, Bob had headed for Modena and became a racing mechanic with the Camoradi and Serenissima racing teams, where he gained practical experience of Ferrari and Maserati competition cars. Wallace's driving expertise perfectly complemented Dallara's and Stanzani's essentially theoretical approach. He was to test the Lamborghini prototypes endlessly over every imaginable road conditions: along the hot, straight *autostrade*; down twisting mountain tracks; and over punishing, potholed, dusty tracks. Yet he, like Dallara, cherished a hope that Lamborghini would decide to go motor racing. The average age of Lamborghini's design and development team was now 24.6 years: surely the youngest team in the business!

As Lamborghini was determined that his car would make its public début at the Turin Motor Show that opened on 30 October, styling and bodywork had become a matter of urgency. He therefore contacted Franco Scaglione, Bertone's chief stylist until 1959, who was then running the Sargiotto coachworks in Turin, to design the first Lamborghini body. As the only completed chassis at this time was the lightweight Bizzarrini-designed model, this was the recipient of Scaglione's handiwork.

The car was built at a plastics factory that Lamborghini had purchased near Turin, and the Grand Tourer was ready just in time for the show, although it did not make an appearance until late on the opening day. The shortage of time meant that this first car had to be fitted with Bizzarrini's original V12 in its raucous 360 bhp state, and the car was consequently named GTV (V for *veloce* 'fast').

Ferruccio Lamborghini's car generated considerable interest at Turin, although undoubtedly its appearance attracted less attention than its advanced mechanical specification. Stylistically, the GTV left much to be desired, and its poor finish reflected the speed of its construction. In following Lamborghini's instructions, Scaglione had come up with an uneasy amalgam of styles. At the front, the car resembled Chevrolet's recently introduced Corvette Sting Ray, while its concealed headlamps recalled those of the Ferrari Superfast II. As for the window line, this reminded one of the Karmann Ghia Volkswagen, but the gentle curves of the front of the car were not carried through to the rear, which was clipped and angular. The GTV bore a 'Lamborghini' scroll on the offside of the bonnet, close to an insignificant badge bearing a charging bull motif. (The reason for the bull was that Lamborghini was born on 28 April 1916 under the sign of Taurus.) The badly fitting bonnet hinged at its forward end, like an E-type Jaguar. However, if visitors to Turin wanted to inspect the GTV's engine, one had been put on display behind the car.

The GTV V12

As the GTV's V12 engine has powered every mainstream Lamborghini since 1963, we should take a close look at this remarkable power unit. It is an all-aluminium engine; that is to say, the combined crankcase and block, as well as the cylinder heads, are made from aluminium.

Beginning at the bottom of the engine, the seven-bearing crankshaft was not a forging, as it would have been in most other engines, but was machined from a solid 92.5 kg (204 lb) steel billet. As the finished shaft weighed only 24 kg (53 lb), the wastage in its manufacture was colossal. This particular engine

also betrayed Bizzarrini's ambitious hopes for it, because a dry –
rather than the usual wet – sump lubrication system was used.
The pistons ran in cast-iron wet cylinder liners, although the
cylinder banks were closed at the top, rather than being left
open in Ferrari and Maserati style. The aluminium cylinder
heads contained the twin overhead camshafts which ran,
Maserati-fashion, straight into the head. Each pair of camshafts
was driven by its own chain and half-engine-speed sprocket.
There were two valves per cylinder, at a 70-degree angle to each
other. The engine was unusual in that the inlet tracts emerged
between the camshafts rather than within the V – as they would
have in a Ferrari racing engine – and each cylinder bank
contained no less than three vertically mounted 36IDL Weber
carburettors, adding to the height of the engine.

Lamborghini had considered adopting a fuel injection
system. Two had been considered – one courtesy of his tractor
factory, and the other produced by Lucas in Britain. However,
as Lamborghini explained on the GTV's launch, since a system
did not yet exist for 12-cylinder units, it would have been a case
of fitting two six-cylinder components, which would have put
about 622,000 lire (£357) on the car's price. Marelli distributors
were driven off the rear end of each inlet camshaft.

Once the Lamborghini factory had been completed and its
testing facilities were ready, each engine was run for about 20
hours and detailed performance records were kept. For
approximately half the test time the V12 was driven by an
electric motor and then run for about four hours on a light
throttle opening. For the remainder of the test, the speed was
gradually increased so that, by the time the engine was installed
in its chassis, it was run in and all set for the road.

This visually and aurally impressive engine was mated to a
five-speed German ZF gearbox, while final drive, courtesy of
independent rear suspension, was via a Salisbury limited-slip
differential. Borrani wire wheels, with knock-off hubs, were
fitted, shod with Pirelli Cinturato HS205 tyres.

When compared with the contemporary Ferrari 250 GTE,
the Lamborghini had the mechanical edge with the twin-cam
heads and all-independent suspension. However, the Maranello
car's Pininfarina bodywork was infinitely superior to the
GTV's. In its defence, it should be remembered that the GTV's
body had been a very hurried production. Meanwhile, Dallara's
heavier and more substantial GT chassis was waiting in the
wings.

With the mechanical modifications to the design well in
hand, Lamborghini turned his attention to the all-important
business of resolving the model's styling and bodywork
production. At the Turin Show, Lamborghini had his first
meeting with representatives of the respected Touring
coachbuilding company of Milan, with a view to that company
refining Scaglione's design.

A Touring body

Although Touring had been one of Italy's most famous
coachbuilding companies, it was experiencing severe financial
problems at the time of the initial negotiations with
Lamborghini.

In October 1961, Touring had signed an important contract
with the British Rootes Group for the assembly of the Sunbeam
Alpine sports car and Hillman Super Minx saloon in Italy. They
also undertook the styling and production of the luxury
Humber Sceptre-based Venezia coupé. Because of these heavy
commitments, Touring decided to leave its old premises in
Milan's Via Ludovico da Breme, and to transfer production to a
much larger, purpose-built works at Nova Milanese to the north
of the city.

Touring moved into these new headquarters early in 1962.
Unfortunately, in July of that year, the firm suffered a
damaging strike which lasted until February 1963. In addition,
Rootes, whose 1961 order had triggered the move, were finding
themselves in financial deep water and cancelled the Minx and
Venezia contracts. The only good news was that the Alpine
contract remained, and the first of these cars left the Nova

LEFT *A 350 GT in the service department at the Lamborghini factory. The firm also runs a restoration department for the rejuvenation of its older models.*

RIGHT *The 1963 GTV's styling was greatly improved by Touring, who were awarded the body contract. The results of the coachbuilder's efforts first appeared at the 1964 Geneva Motor Show as the 350 GT. This example has been fitted with optional bumper over-riders. Note the single windscreen wiper and Touring badge on the side of the front wing. This model evolved to become the 400 GT 2+2 in 1966. Its bodywork was mildly reworked and that model is instantly identifiable by its quadruple headlights. It remained in production until 1968.*

Milanese works in the autumn of 1963. It was in this increasingly gloomy climate that the first official meeting with Lamborghini and Dallara took place at Touring's Nova Milanese headquarters on 1 February 1964. Obviously, Touring were relying on the 350 GT contract for their survival and the first example appeared at the Geneva Show in March.

When the 350 GT (the V suffix had been deleted) made its Geneva début, it represented an enormous visual advance over the GTV prototype of five months earlier. The front of the car had been completely revised: the original grille was dispensed with, along with the concealed headlights which were replaced by two prominently mounted Cibié units. The Lamborghini charging bull badge, now centrally located, was also enlarged. The bonnet line was also about 38 mm (1.5 in) lower than previously: this was made possible by the replacement of vertically mounted Weber carburettors by six side-mounted twin-choke units. Also noteworthy was the single, centrally located windscreen wiper. The rear of the body had received all-important refinements and now there were only four exhaust pipes, instead of the original six. The light, aluminium bodywork conformed to Touring's established *Superleggera* principles: a network of small diameter tubes was clad in a light aluminium covering, giving a strong but expensive structure.

The main mechanical difference on this car, when compared

with the GTV, was Dallara's detuning of the engine. The V12 now developed 270 bhp at 6500 rpm, rather than 360 bhp at 8000 rpm, giving the GT a top speed of around 265 km/h (165 mph). This lowered output had been achieved by the new carburettors and milder camshafts. Yet another modification, more in the interests of everyday running than performance, was the repositioning of the Marelli distributors, which were moved from the rear of the engine to the front. There, driven by the exhaust camshafts, they were far more accessible than before. In addition, the dry sump layout of the original car was replaced by a more conventional wet sump system.

There were also interior changes as the car's wheelbase had been increased from 2450 mm (8 ft) to 2550 mm (8 ft 4 in) and this permitted the fitment of a centrally located rear seat, although, as it happened, this feature was not perpetuated on the production cars. The 350 GT was priced at 5,500,000 lire (£3157) which would undercut the new 275 GTB Ferrari (unveiled at the Paris Motor Show later in the year) by some 3,000,000 lire (£1700). Maranello responded to Sant'Agata by introducing all-independent suspension with this model, but it would be 1966 before the car, retitled the GTB/4, attained four-camshaft status.

Getting the model into anything resembling production was a slow procedure. The magnificently equipped Sant'Agata factory, with its spotless interior, had only just been completed, and there were the inevitable teething troubles. So production proper did not begin until late in the year and a mere 13 examples of the 350 GT had been built by the end of 1964.

Production did not in fact begin in earnest until 1965, and in that year 76 cars were delivered. Although this was a reasonable start, the appearance of the model's bodywork still irked Ferruccio Lamborghini. He approached Nuccio Bertone but the designer was reluctant to commit his *carrozzeria* until it had something special to offer. Lamborghini's next appointment was with the Zagato bodybuilding concern and there he commissioned a one-off body on the 350 GT chassis. Designated the GTZ (for Zagato), it appeared on the Lamborghini stands at the 1965 Paris and London Motor Shows but, perhaps inevitably, had the appearance of a Ferrari 'look-alike'. . . and *that* Lamborghini did not want.

In the meantime, Touring's financial position had steadily deteriorated. In February 1965 the firm's creditors had applied to the courts for a winding-up order, and this was confirmed in the following month. However, Touring continued to operate while existing contracts were being fulfilled. Against this precarious background the firm conceived a spider two-seater body for the Lamborghini, which bore a strong resemblance to the GT. There was also a hardtop version and, although the open car was exhibited at the 1965 Turin Show, it did not enter production. A second example was built but not displayed.

Enlarging the 350

The Geneva Motor Show was again the venue for the announcement of a new Lamborghini offering. The 1966 event witnessed the arrival of the 400GT 2+2, which was a development of the original 350 GT theme. Although the car resembled its predecessor, practically every body panel had been changed – although the 2550 mm wheelbase remained inviolate. Despite this, the model did indeed emerge as a two-plus-two, which had involved raising the roof line slightly and lowering the floor. For this car Touring abandoned its celebrated *Superleggera* body

construction, with the result that the 400 was heavier than the 350, turning the scales at 1380 kg (3036 lb), rather than 1050 kg (2310 lb). The most obvious difference between the two cars was their headlamps, the single Cibiés being replaced by twin sealed-beam Hella units.

As the new car's title suggested, the engine was an enlarged version of the 3464 cc unit, the 3929 cc capacity being achieved by enlarging the bore from 77 to 82 mm, while the compression ratio was increased to 10.2:1. Consequently, the power output rose to 320 bhp. In addition to fitting this larger capacity engine, Lamborghini introduced his own purpose-built five-speed gearbox with Porsche baulk-ring synchromesh, which was even fitted to the reverse gear. The 400 also saw the début of a Lamborghini-built final-drive ratio. Both components had been prompted by Ferruccio's dissatisfaction with the noise levels of the ZF and Salisbury units respectively. That being said, his own gearbox was somewhat stiff in action, particularly when it was cold. Despite the fitment of the more powerful version of the V12, any potential increase in performance was cancelled out by the heavier bodywork, so that the 400 was about 16 km/h (10 mph) slower than its predecessor, with a 249 km/h (155 mph) top speed. The new engine was also fitted in the 350 bodyshell, the resulting car being known as the 400 GT. In addition there was a top-line 350 bhp GTV.

Touring exhibited a convertible version of the 400, carrying the 400GTS designation, at the 1966 Turin Show. By this time

the once great Touring name was in its death throes, but at the same event it unveiled the Flying Star II. The front end of this model's two-door body bore a close resemblance to Zagato's 350GTZ of the previous year. At the rear the resemblance ended, for the Flying Star II was a small hatchback. Handsome Campagnolo alloy wheels were fitted but the car, with its evocative name which harked back to Touring's golden days of the 1930s, sadly never entered production.

The Milan coachbuilding company finally closed its doors on 31 January 1967 after 41 years in the business. Practically all existing orders had been seen through, with the exception of the Lamborghini contract. A group of ex-Touring workers were determined to complete the order and established themselves at the works of Mario Marazzi. a former Touring sub-contractor, with premises at Caronno Pertusella, just to the north of Milan. Not only was the Lamborghini order filled, but also Marazzi was able to undertake such projects as the Alfa Romeo 33 Strada and ASA 1000 berlinetta.

The Lamborghini 350 series was finally discontinued in 1967, after 123 examples had been built, plus an additional 23 with the 4-litre engine. As body supplies were assured, the 400 GT series continued until 1968, by which time 247 examples had been built. Clearly, by this time the body required a radical redesign, and Marazzi came up with a rather anonymous two-door coupé built on the 400GT 2+2 chassis. Called the Islero, after a Spanish fighting bull – this naming system was by then

becoming standard Lamborghini practice – its concealed headlamps were a distinctive feature. A 350 bhp S version arrived in mid-1969, and the model remained in production until 1970.

Although the Islero, with its 257 km/h (160 mph) top speed, performed better than its predecessor, it lacked the glamour that Ferruccio wanted to be associated with the Lamborghini name. The same could never be said of the model that Lamborghini introduced at the 1966 Geneva Motor Show. It was there that the Miura, the world's first series-production mid-engined car, made its sensational début.

Miura magic

It is fair to say that before the Miura, Lamborghini produced some outstanding Grand Touring cars which, despite their superlative mechanical specifications, somehow lacked a definable persona. All this changed with the Miura, and to find the origins of this extraordinary model we must retrace our steps to

BELOW *The Islero of 1968 used the mechanics of the 400 GT and was built until 1970. But the bodywork, styled and built by Marazzi, somehow lacked the usual Lamborghini flair.*

OVERLEAF *The Lamborghini Miura, the world's first series-production mid-engined car, was introduced at the 1966 Geneva Show. Its transversely located V12 engine is shown to effect.*

November 1964 when Dallara, Stanzani and Wallace began thinking about a prestigious road car which they hoped would, in the long term, have the makings of a Lamborghini sports racer. Dallara had been much impressed by the mid-engined Lola GT-based Ford GT40, of 1964. But this had its V8 engine mounted longitudinally and, if the Lamborghini V12 had been so located, the resulting car would have been too long.

What Dallara did was to follow Alec Issigonis' example – there were plenty of Innocenti-built Minis and 1100s around to act as reminders – by positioning the engine transversely across the chassis. However, the combined engine/gearbox unit would have been unacceptably wide, so Dallara also imitated Issigonis by locating the five-speed gearbox in the V12's sump so that, just like the Mini's, it shared the engine's oil.

When this concept was put to Lamborghini he responded positively for, although the mid-engine location was by then standard Grand Prix and popular sports racing practice, no one had yet offered a roadgoing car with this configuration. This prestige model would also generate welcome publicity for the marque and, above all, stimulate sales of the other models in the Lamborghini range.

The project was given the P400 designation, 'P' for *posteriore* (rear), and '400' for 4 litres. Once he had been given the go-ahead, Dallara and his team set to work on the model's engine. Fortunately, the 3929 cc version of the V12 (for the 400 GT 2 + 2) was in the offing, although a new cylinder block was required for the Miura, because it had to contain the gearbox and final drive. Apart from this the engine was much the same as the 400GT unit. However, as bonnet height would not represent a problem with the mid-engined arrangement, four vertically mounted Weber carburettors were fitted, echoing the layout of the original GTV Lamborghini of 1963.

Work on the construction of the P400 chassis began in the summer of 1965 and proceeded apace throughout the autumn,

with a view to the new model making its début at that year's Turin Show. Fortunately the task was completed in time, and the mid-engined chassis took its place on the Lamborghini stand. At the show, Lamborghini found speculation that he might be entering the Grand Prix field. He thought that he might produce around 20 P400s a year, and also predicted that the mid-engined chassis would give birth to not one, but two, cars. The second would be powered by a transversely mounted derivative of the V12.

Bertone takes over

Lamborghini's main preoccupation was with finding a body designer of sufficient skill to reflect the new model's unconventional specifications: he did not want to experience the dissatisfaction he still felt with the 350/400 styling. Nevertheless, Touring did produce some designs for the P400's bodywork. There were at least two of them: one had a rear end which was clearly borrowed from Ferrari's mid-engined experimental 206S Dino, exhibited at the previous year's Paris Show, while the second bore a striking similarity to the styling which Lamborghini eventually adopted.

As for the other coachbuilders, Pininfarina was deeply committed to Ferrari, while Frua and Ghia maintained close relationships with Maserati. Of the first division stylists this left only Bertone. Although that company had strong ties with Alfa Romeo and Fiat, it had no significant sporting commitments, apart from Iso.

Bertone's chief stylist was 26-year-old Marcello Gandini, who had a musical, rather than a coachbuilding background. Immediately after the Turin Show, Gandini began work on the project. A second, slightly longer chassis was dispatched to Bertone and work on marrying it to the first body began early in the year. The coachbuilders had to have the car completed by

LAMBORGHINI MIURA 1967–9
ENGINE
No. of cylinders V12
Bore/stroke 82 × 62 mm
Displacement 3929 cc
Valve operation Twin overhead camshafts per cylinder bank
Compression ratio 9.5:1
Induction 4 Weber downdraught carburettors
BHP 350 at 7000 rpm
Transmission Five-speed sump-mounted gearbox
CHASSIS
Frame Box section
Wheelbase 2500 mm (8 ft 2 in)
Track – front 1400 mm (4 ft 7 in)
Track – rear 1400 mm (4 ft 7 in)
Suspension – front Independent, wishbones and coil springs
Suspension – rear Independent, wishbones and coil springs
PERFORMANCE
Maximum speed 273 km/h (170 mph)

LEFT *The Miura's chassis displayed at the 1965 Turin Show with a 350 GT in the background.* ABOVE *The Miura's 3929 cc V12 engine. Its proximity to the driver and passenger is readily apparent.* TOP *A 1967 Miura with its magnificent Bertone bodywork. Provided by Michael Gertner.*

the first week in March 1966, as the Geneva Motor Show opened its doors to the public on the 10th of that month. Happily, the car was finished on time, placed in a truck and dispatched over the Alps to Geneva.

It was there that the P400 officially became the Miura, introducing Ferruccio Lamborghini's practice of complementing his 'charging bull' badge (although he would never describe it as such) by giving his cars names with bullfighting associations. The Miura was named after Don Eduardo Miura, a famous breeder of fighting bulls. Finished in a striking orange-red hue, the car sold for 7,700,000 lire (£4425), which was 1,850,000 lire (£1063) more than the 400GT 2 + 2, with which it shared the Lamborghini company's stand.

Not surprisingly, the Miura caused a sensation. Gandini had produced a magnificent body which triumphantly reflected the model's revolutionary mechanics. Only 1050 mm (3 ft 5 in) high, the Miura was outstandingly impressive from practically every angle. At the front of the car, the headlamps lay exposed and flush with the body contours while not in use. When required, they could be activated by electric motors. A striking feature was the 'eyelashes' above and below the light pods. These concealed cold air ducts to cool the front disc brakes. In the centre of the bonnet were two grilles which acted as exit routes for the air that flowed through the radiator. One of these grilles could be raised to gain access to the petrol tank. Both these features made important functional and visual contributions to the charisma of the 273 km/h (170 mph) Miura.

Bob Wallace spent the next 12 months turning the show car into a production model. Most of the problems were associated with the engine overheating, while roadholding could be unpredictable.

The first production Miura, in the same orange as the prototype, was completed on 24 March 1967, just over a year after the model's Geneva début. The most obvious visual difference was the replacement of the Plexiglass rear window with a 'venetian blind' to provide rear visibility and keep the engine sufficiently cool. Output soon built up and 1967's Miura production stood at 111. By this time the model's internal dimensions had altered slightly. The roof line had been raised by 10 mm (0.39 in) and the seats lowered by the same amount to give a more roomy interior. In 1968, Miura sales reached a record of 184. A few more modifications had been made by this time. At the beginning of the year, the gauge of the chassis metal had been increased by 1 mm (0.03 in) and later that year, with the 200th car, the front chassis member had been reinforced.

Behind the scenes, the Lamborghini team was continuing a policy of refinement. The results of this work were displayed at the 1968 Turin Motor Show, and the Miura S entered production on 29 January of the following year. This model boasted a more powerful 370 bhp engine with larger inlet ports and modified combustion chambers. Outwardly the model was identifiable by its wider 70 section Pirelli Cinturato tyres, although the lovely Campagnolo magnesium alloy wheels of the original Miura were continued. Lamborghini had an excellent relationship with Pirelli, and the new tyres were certainly good for the model's roadholding. However, they tended to absorb much of the extra power from the engine, so the Miura's top speed remained about the same. Modest changes were made to the interior, and air-conditioning became a popular option.

The ultimate Miura

Miura production held up well in 1969 with 150 cars built, and 1970's output was only slightly down, at 138. Then, at the 1971 Geneva Motor Show, Lamborghini exhibited what was the ultimate version of the Miura. This was the SV (the 'V' for *veloce*). External changes were obvious with this model: the familiar headlamp 'eyelashes' were dispensed with, while the rear wheel arches were extended to cater for new 60 section Pirelli tyres. Changes were also made to the rear suspension, the original layout being replaced by an improved quadrilateral layout. Power was up once more, this time to 385 bhp, by again increasing the size of the inlet ports, and the camshafts were also modified. Yet another improvement was the option of a ZF limited-slip differential, but this required its own lubrication system rather than relying on the engine's. Consequently, the unit could not be offered until the autumn of 1971. Even then, only a few cars were so equipped.

Ninety-two Miuras were built in 1971 and the production figure dropped to 76 the following year. It was then that Lamborghini took what was, in retrospect, a disastrous decision – to discontinue the model, just when so many of its shortcomings had been resolved. Total production amounted to 763 cars. In theory, the Miura was due to be replaced by the

Countach, but in reality the new model would not enter production until 1974, three years after the prototype had shared the 1971 Geneva Show stand with the Miura SV.

Good as the Miura looked, it was considered to be only a matter of time before Bertone came up with an open version. This appeared on Bertone's stand at the 1968 Brussels Show, but was rather more subtle than a coupé with the top cut off. The rear of the car, in particular, was reworked aerodynamically, was more robust than the coupé's and incorporated a modest spoiler. This Bertone Miura was purchased by ILZRO, the International Lead Zinc Research Organization. Named ZN 75, it was used – after appropriate modifications – to promote the organization's alloys and coatings at shows and exhibitions throughout the world.

After the Miura had made its sensational 1966 début, the Sant'Agata design team turned its attention to a second project:

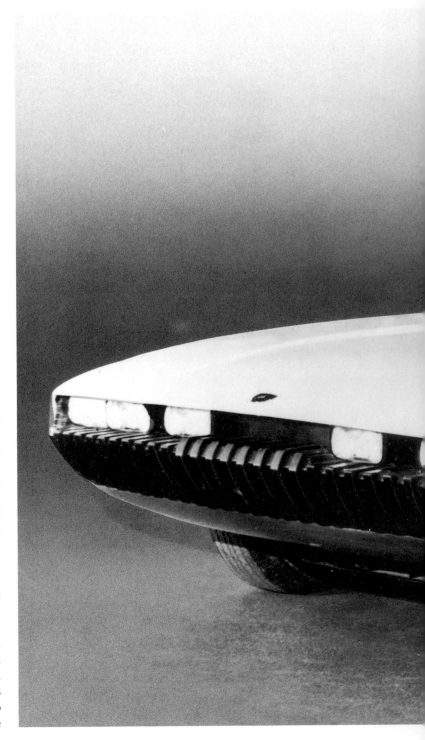

to create a genuine four-seater, but with the looks and performance of a Grand Tourer.

A six-cylinder version of the Lamborghini's 12-cylinder engine had been mooted right at the start of the entire project, and a 1997 cc twin-overhead-camshaft six was produced with relative ease. As the car had to seat four people in reasonable comfort, it was decided that, to save space, the unit would be mounted at the back, behind the rear axle line, rather than in the middle of the car, as on the Miura. Marcello Gandini came up with an extraordinary body which was built on an extended Miura chassis with a 2620 mm (103 in) wheelbase and borrowing the Miura's suspension and steering systems.

The prototype was exhibited at the 1967 Geneva Show (significantly, on the Bertone rather than the Lamborghini stand) and was christened Marzal, 'the raging bull of March'. Although the mechanics were conventional enough, the same could not be said of the bodywork. This was finished in silver and was sharply angular, instead of being gently curved like the Miura. But the most extraordinary aspect of the design was the transparent gullwing doors, tinted to protect the driver and passengers from the sun's rays.

The Marzal was thought to be capable of only around 190 km/h (118 mph) and weighed 1200 kg (2645 lb). Lamborghini therefore decided to drop the idea of developing a six-cylinder version of the V12 and to use the production engine instead. However, if this was going to power a four-seater car then, as in the 350/400 series, it would have to be front-mounted to avoid encroaching on passenger space.

BELOW *The extraordinary Marzal, with rear-mounted 1965 cc six-cylinder engine, was created by Marcello Gandini and displayed by Bertone at Geneva in 1967. It never entered production.*

Once the decision had been made to change the engine and its location, work on the project proceeded with great speed, and the new car was announced at the 1968 Geneva Show, exactly a year after the Marzal had raised so many eyebrows there.

When compared with the Marzal, this Espada (named after the sword used by matadors to kill fighting bulls) was relatively conventional. It was also slightly longer than the Marzal with a 2650 mm (104 in) wheelbase. Its chassis was completely new and a semi-monocoque, with the underframe produced by Marchesi. The 3929 cc V12 was effectively that of the 400GT which had just been phased out and was shared with the latter's Islero replacement, also announced at the '68 Geneva Show.

Espada production began in the summer of 1968 and 186 examples had been built by the end of 1969. The first changes to the design appeared in the retrospectively titled 2nd Series cars, which were seen at the Brussels Motor Show in January 1970. Lamborghini took the opportunity to boost the power of the engine to 350 bhp at 7500 rpm, while the instrument panel was also improved.

The Espada improved

The ultimate version of the Espada was the 3rd Series, announced at the 1972 Turin Show. The instrument panel was again changed for the better and power steering became an optional extra. External changes included a new square-holed radiator grille and the long-running Campagnolo wheels were replaced by a new design. More powerful brakes and minor suspension changes completed the package. Chrysler Torqueflite power steering could be specified on the Espada from March 1974 onwards, but thereafter the increasingly unsettled atmosphere at the Sant'Agata factory resulted in the Espada's development being curtailed. Production of the model ceased in 1978, with the total output standing at 1217 cars, which is still a record for any Lamborghini.

The Espada was, of course, a two-door car, but at the 1978 Turin show Frua exhibited the one and only four-door Espada, which it called the Faena. This one-off car was based on a 2nd Series Espada with its chassis lengthened by 175 mm (6.8 in). In this context it should be noted that Touring had completed designs for a four-door Lamborghini back in 1966, but this car never saw the light of day.

During the Espada's 10-year production span, Ferruccio Lamborghini became disenchanted with car production; so much so that, in 1974, he was to sell all his remaining shares in the company that he had created.

As early as 1967/8 he began spending less time at the Sant'Agata factory and, in the latter year, he asked Paolo Stanzani – who it will be recalled, was Giampaolo Dallara's assistant – to take over the day-to-day running of the factory. Not unnaturally, this irked Dallara, who was still nursing ambitions to be involved in a racing car project. He left Lamborghini in September 1968, seduced by an invitation from Alessandro de Tomaso to design a Formula 1 car. However, this was not to be Dallara's last contact with Sant' Agata.

Perhaps significantly, Lamborghini had decided to start another company and, in 1969, Oleodinamica SpA, specializing in earth-moving equipment, hydraulic machinery and oil drilling aparatus, was established in Cento. It was subsequently run by Ferruccio's son, Dr Tonino Lamborghini.

By this time Ferruccio had, in addition to his industrial activities, bought a 305-hectare (750-acre) farm, called La Fiorita, at Panicarola in the Umbrian region of central Italy, about 193 km (120 miles) south of Sant'Agata. He used it at first as a hunting reserve and for growing corn and maize. Subsequently, 77 hectares (190 acres) were developed as a vineyard, from which Lamborghini would ultimately produce wines under his own name.

Ferruccio Lamborghini's home, by contrast, was at Casalecchio, on one of the hills overlooking Bologna. He had designed the house himself and it contained an indoor swimming pool and gymnasium: Lamborghini likes to keep fit! By this time he had also remarried and in 1974, at the age of 58, he became a father for a second time when his wife, Maria Teresa, bore him a daughter, Patrizia.

Before this happy event, Ferruccio received a body blow when, in 1972, at a time of economic recession in Italy, a valuable export order for 5000 tractors destined for Bolivia was cancelled following a revolution in that country. Unfortunately, Lamborghini Trattrici had only just moved into a new, larger factory at Pieve the previous year and was, consequently, financially stretched. Lamborghini decided to cut his losses and to sell out to Fiat, the market leaders.

In the same year Ferruccio ceded overall control of the car company that bore his name by selling 51 per cent of the firm to Georges Rossetti, from Neuchâtel, Switzerland, who ran a watch component business and was a partner in a Lamborghini distributorship. The sum was reputedly in the region of 1216 million lire (£800,000). Then, in 1974, he disposed of his remaining 49 per cent holding to René Leimer, another Swiss businessman.

Unaware of all the corporate upheavals to come, back in the late 1960s Stanzani was turning his attention to the Islero's replacement. One of that model's weak points had been its Marazzi-designed body, so Bertone styled the new car, although Marazzi still retained the body-building contract. The replacement which appeared at the 1970 Geneva Show was called the Jarama, named after an area of Spain famous for its fighting bulls. It was certainly better looking than the Islero but, on the debit side, the Jarama was a heavy car weighing 1540 kg (3395 lb). This was because, unlike its predecessor's, the Jarama's chassis was not tubular, but instead was based on the Espada's semi-monocoque. Although the V12, carried over from the Islero S, was mounted as far forward as possible, rear accommodation in this two-plus-two was somewhat cramped due to the relatively short 2380 mm (94 in) wheelbase, dictated by the ever-present weight considerations. This weight problem was exacerbated by the use of steel, rather than aluminium, body panels. Although the model was capable of around 257 km/h (160 mph), it was no great flier by Lamborghini standards, and this was reflected in the somewhat modest sales figures. An S version with 365 bhp on tap and new road wheels was announced at the 1972 Geneva Show. This helped the model to survive until 1978 but, like the Espada, it suffered from lack of development during its last years.

BELOW *The sensational four-seater Espada of 1968 with the forward location of the 3929 cc V12 engine revealed by the cooling vents on the side and top of the bonnet. Styling influences were the Marzal and the 1967 Jaguar E-type-based, Bertone-styled, one-off Pirana.*

OVERLEAF *The two-plus-two Jarama of 1970, designed by Bertone and built by Marazzi, was stylish but heavy. The 3929 cc V12 engine was much the same as that used in the Espada and the Jarama's chassis also had much in common with the Espada's.*

The 'little bull'

Yet the Jarama was not the only new Lamborghini to make its appearance in 1970; for that year's Turin Motor Show revealed the first production Lamborghini not to use the magnificent V12. The mid-engined Urraco, or 'little bull', boasted a new V8 power unit of 2463 cc with belt-driven single overhead camshafts. Like the straight-six engine, used in the one-off Marzal, a V8 version of the V12 had been mooted back in 1963. However, when the unit was finally built, it bore little resemblance to the 12 because, for once, the new Lamborghini was to be a cost-conscious car.

When he came to design the Urraco's suspension, Stanzani dispensed with the established all-independent coil spring and wishbones, and chose simpler MacPherson struts with lower transverse arms instead. Disc brakes were fitted all round, while steering was by Lamborghini's proven rack and pinion system.

The period of the Urraco's development regrettably coincided with Lamborghini's growing disillusionment with his

car company, a state of mind that was compounded by strikes and labour unrest throughout the Italian industry which affected Bertone and even the Sant'Agata plant itself. Despite this, Lamborghini car production was holding up relatively well. The 400 barrier was broken for the first time in 1970, and in the following year 421 cars were built, although production dropped slightly to 409 in 1972. This was the year, it will be recalled, in which Lamborghini sold a controlling interest in his business to Georges Rossetti.

The Urraco finally entered production in the autumn of 1972 and a mere 35 cars were built. There was a considerable improvement in 1973, however, when 285 examples were produced – a record for a Lamborghini model. Unfortunately the Urraco developed a reputation for unreliability, which smacked of underdevelopment. The principal problem lay in the crucial area of the single belt which drove the overhead camshafts. On occasions the belt would snap, to the extreme detriment of the engine, and the same thing could happen if the car was tow-started and the driver let the clutch out too smartly.

Then, late in 1973, the oil crisis arrived, and Lamborghini

disposed of the remainder of his company in the dark days of 1974. Despite this era of corporate uncertainty, that year's Turin Show stand radiated optimism for the future. A new version of the Urraco, the P200, was on display. This was a 2-litre car, developed from the original larger-capacity engine and intended for the Italian market, which charged a higher VAT rate on cars above this capacity. But the really significant arrival was the Urraco P300, powered by a 3-litre derivative of the V8. The extra volume was achieved by retaining the 86 mm bore but lengthening the stroke from 53 to 64 mm, which called for a new crankshaft although the original connecting rods were preserved. Even more significantly, Stanzani reverted to Lamborghini's beloved twin overhead camshafts, while the troublesome belt was replaced by reliable chains. Four twin-choke Weber carburettors were fitted and the new engine developed 250 bhp at 7500 rpm. The Urraco had been capable of approximately 209 km/h (130 mph) in its original form, but this larger capacity version was a 249 km/h (155 mph) car.

It was decided that a 2.5-litre Urraco would be sold on the American market. This Tipo 111 was produced from the autumn of 1974 and was based on the original 2.5-litre car, but with the slightly different P300 body and the earlier version's forward end. Yet transatlantic sales did not take off and never attained the projected 500 cars a year. Eventually both models merged and retained the later 3-litre bodyshell and interior. But the P250 Urraco, under production in a crucial era of Lamborghini's history, was discontinued in 1976 after a mere 520 had been built — a far cry from the projected 2000 per annum. Happily, the 3-litre version lasted somewhat longer and remained available until 1979.

The 1974 Turin Show was notable also for the display of a Bertone dream car, the Bravo. Based on the Urraco's 3-litre monocoque chassis, shortened by 200 mm (7.8 in), the Bravo represented another styling masterpiece by Marcello Gandini. Wedge-shaped, it bore more than a passing resemblance to the Lancia Stratos; also the result of a Bertone styling exercise.

BELOW *The Urraco combined a mid-engined location with four seats. In its original 1970 form it had a 2462 cc V8, although a 2995 cc derivative, shown here, was introduced in 1974.*

On 2 January 1975, just six weeks after the end of the Turin Show, Paolo Stanzani resigned from Lamborghini, to set up his own design consultancy business in nearby Bologna. Stanzani was the second of the original 1963 triumvirate to leave Sant'Agata and his departure enabled Giampaolo Dallara to return to Lamborghini in a consultancy role. The position of chief engineer was held by Franco Baraldini, who was subsequently to be replaced by Marco Raimondi. Yet these were difficult days for the company and Stanzani was not the only member of the original team to depart as Bob Wallace, who had untiringly put Lamborghinis through their paces for 12 years, also left the firm.

In an increasingly fraught financial climate, Luigi Capellini from De Tomaso was appointed to bring some sense of order to the company. He recognized the importance of the American market — not surprisingly in view of his experiences with the Italian-American De Tomaso Pantera, which had been aimed at transatlantic buyers. Plans were therefore immediately put in hand for a new 3-litre Urraco-derived Lamborghini. The result was the mid-engined V8 Silhouette, announced in 1976. This was Lamborghini's first open car, but only 54 examples were built during its two-year production life.

As the western world reeled from the effects of the 1973 oil crisis, Lamborghini was desperately short of money. A useful project, obtained by Baraldini, was a contract from BMW for Lamborghini to develop a sports racer, which carried the E26 code. BMW had conceived the project as a potential Porsche-beater and the car was built to Group 4 specifications, powered by a longitudinally mounted twin-overhead-camshaft version of BMW's faithful six-cylinder 3435 cc engine. As luck would have it, this work coincided with a particularly difficult time for Lamborghini, which was sliding towards insolvency. Finally Baraldini departed and Capellini set up Ital Engineering. This new company took over the components already produced for the car — known as the M1 — and these were then dispatched to the Stuttgart works of the Baur body company where they were completed.

One of the reasons for Lamborghini's cash problems was the company's decision to simultaneously develop a Chrysler V8-engined off-road vehicle which, it was hoped, would win a valuable American Army contract. Just one Cheetah, as the vehicle was called, was built in 1977, but it was subsequently badly damaged in a crash during Californian trials.

A government take-over

The Rossetti/Leimer ownership of Lamborghini finally reached the end of the road in August 1978, and the Italian government had no alternative but to take responsibility for the firm to prevent it closing. In came Dr Artese, to take over the running of the company and his great achievement was to convince no less than Giulio Alfieri, formerly technical director of Maserati and Dallara's cousin, to join Lamborghini.

In September 1979, an era of stability appeared to have arrived when a German consortium, headed by financier Dr Raymund Neumann, took over. He became Lamborghini's president while Klaus Steinmetz, formerly of Porsche, Abarth and BMW, came in as development engineer. Alfieri also took over the role of plant manager.

Although Lamborghini now appeared to be on an even keel, the Bologna bankruptcy court finally ruled the German combine as unsuitable to run Lamborghini. The government's stewardship of the firm was due to run out in 1980 and, in the summer of that year, Artese began talks with the Swiss/French Mimran Group, whose interests included shipping, property and sugar refining. As a public gesture of goodwill to Lamborghini and of faith in its future, Bertone produced the one-off Silhouette-based Athon 'Hymn to the Sun' open two-seater, which appeared at the 1980 Turin Show, though there was never any intention of putting it in production.

Mimran's lease on the Sant' Agata factory was confirmed in 1981 for, in September 1980, the company had entered a new phase with the creation of Nuova Automobili Ferruccio Lamborghini SpA. A sign of the times was that a new Lamborghini had arrived at the 1981 Geneva Show – the Jalpa, named after a breed of Mexican bull. It was by Urraco out of Silhouette, and a development of the latter concept. Alfieri had succeeded in stretching the capacity of the V8 to 3485 cc by again lengthening the stroke, this time to 75 mm; twin overhead camshafts were perpetuated. The Jalpa remains in production at the time of writing, alongside . . . the Countach. The Countach and Miura must be the greatest of all Lamborghinis: the marque's place in motoring history is secure.

Classic Countach

To discover the Countach's origins, we must retrace our steps to 1970, for what was to become the Miura's successor started life as a Bertone concept car.

From the outset, Paolo Stanzani had decided that, rather than place the V12 engine transversely, as he had done with the Miura, he would retain the central location but mount the unit longitudinally. However, rather than putting the five-speed gearbox and the differential at the rear of the car, Stanzani decided on the ingenious, expensive, uncompromising approach of locating the gearbox at one end of the engine alongside the driver, with the differential at the other end of the power unit. This he achieved by taking the drive from the gearbox, via a sealed tube, through the sump of the engine, to its rear end. The result was a far more balanced car – the Miura had always had a tendency for nose lightness – with an impeccable gearchange. The engine itself was an enlarged version of the Miura's V12 with the 4971 cc achieved by increasing the bore

ABOVE AND LEFT *The mid-engined Silouette was Lamborghini's first convertible model and, being built on a strengthened Urraco chassis, it was approriately V8-engined, with a 2995 cc power unit. The body was both styled and built by Bertone. Introduced at the 1976 Geneva Motor Show, it unfortunately lasted only until 1978.*

RIGHT *Not a Lamborghini but designed at Sant'Agata Bolognese, the BMW M1 was a German/Italian confection, with a mid-located version of BMW's 3.5-litre 32-valve twin-overhead-camshaft six-cylinder engine. Styling was by Ital Design. The M1 eventually reached production in 1978. This is the road version, produced so that the 400 cars required for racing homologation could be built.*

LAMBORGHINI COUNTACH
LP 500S 1982–5

ENGINE

No. of cylinders V12

Bore/stroke 85 × 69 mm

Displacement 4754 cc

Valve operation Twin overhead camshafts per cylinder bank

Compression ratio 9.2:1

Induction Six horizontal Weber twin-choke carburettors

BHP 375 at 7000 rpm

Transmission Five-speed gearbox

CHASSIS

Frame Tubular

Wheelbase 2450 mm (8 ft)

Track – front 1492 mm (4 ft 11 in)

Track – rear 1606 mm (5 ft 3 in)

Suspension – front Independent, wishbones, coil springs and telescopic shock absorbers

Suspension – rear Independent, wishbones, coil springs and telescopic shock absorbers

PERFORMANCE

Maximum speed 289 km/h (180 mph)

ABOVE *The Countach finally reached production status in 1974, and in 1979 came the improved LP 400S. At the 1982 Geneva Show this 4754cc LP 500S derivative appeared.*

and stroke to 85 × 73 mm. As the LP 500 (*Longitudinal Posteriore 5 litri*) was intended only to be a show car, it had a simple chassis, made of square tubing and sheet metal, which resulted in a semi-monocoque.

Now it was the turn of Bertone's Marcello Gandini to lavish his stylistic genius on the LP 500. As he already had the Miura to his credit, it seemed to be tempting providence to expect him to produce something even more sensational, but he did. In 1968 Gandini had designed the Alfa Romeo Tipo 33 sports racing based 'Carabo' (scarab beetle) show car, so named because its doors opened like a beetle's wings. This represented his starting point for the Lamborghini project which was completed just in time for the 1971 Geneva Motor Show. As Bertone was rushing to complete the lemon-yellow car, one of the Torinese workers is said to have exclaimed: 'Countach!' This is a Piedmontese slang word of praise and astonishment and the highly appropriate name stuck. It was the first Lamborghini car not to have bullfighting associations which was, perhaps, a reflection of Ferruccio Lamborghini's growing lack of interest in his car company and its products.

As the Countach was completed on the very eve of the show, Bob Wallace had to drive the car over the Alps to Geneva. To underline the fact that the Countach was a concept, rather than a production model, it was displayed on Bertone's stand, instead of Lamborghini's.

As the Miura had on its début, the Countach caused a sensation. Only 1030 mm (40 in) high, it probably represented the ultimate development of the wedge shape while the doors, actuated by an expensive servo-hydropneumatic mechanism which opened them parallel to the bodywork, came in for particular comment.

The reception given to the Countach at Geneva was sufficient incentive for Lamborghini to put the model into production, although it was to be another three years before the car reached the public. This was partly due to the refinements that had to be made and partly to the increasingly uncertain state of the Lamborghini company's ownership.

When the first production car was displayed at the 1974 Geneva Show, some significant changes were apparent both above, and below, the surface. The most obvious modification was the intrusion of radiators on either side of the car, just behind the side windows, with additional cooling ducts adjacent to the recessed door handles. The aluminium alloy body, although the work of Bertone, was not built at Grugliasco but by

RIGHT *The Silouette theme appeared in updated form as the current Jalpa P350 at the 1981 Geneva Show. It is accordingly mid-engined with a 3485 cc V8.*

BELOW *The ultimate off-road car, the LM-002 with optional four-wheel drive, has the 4754 cc V12 mounted at the front of the vehicle. Another version is the LM-004/7000 with a 7-litre V12 unit which is also available for power boats. The interior is appropriately luxurious.*

FAR RIGHT *The Countach's magnificent V12 engine, unlike the Miura's which was transversely mounted, is longitudinally located. Consequently, as the gearbox is next to the driver, the drive runs back through the power unit's sump and emerges, via the ZF limited-slip differential, at the rear. The magnificent aluminium casting is an impressive sight.*

RIGHT *Unlike the bodywork on other Lamborghini models, the Countach's, although styled by Bertone, is built by the works. Its chassis is a complex tubular one which is then mounted in a jig for the individual body panels to be attached.*

Lamborghini itself at Sant'Agata. In addition, the original makeshift chassis had been dispensed with and replaced by a light, but complex, tubular one. Despite this, the weight had risen from the concept car's 1075 kg (2369 lb) to the 1100 kg (2425 lb) mark.

The main difference between the prototype and the production car was the reversion to the current 3929 cc engine, which resulted in a new LP400 designation: the larger capacity unit had been dispensed with on the grounds of unreliability. The Countach's top speed was around 281 km/h (175 mph) and this model sold for 23,400,000 lire (£15,184).

Only 23 Countachs were built in 1974, although the figure rose to 60 in 1975 – the year in which Paolo Stanzani, who had engineered it with such daring and originality, left Lamborghini. Dallara was soon to follow him for a second and final time, but before he went he undertook some refinements to the Countach which emerged as the LP400S derivative of 1978. The engine was virtually unchanged, for Dallara had concentrated his talents on chassis refinement. There were changes to the suspension rates and the rear system was revised, with the lower A arms being replaced by twin parallel links. The brakes were improved and new wheels fitted, but the most significant change was the introduction of new, wider Pirelli P7 tyres which demanded larger wheel-arches than hitherto.

In the dark days of 1978 only 16 Countachs had been built, but output perked up to 40 in 1979 and trebled to 120 in 1980. Giulio Alfieri had, in the meantime, been turning his attention to the Countach's engine, as its 3929 cc capacity had been unchanged since 1966. He therefore enlarged the capacity, not to the 4971 cc of the 1971 original, but to 4754 cc, achieved by increasing the bore and stroke to 85 × 69 mm. The gearbox ratios were changed at the same time. There were no major external modifications to indicate this change, apart from the new Ozeta wheels which replaced the Campagnolo originals.

Yet another development took place in 1985. This was the first radical alteration made to the V12 since its conception some 25 years before. Rather than risk turbocharging, which he thought would sacrifice reliability, Alfieri decided to follow Maserati's and Ferrari's example by introducing four-valve cylinder heads while, at the same time, slightly increasing the engine's capacity. This is now 5167 cc and was attained by enlarging the stroke to 75 mm. The results of these ministrations pushed the engine's power up to 455 bhp at 7000 rpm. The Countach is now a 289 km/h (180 mph) car and the only outward evidence of the improved power arrangements is a slightly enlarged engine cover to accommodate the new carburettors.

With demand for this sensational 'supercar' still strong, and along with the Jalpa- and Cheetah-like V12-powered LM off-road vehicle introduced in 1982, Sant'Agata looks set for the future, under-pinned by Chrysler who bought the firm in 1987.

And what of Ferruccio Lamborghini, who saw his ambitions become reality back in 1963? Now aged 71, still as energetic and optimistic as ever, he tends his vines at La Fiorita and dreams of creating a new make which would, once again, set new standards of excellence to shock, amaze and delight Italy and the world.

LANCIA

Of all Italy's great marques, none has maintained such a high technological profile, and for so long, as Lancia. Established by Vincenzo Lancia in 1906, the firm grew rapidly to become Italy's second-largest car company during the 1920s and '30s. Yet, after the Second World War, in the wake of competition from a revitalized Alfa Romeo and the ever-powerful Fiat, Lancia's fortunes waned. In 1969 it was taken over by Fiat; an appropriate move, as Vincenzo Lancia had worked for the firm before founding his own company.

Vincenzo Lancia was born on 24 August 1881 in the village of Fobello, about 100 km (62 miles) north-east of Turin. He grew up in comfortable circumstances for his father Giuseppe owned a prosperous Turin-based canning business. At an early age, Vincenzo was showing a precocious interest in mechanical matters: he dammed a stream near the family's Alpine summer home and built a water wheel, which made rather too much noise for his parents' liking!

In 1892, when he was 11, young Lancia was sent to the Niccolo Tomaseo school in Turin where he made a firm friend of Fausto Carello. Lancia was no academic and the pair were soon playing truant, often spending their time at the Carello family business. Founded in 1875 it specialized in the manufacture of carriage lamps, and was to grow into one of Italy's largest companies by progressing to the production of car headlights and electrical equipment. Matters came to a head one day when Vincenzo returned home, soaking wet, having fallen into the river when he should have been at his lessons. Giuseppe Lancia had come to the end of his tether and sent his errant son off to boarding school at Varello, just 12 km (7 miles) south of the family's summer retreat at Fobello. Lancia senior was anxious that his youngest son should enter the family business and, as Vincenzo was showing some mathematical prowess, his father decided that he should study commercial bookkeeping.

LEFT *Lancia's most successful competition car, the Ferrari-engined Stratos of 1972–9 which gave the Turin company no less than three World Rally Championships.*

While at boarding school young Lancia was admired by the other pupils for his proficient bicycle-riding and with good reason. Giuseppe Lancia had rented the ground floor of the family's Turin home to Giovanni Ceirano, who first imported British Rudge bicycles and then produced his own two-wheelers, marketed under the Welleyes name. This workshop at 9 Corso Vittorio Emanuele II had drawn young Lancia like a magnet, and he soon mastered Ceirano's machines.

Back to Turin

When he was 15, in 1896, Lancia left Varello for the Giuseppe Lagrange Technical School, which had recently opened in Turin and where he met up again with Fausto Carello. But, although Vincenzo was as keen as ever on mechanics, his father insisted that he take a course in bookkeeping with the result that there was increasing friction between father and son. Eventually a compromise was reached, and in 1898 Lancia went to work for Ceirano in his bicycle business, ostensibly as a bookkeeper.

He could not have joined the firm at a more opportune moment for, as recounted earlier, Ceirano and his engineer Aristide Faccioli were hard at work producing the Welleyes car. When Ceirano's business was put on a corporate footing as the Ceirano Motor and Bicycle Works in October 1898, Lancia was listed as bookkeeper and Giuseppe Gallo as storekeeper: in truth the latter did both jobs, for Lancia was totally absorbed in mechanical matters and was seldom seen out of his overalls!

But Ceirano's was a short-lived enterprise for he sold out to the local F.I.A.T. company, which had only recently been created. For the 30,000 lire (£1190) purchase price, F.I.A.T. acquired not only the services of engineer Faccioli (who went on to become F.I.A.T.'s first technical director), but also those of Vincenzo Lancia and Felice Nazzaro, another youngster who worked for Ceirano.

Eighteen-year-old Lancia must have impressed the directors of the new company in Corso Dante, for he was appointed chief inspector in the factory. By this time Lancia had established a good rapport with Aristide Faccioli, who was an excellent pianist, and they often spent evenings together. Technical

problems were set aside and Lancia, a great music-lover, would break into song, with Faccioli accompanying him on the piano. But, by 1901, Aristide had left F.I.A.T. after clashing with the formidable company secretary, Giovanni Agnelli.

Lancia, by contrast, enjoyed Agnelli's confidence. Early on, the F.I.A.T. board had decided that valuable publicity could be obtained from racing, and both Lancia and Nazzaro were soon in the fray. Vincenzo's racing career began at Padua on 1 July 1900 when he won his class in a 6 hp racing F.I.A.T., with Nazzaro placed second in a similar car. These original two-cylinder models were soon replaced by more powerful four-cylinder machines and, in 1903, Lancia found himself competing in the Paris–Madrid race, but unfortunately retired in the early stages. However, in 1904 he was placed eighth in the prestigious Gordon Bennett Cup, then finished the year in style by winning the Coppa Florio event for F.I.A.T.

By this time Felice Nazzaro had left the firm to drive for the wealthy Vincenzo Florio, but he returned in 1905 to head the F.I.A.T. racing team, which was entered in that year's Gordon Bennett Cup. Lancia led for a time, but unluckily had to drop out after a stone penetrated his radiator. Although a French Richard Brasier won the event, Nazzaro drove his F.I.A.T. into second place.

Lancia is said to have possessed such a fine musical ear that any mechanical irregularities jarred. But he also had a reputation for driving his cars flat out, and therefore tended to suffer from more mechanical problems than Nazzaro, who usually kept something in reserve.

In 1905 the increasingly ambitious F.I.A.T. company took a team of cars across the Atlantic for the Vanderbilt Cup race at Long Island, New York. Although Vincenzo characteristically put up a fastest lap, he had to settle for a disappointing fourth place after colliding with an American Christie car.

In 1906, Lancia won the Coppa d'Oro race in Milan, making up for his retirement in the Targa Florio, and achieved a laudable fifth position in the French Grand Prix, held for the first time that year. Also in 1906, he had a close-fought tussle in the American Vanderbilt Cup race, coming home second behind Wagner who was in another F.I.A.T.

LANCIA (Italie) sur sa F·I·A·T.

ABOVE RIGHT *This lofty carriage is the oldest surviving Lancia and is a 12 hp model, retrospectively titled Alpha, of 1908. It is powered by a four-cylinder fixed-head side-valve engine of 2543 cc, with a 90 × 100 mm bore and stroke.*

LEFT *One of the earliest pictures of Vincenzo Lancia as a racing driver. He is shown here at the wheel of a 24 hp F.I.A.T. Corsa on 27 July 1902 at the Susa–Monteceniso hill-climb which he won. Along with Felice Nazzaro, he was F.I.A.T.'s most successful racing driver and consequently his name was already world famous when the first Lancia car appeared in 1907.*

Going solo

Nineteen hundred and six proved a pivotal year in Lancia's life. He was only 25, yet already he was thinking about setting up his own car manufacturing business. Because of his racing exploits the name Lancia was now world-famous and Vincenzo believed that the time had come to leave F.I.A.T. He had discussed the matter in detail with two friends, Claudio Fogolin from San Vito al Tagliamento, who had joined F.I.A.T. as a tester in 1902, and Francesco Contin. Unfortunately Contin died suddenly, but Lancia and Fogolin decided, nevertheless, to set up in business together.

Not surprisingly, Giovanni Agnelli did not want to lose his number two racing driver, and managed to convince Lancia to continue driving for Fiat. The agreement was ratified in March 1907, but Lancia had little success either in that year or in the following season. (Interestingly, Nazzaro followed Lancia's example and left Fiat in 1911 to produce his own car – the Nazzaro. This was initially built in Turin and was then produced at a Florence factory from 1919 until 1923.)

So, on 29 November 1906, only five weeks after Vincenzo's Vanderbilt Cup victory, *Lancia et Cie Fabbrica Automobili* (Lancia and Company Car Manufacturers) was registered for business. Lancia and Fogolin each contributed 50,000 lire (£1982), with Vincenzo being responsible for engineering and design, while his colleague was to look after the sales and administrative side of the business.

But first the young firm needed a factory: the young men found one on the corner of the Via Ormea and Via Donizetti in Turin. These small, two-storey premises had previously been occupied by the Itala company, established in 1904 by Giovanni Ceirano's brother Matteo.

It may be that work on the design of the first Lancia had begun prior to the firm's creation but, whatever the case, in February 1907 disaster struck when oil dripped from a lamp on to a stove resulting in a fire that destroyed the prototype, drawings and tools. Vincenzo's sister Maria later said that this was the only occasion on which she ever saw her brother in tears.

Lancia began working on the car with a staff of about 30. Engine design was vested in Rocco, while Zeppegno was responsible for the frame, gearbox and rear axle. Rocca was shop foreman and Allevi mechanical-assembly foreman.

Because of the fire, the first Lancia was not completed until September 1907. In was a straightforward 12 hp car, designated Tipo 51, and had a 2543 cc side-valve four-cylinder engine which developed 24 hp at a respectable 1450 rpm. (In 1919, at the suggestion of his brother Giovanni, Vincenzo decided to name his cars after the letters of the Greek alphabet, so his earlier models were titled retrospectively, beginning with the Tipo 51, which was named Alpha.)

When the car was finished and ready to be driven on to the Via Ormea, there was one big problem: the doorway was too narrow! It was only when the sides had been removed with picks that the Alpha could emerge, with Vincenzo at the wheel and Luigi 'Vigin' Gismondi, a young mechanic, at his side. There was a second prototype, while the third example became the first production Lancia and, by the end of the year, an impressive total of 16 cars had been built.

The Alpha was joined, in the summer of 1908, by an additional six-cylinder car, which was a lengthened 12 with a 3815 cc engine – effectively the four with two extra cylinders. This Dialpha was not a success, however, and only 23 examples were built. The four, by contrast, fared somewhat better and, when it ceased production in 1909, no less than 108 Alphas had been built. It was a good start in a difficult economic climate.

It comes as no surprise to find that Lancia raced his cars: he drove one to victory in the 1908 Padua Bovalenta race. Some were even sent to America, where the new racing models fared well. The factory prepared some special *Tipo de Corsa* (competition) cars, one of which, driven by Jim Hillard, won the International Light Car Race of the Automobile Club of America at Savannah, Georgia in November 1908; 1909 saw a repeat performance. Back in Europe, Lancias won impressive second places in the Targa Florios of 1911 and 1912, although thereafter Lancia's commitment to racing waned.

Meanwhile, Lancia had decided to discontinue the 12 hp and to replace it by a more powerful 3120 cc 15–20 hp, designated Tipo 54. Vincenzo followed the design profile of the Alpha, reflecting contemporary trends rather than anticipating them. Consequently the Beta, as it was later known, had its cylinders

cast in one piece and boasted a pressurized lubrication system: this sturdy design was to form the basis of all future Lancia engines until the Dikappa of 1921.

Lancias were beginning to sell. One hundred and fifty cars were made in 1909 and demand began to outstrip the confines of the original works. More factory space was found in the Corso Dante, where Fiat was also based and, with the development section transferred there, along with chassis testing, valuable space was released. As a result, in 1910 production rose to around 300 cars. The Beta's engine was uprated that year and the car renamed the Gamma. Capacity was increased to 3460 cc, but the Gamma was produced for only one year.

A new factory

Lancia's search for larger premises was finally resolved when the firm bought a 10,000 sq m factory in Turin's Via Monginevro, with room for a further 40,000 sq m to cope with future expansion. The company moved in on 14 January 1911, and the first models built there were the 20–30 hp Delta with 4080 cc unit, its Epsilon derivative (which shared the same capacity engine though somewhat refined) and the overhead-camshaft Eta of 5030 cc. All these cars featured a striking new radiator badge to mark a new chapter in Lancia's history.

Until 1911 the Lancia radiator had borne just the marque's name. But, soon after the move to the new factory, Count Biscaretti di Ruffia, an old friend of Vincenzo's, was invited to call. Lancia wanted a new radiator badge and di Ruffia, who was something of an artist, sent six designs on a sheet of paper 'as I understood his tastes and character well'. The one Vincento immediately opted for has featured as Lancia's badge ever since:

LEFT *W.L. Stewart held the Lancia concession for Britain and is seen here at the wheel of a 1909 20 hp Lancia at Brooklands track, circa 1911.*

BELOW *The Lancia Beta of 1909 with its engine block progressively cast in one piece. A 3120 cc four, it also boasted a pressurized lubrication system.*

against the background of a four-spoked steering wheel is a lance bearing a standard simply proclaiming one word: 'Lancia'. The use of the lance was an ingenious reference to Vincenzo's surname, because lance in Italian is . . . *lancia*.

Prior to 1912 most Lancias, with the exception of the Alpha, had been large cars of over 3 litres capacity. However, in that year the firm introduced a smaller model, probably called the Zeta. It departed radically from previous Lancia practice in that the 2620 cc engine boasted roller rather than plain bearings, there was an ingenious spring-loaded clutch, and the rear axle also incorporated a four-speed gearbox. The model, which lingered on until 1916, was hardly a success – only 34 were built. Nevertheless, the Zeta did reflect Vincenzo's penchant for experimentation, a side of his character which was not discernible in his mainstream models at that time.

In 1913, Lancia introduced his most popular car yet, the 4940 cc Theta, which was to sell 1696 examples by the time that production ceased in 1918. Strangely, the Theta had its origins in Lancia's growing commercial vehicle section. Some van bodies had already been offered on car chassis, but it was not until 1911 that Lancia laid down his first purpose-built commercial vehicle frame. This was the IZ, and its engine was derived from the Delta and Epsilon fours with the capacity increased to 4940 cc.

The IZ entered production in 1912 and the engine featured in the Theta, introduced at the London Motor Show at Olympia in November 1913. The straightforward chassis frame employed simple half-elliptic springs all round and the really significant aspect of the Theta was that it was the first European car to offer electric starting as standard equipment. An electric starter motor, by Delco, had first appeared on the Cadillac Model 30 of 1912 so, perhaps inevitably, the Theta's system was an American 6-volt Rushmore set.

Once Italy had entered World War 1, in 1915, all Theta output was snapped up by the military. A significant number of Thetas found their way to Britain where they were used by the Royal Navy as balloon carriers and in France as staff cars, while some were converted to ambulance duty. The Theta's IZ forebear also formed the basis of the armoured Autoblinda. This Lancia armoured car, built by Ansaldo of Genoa, was based on the IZ M (for military) chassis, and saw service well into the 1930s, and beyond, in Somalia, Albania, and even as far afield as China.

Although Lancia's factory almost doubled in size during the war, Vincenzo still had time to rethink completely his design strategy, the results of which were to appear in the early post-war years. As will already be apparent, Vincenzo kept a close watch on transatlantic design trends and, in September 1914, Cadillac introduced its Model 51, America's first series-production V8-engined car, although de Dion Bouton had introduced the concept in Europe in 1910.

Such an important design development would not have escaped Vincenzo's attention and consequently, on 1 July 1915, he applied for a patent for a V8 engine with an included angle of 60 degrees between the cylinders. It was the first outward expression of a commitment to V engines which was to come to dominate Lancia car design from 1922 until 1976. After two years of building experimental aero engines, in 1917 he actually produced the Tipo 4 350 hp V12 engine of 24 litres capacity and with overhead horizontally mounted valves. This was followed by a Tipo 5 derivative of 32 litres capacity. Neither of these engines entered series production, although one of them was used in a Caproni aeroplane.

An exotic V12

Then, on 9 September, 1918, Lancia patented two further V car engines. Both were side-valvers – a 45-degree V8 and a V12 of 30 degrees. The latter's 6032 cc 1919 derivative had the cylinders modestly staggered at only 22 degrees, resulting in an extremely compact unit, as it was possible to cast the cylinder block in one piece. The cylinder head was detachable, while the vertical overhead valves were operated, through rockers, by a single overhead camshaft.

On the prototype car this neat unit was mounted in a straightforward chassis frame, but the suspension was unusual. Half elliptics featured at the front, although the rear was unnecessarily elaborate, consisting of two cantilever springs mounted ahead of two single-leaf semi-elliptic ones. The live

axle was attached directly to the half-leaves and, via a short cable, to the extremity of the cantilever. The model was displayed, in chassis form, at the 1919 Paris and London Motor Shows. Perhaps fortunately, this V12 Lancia never went into production because it was too complex, and therefore much too expensive.

The model produced in 1919 was the Kappa – effectively an updated Theta. The Theta engine was used, though with a detachable cylinder head, and the gear lever was moved from the driver's right to the centre of the car: both these features followed American practice. The Kappa continued in production until 1922. Lancia's next model, the Dikappa, of 1921, was a sports version, most of which were produced with wire wheels and four-seater touring bodywork. This model used the Kappa's 4940cc engine but with overhead rather than side valves, boosting the power from 70 to 87 bhp.

The Trikappa, the first of a new generation of Lancia designs, appeared in 1922. Although outwardly this was a traditional car, under the bonnet was Lancia's first production V configuration engine, a 22-degree V8 derived from the 1919 still-born V12, and the single-overhead-camshaft 4594cc unit developed 98 bhp at 2500 rpm. More than 800 Trikappas were made and it was with this model that Lancia introduced its series designation. Fifty 1st Series cars were built, followed by 450 of the 2nd Series, and front-wheel brakes arrived with the 3rd Series Trikappa, following experiments with Vincenzo's *tour de force* – the Lambda.

Genesis of a masterpiece

In October 1922, Lancia introduced what was probably one of the most technically advanced cars in the world. The Lambda bristled with ingenuity and was, without doubt, Vincenzo Lancia's masterpiece.

The idea for the Lambda was born during a sea journey Lancia took after the end of World War 1. As the ship carved through the waves, Vincenzo began musing on the differences between a car's chassis frame, with its separate bodywork – a legacy of coaching days – and the strength to be found in the hull of a ship. These thoughts were translated into a patent for a chassis-less car, applied for on 31 December 1918 and granted on 28 March of the following year. The patent showed transverse leaf-spring suspension at the front and quarter-elliptic springs at the back.

It was not until 15 March 1921 that Vincenzo gathered his design team together. Having floated the idea of a unitary construction car, Vincenzo listened as draughtsman Falchetto and chassis engineeer Zeppegno pointed out the advantages of such a light and strong structure. However, Lancia was keen that the car should also have independent front suspension, another revolutionary feature for its day.

Lancia therefore asked Falchetto to produce a number of alternative designs, and the enthusiastic draughtsman worked through the night returning with 14 suspension options. Falchetto's starting point had been the transverse system described in Lancia's 1918 patent, but Vincenzo immediately selected a system in which the suspension medium was helical springs, where the hub carriers slid up and down on pillars that also acted as steering kingposts. However, this meant that even greater stresses would be placed on the unitary hull so, in Falchetto's words, 'The idea was born of extending the rear of the car with a tapered tail functioning as a closed box to resist torsional strain and acting at the same time as a luggage compartment.'

LEFT *The Theta, the best-selling Lancia of the pre-World War 1 years. Introduced in 1913, it was the first European car to be offered with electric starting as standard equipment, although this was an American 6-volt Rushmore unit. The model's 4940cc four-cylinder engine was rooted in the IZ commercial vehicle of 1911, the firm's first truck chassis. The Theta also echoed the IZ's simpler all-round half-elliptic springs.*

RIGHT *Lancia's revolutionary Lambda of 1922 is best remembered for its independent front suspension, V4 engine and unitary construction hull, but yet another innovative feature was this boot, which provided reinforcement for the rear end of the body. Not that The Autocar magazine called it a boot when it road-tested this Lambda in January 1924. After pointing out that it contained the petrol tank, the report described it as 'a large felt-lined compartment for luggage'. 'Boot' only meant footwear in those days!*

Meanwhile work was proceeding apace on the rest of the car. The all-important engine, the responsibility of Rocco and Cantarini, was even narrower than the Trikappa's with only a 13-degree angle between the cylinder centres. The 75 mm bores were, however, shared with the contemporary V8 and the shaft-driven overhead camshaft followed the same valve layout pioneered on the 1919 V12.

The eight-strong Lancia drawing office was soon working round the clock on the design and the prototype Lambda was completed by August. It was a four-seater tourer with two door recesses and a unique horseshoe-shaped radiator. As Lancia was keen to keep the car's weight down to below 700 kg (1543 lb), a differential unit was not included in the specification. Only after a half-shaft broke a few months later did Vincenzo agree to the feature being incorporated. (Fortunately, Falchetto had taken the precautions of preparing drawings for one just in case it was needed . . .) Lancia was also sceptical of the advantages of front-wheel brakes so the prototype only had rear ones, although front brakes were subsequently adopted on the production cars.

Once this first Lambda had been completed, it was taken on an inaugural run through the Via Salbertand Pass. Then, on 1 September 1921, Lancia himself took the wheel and gave the Lambda a rigorous baptism on the demanding gradients of the Monte Cenissimo.

During the subsequent 12 months of prototype testing, romance blossomed for Vincenzo and in October 1922, at the age of 41, he married Adele Miglietti, his secretary. They were to have three children; a son Gianni, and two daughters, Maria and

ABOVE Vincenzo Lancia's Lambda of 1922 with independent front suspension and unitary hull. The front-wheel brakes were another advanced feature. Lancia's name thereafter became associated with a policy of technical innovation.

Nori. The couple's honeymoon was something of a 'busman's holiday' for they spent it at the 1922 Paris and London Motor Shows, where the Lambda made its début.

Needless to say, the Lambda as unveiled to the public was considerably changed from the original prototype. The most obvious difference lay in the radiator, which now followed the more traditional, angular Lancia lines. The body construction had also been altered and consisted of a complete skeleton incorporating the radiator mounting and lower-engine compartment sides. Reinforcement came from bulkheads at the scuttle and behind the front seat, with longitudinal support coming from a propeller shaft tunnel — a feature inherited from the 1919 patent specification. Sheet-steel cladding was then welded, or riveted into position. The only non-stressed parts of the bodywork were the doors, bonnet and boot lid. (A boot was another unusual feature in those days.)

Initially, only a four-seater tourer was on offer, and very roomy it was with its 3100 mm (10 ft 2 in) wheelbase. In this form the Lambda turned the scales at 1066 kg (2350 lb), which was rather more than Vincenzo had hoped but, despite its weight, this supremely elegant car was capable of about 110 km/h (68 mph). The Lambda sold for £725 in Britain, which put it in the Aston Martin class.

RIGHT *The Lambda's unusual 13-degree V4 engine. The 2120 cc unit has an aluminium block with cast-iron liners.*

BELOW *The Lambda's driving compartment. Note the right-hand steering, a Lancia feature until the 1950s.*

LANCIA LAMBDA (1st series) 1922–4

ENGINE	
No. of cylinders	V4
Bore/stroke mm	75 × 120
Displacement cc	2120
Valve operation	Single ohc
Compression ratio	5.1:1
Induction	Single Zenith carburettor
BHP	49 at 3250 rpm
Transmission	Three-speed
CHASSIS	
Frame	Unitary
Wheelbase mm	3100
Track – front mm	1332
Track – rear mm	1366
Suspension – front	Independent sliding pillar
Suspension – rear	Half-elliptic
PERFORMANCE	
Maximum speed	110 km/h (68 mph)

Changes introduced as the design evolved were reflected in the series designations. By 1925 the 5th Series had appeared, incorporating the first significant departure from the original design – the introduction of a four-speed, instead of three-speed, gearbox. The 6th Series Lambda of September 1925 had wider door recesses which meant that the wheelbase had to be extended to 3420 mm (11 ft 2 in), to the detriment of the model's proportions. The new, heavier, Lambda was offered with the usual four-door touring bodywork, but at the same time a variation was made available with a platform chassis. The factory offered a four-door Weymann saloon, while the variant

was ideal for bespoke coachwork. This 6th Series Lambda was a great success, with more than 1000 built within 18 months.

Next, in May 1926, came the 7th Series cars with the capacity of the V4 engine increased from 2120 to 2370 cc to counter the increased weight. Then, with the introduction of the 8th Series in 1929, the ingenious unitary construction was finally abandoned, and all the Lambdas had conventional chassis. Engine capacity was again increased, with a new 82 mm bore giving 2570 cc.

Although the Lancia factory had eschewed competition in the 1920s, the creation of the Mille Miglia road race in 1927 tempted Vincenzo, and he entered two special Lambdas for the inaugural event. These featured high-compression engines with oil-coolers, skimpy bodywork and side-mounted spare wheels, and they attained creditable third and fourth places. In the following year's event, the works entered a trio of Casaro-bodied short-chassis Lambda spiders and also special Series MM (for Mille Miglia) 'torpedoes'. Their engines were fitted with special Pirotta cylinder heads, with wedge-shaped combustion chambers and external exhaust manifolds. In the 1928 race a Lambda driven by Gismondi harried the eventual winner – the Campari Alfa Romeo – before being put out of the running by an accident. However, another Lambda achieved a well-earned third place.

Sales of the 8th Series cars held up well and 3900 examples were sold between its introduction and August 1930. The last of the Lambda line was the 9th Series of 1930 which survived until November 1931. The first of Vincenzo Lancia's historic designs had run its course after more than 12,530 had been built.

Luxury from Lancia

Once Lancia had seen the Lambda safely into production, he began to turn his thoughts towards a complementary model. When work on the project – a 3-litre V8-engined successor to the Trikappa – started in 1926, Vincenzo received a visit from a Mr Flocker, of American/Italian origins, who had ambitious ideas about building Lancias in the United States. Lancia was keen to gain a foothold in the booming American market so, in mid-1927, Lancia Motors of America Inc was established. The plan was that a 4-litre V8-engined car would be built at a rate of about 20 a day, using engines and gearboxes imported from Italy. Lancia completed 10 prototypes for Flocker and these were shipped to New York at the end of 1927. When Lancia arrived to see them on display and to meet his American colleagues he soon realized that things were far from well and that the Lancia flotation had involved some very dubious characters. The unhappy affair culminated with the luckless Vincenzo being chased through the streets of the American capital by a group of highly unsavoury individuals, and he was mightily relieved to board ship and return to Italy. Fortunately, the cars eventually found their way back to the factory.

The design that had been planned as an American-built Lancia eventually made its début at the 1929 Paris Motor Show; an event that, alas, coincided with the Wall Street Crash. The Dilambda, as the model was called, was Lancia's most luxurious car to date. The engine was a very up-to-date completely new 24-degree V8 of 3960 cc. The overhead camshaft was chain- rather than shaft-driven and, unlike earlier Lancia engines, the Dilambda's camshaft operated the overhead valves via short pushrods and rockers so that, when the cylinder head was removed, the camshaft and timing would remain untouched. This engine and its in-unit four-speed gearbox were mounted in a substantial box-section chassis which was notable for its exceptionally deep side-members adjoining the engine, giving the front of the car sufficient strength to counter the stresses of the Lancia independent front suspension. Beyond the bulkhead

ABOVE *The Dilambda, powered by a 24-degree 3960 cc V8 engine. This is a 1930 example with coachwork by Stabilimenti Farina, the family firm which Pinin Farina left to open his own carrozzeria.*

BELOW *A stylish fabric-bodied 1930 Dilambda by Weymann in*

Britain. The use of a hypoid rear axle contributed to the model's low look.

RIGHT *The Artena, introduced in 1931, endured until World War 2. It perpetuated the V4 theme of the Lambda with a 1924 cc engine and chain-driven single overhead camshaft.*

the members reverted to more conventional proportions, although at the rear the springs passed below, rather than above, the innovative American hypoid-drive rear axle which helped to give the Dilambda a long, low look.

The Dilambda was obviously aimed at a well-to-do clientele, but it could not have appeared at a worse time as far as the world economy was concerned. However, the model was sold at the very reasonable chassis price of £875 and, although works touring and saloon coachwork was already on offer, the car attracted the attention of specialist coachbuilders. One of the most significant was Battista 'Pinin' Farina, who had known Vincenzo since the early days. Farina opened for business on Turin's Corso Trapini in 1930.

As with the Lambda, series refinements soon appeared. In its original form the Dilambda was offered with a 3475 mm (11 ft 3 in) wheelbase, but a short-chassis version of 3290 mm (10 ft 9 in) was soon available. After 900 cars had been built, the 2nd Series Dilambda appeared, with both wheelbase variants featuring Lancia's new shuttered radiator. Finally, in 1932, came a further revision, distinguished by its handsome angled radiator, while changes were made to the chassis to accommodate the new, lower type of coachwork then gaining popularity. When the Dilambda ceased production in 1932, a respectable 1686 had been built, of which about 70 had left-hand drive.

Italian odyssey

By this time the Lambda had been replaced by two models rather than one, both of which resembled scaled-down Dilambdas. These were the no-frills Artena and the more expensive Astura, introduced together in 1931. As will be apparent, Lancia had abandoned his journey through the Greek alphabet with these models (although the practice continued on the commercial vehicle range and would be revived on Lancia cars in 1972). The new model names were to be Italian rather than Greek and were perhaps thought to be more in keeping with the spirit of Mussolini's new Roman order. So Lancia started to work his way through Italian placenames and landmarks beginning with the letter A.

The smaller Artena had a 2990 mm (9 ft 7 in) wheelbase and, although the usual Lancia front suspension was adopted, both models dispensed with the somewhat unsightly tubular reinforcement between the top of the pillar and the radiator. The Lambda's V4 configuration was perpetuated in the Artena but with a smaller capacity – 1924 cc – and the chain- rather than shaft-driven overhead camshaft was just one of the refinements. The Astura, however, had a V8 engine; effectively a simpler, scaled-down version of the Dilambda design, but with a radically different two-piece cylinder head. On both these

161

models, a feature of the factory four-door saloon bodywork was pillarless construction, which continued as a Lancia speciality until 1963.

Both cars entered a 2nd Series after 500 examples of each had been built, and then, with the 1933 introduction of the 3rd Series cars, both the Artena and the Astura – which was becoming increasingly popular with specialist coachbuilders – were offered in short and long chassis forms. At the same time, the Astura's engine capacity was increased to 2972 cc and hydraulic brakes were fitted. Next came the 4th Series Asturas with new, longer 3475 mm (11 ft 3 in) chassis; these were intended to serve as government state cars and were therefore fitted with a wide variety of specialist coachwork. As for the 4th Series Artena, it had a new platform chassis and hydraulic brakes. In a detuned 51 bhp state it was taken over by the army as a staff car, light van or ambulance and continued to be built in this form until the war years. The Astura, by contrast, remained in production only until 1937.

In the meantime Lancia had been busy creating a new, smaller model more suited to the poor economic climate. Work on the Augusta began in 1930, and with this model Lancia reverted to unitary construction. Under the bonnet was a smaller version of the Artena engine – an 18-degree 1194 cc V4 which propelled the 812 kg (1792 lb) model at a respectable 101 km/h (62 mph). The proven independent front suspension was fitted, while Lockheed hydraulic brakes were in keeping with the model's robust specifications.

The Augusta made its appearance at the 1932 Paris Motor Show. Such was the response to the new car that it was decided to set up a subsidiary company to produce it in France, thus sidestepping import duties. A 50,000 sq m factory was built at Boneuil-sur-Marne and some 2500 Augusta saloons, sold in France as the Belna, were manufactured there.

Although the Augusta was intended to be a cheap car, in 1934 Lancia produced the by-now traditional variant with a platform chassis for the coachbuilding fraternity. By the time it was discontinued in 1937, the Augusta had proved the most popular Lancia to date, with total sales amounting to some 15,000.

Vincenzo's swan-song

The ageing Astura, introduced back in 1931, now needed replacing. The new car, named Aprilia, was the last model to be masterminded by Vincenzo Lancia, and it rightly rivals the Lambda as one of the great Lancias of the inter-war years.

By the mid-1930s, aerodynamic awareness was becoming increasingly fashionable among car designers, especially in Italy with its high-speed *autostrade*. Lancia was thinking in terms of a light, streamlined car, with a relatively small-capacity engine, good acceleration, and superlative roadholding. Work on the Aprilia began in 1934. The engine design followed the proven V4 configuration and had a 1351 cc capacity. However, so that high-efficiency hemispherical combustion chambers could be adopted, the valve gear differed radically from previous Lancia practice: the single overhead camshaft was used in conjunction with no less than three rocker shafts. As

previously, a cast-iron cylinder head was employed, although the engine had an aluminium block.

Vincenzo Lancia was determined that the Aprilia should be a five-seater and that the model's weight should not exceed 900 kg (1980 lb). The design for a pillarless four-door saloon initially incorporated a long tail, but this unattractive rear end had been abandoned by the time that the shape was finalized. In the interests of weight-saving, thinner than normal panels were used for the unitary hull: 1.2 mm for the load-bearing areas and 0.8 mm for the rest.

It soon became apparent that, for excellent roadholding, the car would require all-independent suspension. The front presented no major problems because the well-proven system already existed, but a completely new arrangement was needed at the rear and eventually a transverse leaf spring was used in conjunction with trailing-arm torsion-bar suspension. The rear brakes were mounted inboard, adjacent to the differential housing – yet another progressive feature for its day.

In mid-1936, Lancia asked for a ride in the prototype Aprilia. On the following day he had to make the 240-km (149-mile) journey between Turin and Bologna, so he set off in the Aprilia with Gismondi and the two engineers. It was not until they had almost completed the return journey that Lancia suddenly threw his hands in the air and proclaimed, 'What a magnificent car!' As a result of this trip, minor modifications were made to the design and the car's top speed was reduced slightly to 125 km/h (78 mph).

ABOVE *The Astura, introduced in 1931 along with the Artena, was powered by a 2604 cc V8 engine, although the capacity was increased to 2972 cc for the 3rd Series version. The usual Lancia independent front suspension featured. The position of the door handles indicates that this is a pillarless saloon, a construction technique introduced on this model and a Lancia feature until 1963. This is a factory saloon with a distinctive, and insubstantial, front bumper.*

LEFT *The Augusta, introduced at the 1932 Paris Motor Show, was Lancia's first small car and Europe's first unitary construction saloon. Its engine was a 1196 cc V4 unit. The model was capable of 102 km/h (63 mph).*

The Aprilia was first seen publicly at the 1936 Paris Motor Show (the new car was sold as the Ardennes in France), but did not go into production in Italy until early in 1937. The Aprilia's launch was overshadowed by tragedy, however. By February 1937 Lancia was ill but continued to work, despite medical advice. Then, on Monday 15 February, Vincenzo was unable to get out of bed; the doctor was called but did not arrive in time: Vincenzo Lancia was dead, aged only 55. Large crowds gathered to pay tribute in Turin, and Lancia was buried in his beloved Fobello on 17 February.

After Vincenzo's death his widow, Adele, took over the presidency, while Manlio Gracco was responsible for the day-to-day running of the firm. The Aprilia, meanwhile, had more than lived up to its creator's expectations. Its roadholding, in particular, set a standard by which, for a long time, small European cars were judged. A 2nd Series version appeared in 1939 with the engine's capacity increased to 1486 cc. At the same time, the Lockheed hydraulic brakes were replaced by an Italian-made Sabif system.

The inevitable platform chassis version soon appeared, with a wheelbase 100 mm (4 in) longer than the standard car's 2750 mm (9 ft). There was also an even longer 2950 mm (9 ft 6 in) version, although this had conventional half-elliptic rear springs and live axle in place of the complex independent layout.

Since 1911 the Lancia plant on Turin's Via Monginevro had been the firm's only large factory but, on 15 May 1937, forgings began to arrive from a new works at Bolzano far away in the mountains to the north-east near the Austrian border. Its creation was the result of a 1934 government edict directing industry to establish itself in areas of high unemployment rather than in prosperous Turin. Work on the project began in September 1935, the foundry was operational within two years and, in 1939, component production began at the new plant.

In that year, Lancia's last inter-war model made its appearance: the Ardea. This bore a strong family resemblance to the Aprilia despite its shorter 2440 mm (8 ft) wheelbase and was instantly identifiable by its squat bonnet and truncated tail. There was no outside access to the boot; instead it was reached through the rear passenger compartment. The 903 cc V4 engine followed Aprilia practice except that its valve gear was ingeniously simplified, with the single overhead camshaft actuating the valves through short blocks and longitudinally angled rocker shafts, which resulted in a neat, narrow engine. The front suspension was much the same as the Aprilia's, although that model's rear independent layout was replaced by a simple half-elliptic spring with live axle.

Italy at war

Inevitably, car production was interrupted in 1940 by Italy's involvement in World War 2. A mere 741 Aprilias and 1838 Ardeas were built in that year and most of those went to the army, along with the evergreen Artena. But, as in World War 1, it was commerical vehicles that were in greatest demand. Then there was the Lynx armoured car, built between 1941 and 1945, and powered by an enlarged 1st Series Astura engine.

Until Italy joined the war with Germany in May 1940, Lancia was run by a triumvirate of Sigs Rava, Gracco and Zorzoi, who reported to Adele Lancia. Unfortunately Rava subsequently had to step down because of his Jewish connections. Then, in mid-1944, a Lancia was once again running the firm as general

ABOVE *A Lancia Ardea of 1949; a scaled-down version of the Aprilia, with a 903 cc V4 engine, but a live rear axle. Capable of 108 km/h (67 mph), the model remained in production until 1953 when it was replaced by the Appia.*

RIGHT *The innovative profile of the Lambda was mirrored in the advanced Aprilia of 1937 with its 47 bhp 1352 cc V4 engine, aerodynamic bodywork and all-independent suspension. The Aprilia's roadholding was outstanding for its day.*

manager: he was Arturo Lancia, a cousin of Vincenzo, who had emigrated to America where he had worked for Ford and Continental.

The firm's Turin works had been badly damaged by bombing in October and November 1942, so production moved to Bolzano, which at that stage was out of range of Allied aircraft. The transfer was completed by January 1943, although a small design facility was maintained at Padua.

Lancia was safe, but only for a comparatively short period for the Bolzano factory was bombed for the first time in September 1943 and, with the Italian surrender to the Allies that month and the subsequent German occupation, conditions progressively worsened. There were bombings, deaths and arrests for the workforce, although by May 1945 the war in Europe was nearly at an end. On 2 May, an eyewitness at the factory recorded the scene: 'In the afternoon all work stopped while Wermacht soldiers roamed the factory taking possession of every bicycle that they could lay their hands on'. Peace came five days later.

Slowly Lancia began to pick up the pieces. The Turin factory was rebuilt, but commercial vehicle production stayed on at Bolzano. Only one Aprilia and two Ardeas had been built in 1944, but production proper resumed the following year with 86 Aprilia chassis and one saloon made. Both models were soon updated for the post-war years. The Aprilia had its 6-volt electrics replaced by a 12-volt system, and production continued until 22 October 1949, by which time 23,717 had been built.

ABOVE *Vincenzo's son Gianni, managing director from 1948.*

LEFT *The 1950 Aurelia saloon, the first series-production car in the world to be powered by a V6 engine.*

RIGHT *The B24 Aurelia spider with Pinin Farina coachwork. Most left-hand drive examples were exported to America.*

OVERLEAF *The car that gave birth to the post-war GT movement: the Aurelia Pinin Farina-bodied B20 GT coupé. This is a 1956 car. Provided by Anthony Armstrong.*

The Ardea, a somewhat newer model, lasted rather longer. It also received 12-volt electrics, along with a rear-opening boot, in its 2nd Series form. A 3rd Series arrived in 1948 and was significant for the fitment of a five-speed gearbox, the first series-production road car in the world to be so equipped. Mechanical refinement was also the theme of the 4th Series Ardea when the fitment of an aluminium cylinder head pushed output up from 28 to 30 bhp. The Ardea lasted until 1953, although production was relatively modest at around 22,000. But by then Lancia had produced yet another milestone in automobile design to rival the Lambda and Aprilia. It was named the Aurelia.

Although this revolutionary car did not appear until 1950, it had its inception in the war years. In 1943, Vincenzo's son Gianni, who was beginning to take an increasingly influential role in the firm's affairs, started thinking in terms of a larger-engined version of the Aprilia. By this time the Lancia engineering team had moved from Turin, with the ever-present danger from bombing, to Padua. The engineering director of the day was Giuseppe Vaccarino, but the firm's most important recruit was Vittorio Jano, who had joined Lancia in 1938 as head of the experimental department.

Jano, who was one of Italy's most famous automobile engineers, had been a member of the illustrious Fiat racing car design team of the early 1920s. In 1923 he moved to Alfa Romeo were he created the all-conquering P2 racer, following it in 1932 with the fabled P3 monoposto. However, he left the Milan firm when his V12-engined racer, with all-independent suspension, dropped out of the 1937 Italian Grand Prix with rear axle trouble. This unit also contained the gearbox, the significance

of which will become apparent later. Incredibly, the Alfa Romeo management used this rare failure as an excuse to dispense with his services, saying that at 47 he was 'too old' for the job. So he returned to Turin and joined Lancia, although it seems that, even there, he was never really happy.

A V6 in the making

Young Francesco de Virgilio was head of the Patent and Planning Office in Padua, and to him goes the credit for the idea of extending the concept of the Aprilia's V4 engine to the development of a V6. There was a Lancia precedent for this configuration for, in 1923, the firm had developed an experimental 2649 cc V6 which might even have found its way under the Lambda's bonnet, but never did.

In adopting a V6 layout, young de Virgilio decided to depart from Lancia's traditional single-block shallow V approach, for he realized that an included angle of between 40 and 60 degrees would provide the best balance of inertia forces: he eventually opted for a 45-degree V and six cylinders. Work on the project had begun in November 1943 and by 1947 a 1569 cc unit with 68 × 72 mm bore and stroke had been fitted under the bonnet of an Aprilia, and was undergoing road tests. These were sufficiently encouraging to convince Gianni Lancia that the V6 showed potential – such great potential that it really required a completely new car, as the Aprilia was by then over a decade old and beginning to look its age. By this time Gianni was sharing the firm's managing directorship with Arturo, but in 1948 his cousin died and Gianni was then in sole command.

The new car would perpetuate the well-proven unitary

construction theme and, while work was proceeding on this side of the project, de Virgilio continued his engine experiments. He produced another V6 with a 50-degree angle, which merely served to convince him that an earlier 60-degree design had been correct. So the 60-degree V6 was seen as the finalized unit but, as work proceeded apace on the rest of the car, it soon became clear that a larger engine would be required, so its capacity was increased to 1754 cc.

The Aurelia B10, as it was designated, made its public début at the 1950 Turin Motor Show. Outwardly it was a relatively conventional four-door saloon but below the surface lay de Virgilio's inspired V6 engine . . . and the masterly work of Vittorio Jano.

The Aurelia was the first production car in the world to be fitted with a V6 engine. De Virgilio's creation used short pushrods to operate the overhead valves rather than the more traditional Lancia overhead-camshaft layout. The inclined in-line valves were operated by simple, longitudinal rockers, which kept the width of the engine to a minimum. Both the block and cylinder head were made of aluminium and the 1754 cc unit developed 56 bhp.

But the model's very individual approach did not stop with that remarkable engine. Power was transmitted through a two-piece propeller shaft to the rear axle, which also incorporated a four-speed gearbox. Lancia had first used the arrangement on the 1912 Zeta but, more significantly, it had been a feature of Jano's 1936 Alfa Romeo 12C monoposto and it had been a 1937

development of that design that had triggered his departure from Milan. A further innovative feature, and yet another world first, was the semi-trailing-arm independent rear suspension, while the brakes were carried inboard, as on the Aprilia. Lancia's independent system featured at the front.

Although the four-door pillarless saloon had lightweight aluminium doors, bonnet and boot lid, the Aurelia still turned the scales at 1080 kg (2380 lb). Nevertheless, its top speed was close to 135 km/h (83 mph).

There were, in all, three variations on this original B10 theme: a platform chassis for specialist coachbuilders, and a spider and coupé by Pinin Farina. The coupé not only complemented the Aurelia's advanced mechanical specifications; its two-seater bodywork, with room for luggage, or children in the back, combined the performance of a sports car with the comfort of a saloon. This coupé marked the beginning of a new era, for the Gran Turismo Lancia gave birth to the Grand Touring or GT concept which, in time, was to challenge successfully the supremacy of the open two-seater sports car.

As has been mentioned, Pinin Farina had long-standing associations with the Lancia company. During the 1930s his Turin firm had bodied many of Lancia's products, and after the war he was given the Cisitalia project, a car designed by Fiat's Dante Giacosa for industrialist Piero Dusio (see page 107) which Farina bodied in coupé form. Here Pinin Farina produced a design of such timeless elegance and perfect proportion that it made him world famous.

It was the potential of the Aurelia B10 saloon in competition that convinced Gianni Lancia of the wisdom of producing a purpose-built sports version. Farina applied his incomparable skill to designing the Aurelia coupé, and the result, designated B20, clearly owed much to the Cisitialia and a special-bodied Aprilia coupé, completed in 1947. But the Gran Turismo Lancia offered more than cosmetic changes. In 1951 the Aurelia saloon's engine capacity had been increased to 1991 cc for the B21 model, and the B20 also used this engine, but with a compression ratio of 8.4:1 rather than 6.8:1, and with twin Weber 32 carburettors replacing the B21's single Solex. Consequently output rose from 70 to 75 bhp. In addition the B20 had a shorter – 2660 mm (8 ft 6 in) – wheelbase than the saloon, at 1000 kg (2204 lb) was 80 kg (176 lb) lighter, boasted a higher rear axle ratio, and was capable of over 162 km/h (100 mph).

LEFT *The best selling Lancia of the 1950s was the Appia of 1953 which replaced the Ardea. This example is the standard unitary construction pillarless four-door saloon.*

BELOW *The sports racing D23 spider of 1953 with 2962 cc V6 engine, spaceframe chassis and* de Dion rear axle. The bodywork is by Pinin Farina. This is the only surviving example.*

RIGHT *The 2nd Series Appia. Although it retained a 1009 cc V4 engine, the compression ratio was increased from 7.4 to 7.8:1 and the output was boosted from 38 to 43 bhp.*

In 1952 a 2nd Series B20 arrived, with 80 bhp engine; curiously the saloon by then had a 90 bhp V6. Nineteen fifty-three saw the appearance of the 3rd Series, with a new 118 bhp V6 of 2451 cc. The car was fittingly renamed the GT 2500 and its top speed rose to about 185 km/h (115 mph). The 1954 4th Series followed the saloon in that the semi-trailing arms were replaced by a simpler de Dion unit.

The GT lived up to its good looks, winning the demanding 1952 Targa Florio and, in 1954, the Chiron/Balsadonna GT 2500 gave Lancia its first Monte Carlo Rally victory. But, from the 4th Series cars onwards, the model's weight increased, its performance diminished, and eventually Aurelia GT production ceased, in June 1958, after 3614 had been produced. A noteworthy variation on the GT theme was the Pinin Farina B24 Aurelia Spider of 1954.

Saloon sales were disappointing, with a relatively low figure of about 30,000 purchases by the time that production ceased in 1955. The B10 had developed into the B22 in 1952, with that 90 bhp engine: surprisingly, a mere 1072 B22s were built. In 1954 came the 2nd Series B12 saloon, sharing the GT's de Dion rear axle, but with a 2266 cc version of the B10 engine under the bonnet instead of a detuned GT unit. Lancia was no longer producing its platform chassis for bespoke coachwork, as demand was diminishing, but it did produce some, specially for Pinin Farina, which were built to Aurelia B12 specifications, and these carried the B55 designation. The result of Farina's efforts was the magnificent 1955 Florida two-door coupé, of which just four were produced, one of them a four-door variant.

Appia times

If the Aprilia had been in need of replacement, then the same could be said of its simpler Ardea sister, and this new Lancia arrived in the shape of the 1953 Appia. Although there was a superficial resemblance, more than 90,000 were made during its ten-year production life. The Appia continued the traditional V4 engine theme, but there were some radical changes from previous practice. As on the V6 Aurelia, the long-running single overhead camshaft was replaced by two crankcase-mounted camshafts which actuated the inclined valves through rockers and long pushrods. Suspension followed the Ardea's, and the stylish little car was good for 90 km/h (55 mph). In addition to the customary pillarless saloon, in 1956 Lancia made a platform chassis, the basis for a few special-bodied Appias by Allemano, Vignale and Pinin Farina.

By the time that Appia production had been discontinued in 1963, the firm was no longer in the hands of the Lancia family. Undoubtedly, increased competition from Alfa Romeo and Fiat played its part in this development, but a key factor had been Gianni Lancia's decision to go into motor racing.

The first, relatively modest, step along the racing road had been the B20 GT, but the next was the purpose-built D20 sports racer coupé, which was developed during 1952.

The D20 had a spaceframe chassis with transverse-leaf suspension all round and a 2962 cc V6 Aurelia-derived engine. Interestingly, it was the first Lancia since 1922 not to feature Lancia's independent system, originally seen on the Lambda.

The cars had a good inaugural year in 1953, giving Lancia its third victory in the Targa Florio. A D23 spider version, with de Dion rear suspension, appeared in mid-year and was a great success, winning the Coppa Toscana and the Grand Prix of Portugal. Next came a D24 derivative, with engine capacity increased to 3284 cc, and quarter-elliptic springs with de Dion axle at the rear. Across the Atlantic, D24s swept the board in the 1953 Carrera Pan America race taking first, second and third places. Europe provided equally rich pickings: a D24 finished second in the Sebring 12-Hour Race and another won the Giro di Sicilia, with an Aurelia victorious in the GT class. Ascari also gave Lancia its first Mille Miglia victory, in 1954, and in the same year a D24 took the chequered flag for Lancia yet again in the Targa Florio. A 3.8-litre D25 development appeared later in the year but did not live up to expectations. Then, in October 1954, Lancia announced that it was withdrawing from sports car racing. The kingpin of Gianni Lancia's competition strategy was now ready: the D50, Lancia's own Formula 1 car.

The D50 was masterminded by Vittorio Jano, and was short, low and light compared with its contemporaries. Its engine was a purpose-built 2489 cc V8, developing 260 bhp and with twin overhead camshafts on each cylinder bank. This unit was mounted in a spaceframe chassis while front suspension was by transverse leaf and double wishbone, and a de Dion axle was used at the rear, assisted by yet another transverse spring. However, the D50's most distinctive features were externally mounted panier fuel tanks, positioned either side of the body. The idea was that the car's handling would not be affected as the fuel tanks emptied – this was a source of problems with a rear-mounted tank – while air flow between the wheels would also be improved. The Mercedes-Benz W196 was sweeping all before it. Would Lancia fare any better than Ferrari in its challenge?

The D50s did not appear in public until the last race of the 1954 season when, at the Spanish Grand Prix, Ascari was fastest in practice and led the race for seven laps before retiring. This was an encouraging start but, when the cars appeared at the Argentine Grand Prix, the first race of the 1955 season, all three D50s retired and there had also been handling problems. On home ground, things looked brighter with wins in the Turin and Naples Grand Prix, although these were second-string events.

The prestigious Monaco Grand Prix was full of drama when Ascari, in a D50, plunged into the harbour while leading the field. He was unhurt and, although a Ferrari took the chequered flag, Castellotti in a Lancia was second. Then, four days later, on 26 May, Ascari was killed at Monza after deciding at the last minute to take the wheel of a Ferrari sports car during a practice session. Having lost its star driver, Lancia decided to withdraw 'temporarily' from Formula 1. The costly racing programme was exacerbating Lancia's already precarious financial plight and there followed tripartite negotiations between the firm, Fiat and Ferrari. As recounted on page 51, Fiat agreed to pay Ferrari the sum of 50 million lire annually for five years, and Lancia would pass its promising D50s to Ferrari for further development.

The historic hand-over of six D50s (Lancia retained the remaining two from the eight that had been built) took place on 26 July 1955 on the Via Caraglio. Ferrari went away with not only the cars, but also all the spares, drawings and transporters. Under the Lancia-Ferrari name the modified D50s won five major Grand Prix in 1956 and helped Fangio to his fourth World Championship title. This must have been galling indeed for Gianni Lancia, but by this time control of the company had passed to Carlo Pesenti, a wealthy cement manufacturer.

Pesenti had taken over in 1955 and, in the spring of that year, the firm welcomed a new recruit to its experimental department

BELOW *The Lancia D50 with its distinctive side-mounted pannier fuel tanks and 260 bhp 2480 cc V8 engine. It is seen here on its competitive début at the 1954 Spanish Grand Prix at Barcelona, with Ascari at the wheel, although it retired after nine laps.*

RIGHT *The Flaminia saloon, introduced at the 1957 Geneva Motor Show, with 2.5-litre V6 engine and de Dion rear axle. Two long-time Lancia features disappeared with this model: the distinctive front suspension and pillarless body.*

– Professor Antonio Fessia – who came to Lancia with a wealth of engineering experience behind him. A graduate of the Turin Polytechnic, Fessia had joined Fiat in 1923 and rose, in 1932, to be director of the aero-engine department. In 1936 he held a similar post in Fiat's central design office and the famous Topolino was developed under his aegis.

Fessia left Fiat in 1946 and went on to produce Italy's first front-wheel-drive car, the Cemsa. Powered by a water-cooled 1100 cc four-cylinder horizontally opposed engine, it caused a sensation at the 1947 Paris Motor Show, although it never entered series production. Fessia rejoined Fiat in 1952, and tried to persuade Fiat to follow his front-wheel-drive dream, but without success. He left that company in 1955, and his first task at Lancia was to see the 2nd Series Appia into production. Soon afterwards, Pesenti appointed him Lancia's technical supremo, whereupon Fessia immediately undertook a radical programme of reorganization. One of the first victims of Fessia's shake-up was Vittorio Jano, who followed his D50 Lancias to Maranello and his old associate Enzo Ferrari.

Fessia's Flaminia

The first of the Fessia generation of Lancias appeared at the 1956 Turin Motor Show, but a production version was not ready until the Geneva event of the following year. This was the Flaminia, the first of a new series of Lancias beginning with the letter F (for Fessia?). Pesenti had been impressed by Pinin Farina's experimental Aurelia-based Florida coupés, and the Turin styling house was responsible for the Flaminia's lines.

Although the prototype featured pillarless construction in the usual Lancia manner, the production Flaminia had a conventional door layout. Also new was the unequal-length wishbone independent front suspension, while there was a de Dion axle with inboard brakes at the rear. The 2458 cc V6 engine was less adventurous, as it was derived from the Aurelia unit. Unfortunately, only about 2,600 of these big, luxurious saloons had been sold by 1961. In that year the engine power was boosted from 102 to 110 bhp and, in 1962, its capacity was increased to 2775 cc. Despite these improvements, sales still

LANCIA FLAMINIA
(1st series)
1957–61

ENGINE	
No. of cylinders V6	
Bore/stroke mm 80 × 81	
Displacement cc 2458	
Valve operation Overhead	
Compression ratio 7.8:1	
Induction Solex carburettor	
BHP 102 at 4800 rpm	
Transmission Rear-mounted four-speed gearbox	

CHASSIS	
Frame Unitary	
Wheelbase mm 2870	
Track – front mm 1368	
Track – rear mm 1370	
Suspension – front Independent, wishbones, coil springs, anti-roll bar	
Suspension – rear de Dion rear axle, half-elliptic springs, Panhard rod	

PERFORMANCE	
Maximum speed 160 km/h (99 mph)	

ABOVE *The Flavia convertible by Pininfarina was introduced at the 1962 Turin Show. It was, surprisingly, a real four-seater.*

LEFT *The Zagato-bodied Flaminia Sport appeared at the 1958 Turin Show with the usual 119 bhp engine.*

RIGHT *The Touring-bodied Flaminia GT of 1959. There was a factory hardtop, and 2.5 or 2.8 V6s were on offer.*

moved slowly and had dropped to a trickle by the time that the model was discontinued in 1965. There were, of course, special-bodied variants – coupés from Zagato and Pinin Farina, plus an open two-seater from Touring – available from 1958.

Meanwhile Professor Fessia was pressing ahead with a completely new Lancia which would carry over no features from previous models; this emerged as the Flavia, which was Lancia's, and Italy's, first front-wheel-drive series-production car. Fessia already had a starting point for the design in his still-born Cemsa, and the Flavia bore a close resemblance to it in general, if not precise, terms.

The Flavia was powered by a four-cylinder horizontally opposed engine of exactly 1500 cc which employed two cam-shafts, compared to the Cemsa's one. These actuated short pushrods to angled rockers to obtain the benefits of hemispherical combustion chambers. The 78 bhp power unit was mounted well forward of the front-wheel line, while front suspension was similar to the Flaminia's and featured unequal-length wishbones, but with the addition of a transverse leaf spring. The rear end was more straightforward with a dead rear axle suspended by half-elliptic springs. All-round disc brakes were an advanced feature.

The Flavia's styling was controversial to say the least: a boxy, nose-heavy four-door saloon which had been styled neither by Lancia nor by Pinin Farina but, at Fessia's insistence, by Pietro Castagnero, a freelance consultant.

Production began at Lancia's old Borgo San Paolo works in 1961, but was transferred in the following year to a new factory at Chivasso, alongside the Turin to Milan *autostrada*. Approximately 30,000 Flavias were built in the first two years. A welcome variation arrived in 1962 in the form of a handsome Pininfarina coupé which did wonders for the model. Although the coupés initially used the saloon's 1500 engine, capacity was soon increased to 1727 cc, as the Nardi concern had been offering such a facility ever since the model's introduction. Lancia gave the idea its blessing and the concept was extended to the Flavia proper in 1963, although the 1500 version was still retained. Flavia developments reached their zenith when, in 1966, the 1727 cc was offered with the German Kugelfischer fuel injection which helped to boost engine output to 102 bhp, and the Flavia range continued to be built in this form until 1967. Another, but rarer variation, with only 726 made, was the 1800 cc Flavia Sport of 1963–67 with its distinctive Zagato coachwork.

By this time the Flavia had acquired a scaled-down companion: the Fulvia. Although the model was destined to be the best-selling Lancia ever, with more than 300,000 sold, it did not prove a financial success, and this was a factor in Fiat's taking over the firm in 1969.

The Fulvia shared many components with the Flavia but, although the new model was a front-wheel-drive car, a completely different engine was used. This had the V4 configuration of the Appia and was a 1091 cc twin-overhead-camshaft unit. The suspension was similar to the Flavia's and the styling was again also by Pietro Castagnero. Announced at the 1963 Geneva Motor Show, the Fulvia was capable of 148 km/h (92 mph). However, in the usual Lancia tradition, the car was lacking in power, so in 1964 the Fulvia 2C was born, providing an increased output of 71 bhp compared with the original's 58 bhp. The 2C was not only faster but also possessed far better torque characteristics.

Next came the Fulvia GT, available with 1231 and 1216 cc engine options, and in 1968 yet a further variant appeared – the GTE – with 1298 cc engine and a 20 mm (0.8 in) longer wheelbase. The GTE heralded the arrival of the 2nd Series Fulvia in 1969 and this saloon continued to be built until 1972. There were about 115,000 1st Series and 71,410 2nd Series cars, making a total of 186,410 produced in nine years. But this was far from being the end of the Fulvia model, because a delightful coupé variant continued in production for a further four years.

The coupé was undoubtedly Castagnero's most successful styling exercise. It appeared at the 1965 Turin Motor Show with the saloon's 1216 cc engine, boosted to 80 bhp and good for 160 km/h (99 mph). A host of variants followed over the next three years: the 88 bhp HF; the 1298 cc-engined Rallye; the 90 bhp 1.3 S Rallye; and, in 1968, the impressive 180 km/h (112 mph) 1.6 HF, with a 1584 cc engine and five-speed gearbox. A

2nd Series Fulvia coupé arrived in 1969 and the model continued much as before, although the range was gradually simplified from 1972. The last Fulvia coupé left the Chivasso production line in June 1976, and it was to be the last V-engined Lancia ever built. A very successful Fulvia variant was the Sport, originally of 1.3 litres capacity and later fitted with a 115 bhp 1.6-litre HF engine. Built by Zagato between 1965 and 1972, the Fulvia Sport proved a great success for this styling house, as 7100 were sold.

Fluctuating fortunes

Lancia returned to the competitive fray in 1963, but wisely steered clear of sports and Grand Prix racing, opting, instead, for rallying. To begin with, the firm campaigned the Flavia, achieving a notable victory in the 1965 Alpine Rally. But it was with the arrival of the Fulvia coupé that the rallying programme really began to bite when, in 1966, Lancias were placed second in the Monte Carlo and Three Cities events, in addition to class wins in the Targa Florio and Nürburgring 1000 km race. In 1967 the Lancia lance proved equally sharp with first and second places in the Spanish Rally and the Tour de Corse respectively, and a second in the Acropolis. Nineteen sixty-eight saw Lancia take the Coupe des Dames in the Monte Carlo Rally and a second in the San Remo, while in 1969 the Lancia Rally Team did even better with wins in the San Remo and RAC rallies, repeating the RAC success in 1970. However, by this time Lancia had lost its independence.

BELOW *The last V-engined Lancia, the front-wheel-drive V4 Fulvia of 1963. The boxy styling was by Pietro Castagnero.*

RIGHT *The handsome Fulvia coupé of 1965, also by Castagnero. It remained in production until 1976.*

The sands had been running out for Lancia throughout the 1960s. Nevertheless, in 1958 Carlo Pesenti had still believed that he was witnessing the dawn of a successful new era for the company, and displayed his confidence by erecting the imposing Lancia skyscraper, which straddles the Via Vincenzo Lancia and dominates the Turin skyline to this day. Unfortunately, the cars of the Fessia era were over-engineered and lacked visual appeal. The firm's best-ever post-war year was 1967, when Lancia built 43,172 cars. Then the decline began: sales slipped to 36,668 the following year, and in 1969 slumped to a pitiful 31,556. In the same year, by comparison, Fiat built 1.2 million cars and Alfa Romeo 104,305 – Lancia was obviously ripe for a take-over. Ford, which had been trying to get a toe-hold in Italy since the 1920s, had been spurned in its attempt to buy Ferrari, and was showing an interest in Lancia. However, the Italian government did not want such an old-established car firm to fall into foreign hands, so Fiat was encouraged to buy the ailing company. There were, of course, long-standing historical links between the two concerns and, on 24 October 1969, Fiat bought Lancia for a nominal 1 lira and took over its massive debts, which stood at around £6 million for 1968 alone.

The new management was happy to keep the Fulvia in production, but the Flavia was another matter. This somewhat unfortunate model had been given a facelift in 1967, and by 1969 was being fitted with a new 1991 cc unit. When Fiat took over it was obvious that something radical had to be done with the Flavia if it was going to be salvaged. The car had developed an unfortunate reputation for unreliability, so it was revised yet again and emerged, in 1971, as the Lancia 2000. At the same time Pininfarina came up with a good-looking coupé, which lasted until 1973, while the saloon continued for a further year.

Success with the Stratos

The Lancia name received a much-needed boost with the arrival, in 1972, of the low-production Stratos rally car, which gave the firm a string of World Rally Championship wins in 1974, 1975 and 1976. The basis for the production Stratos appeared on the Bertone stand at the 1970 Turin Motor Show. It had an extraordinarily exaggerated wedge shape, and was called Stratos after a Bertone employee commented that it looked as though it had just come from the stratosphere! A Fulvia 1600 HF engine was mounted behind the driver in the mid-engined position. Although the car was no more than a design exercise in this state, in March 1971 Lancia's management gave its engineers the green light to develop the Stratos as a low-production high-performance rally car.

Bertone was again responsible for the styling, and the result was the far more practical Stratos HF, which retained the wedge theme of the original and appeared at the 1972 Turin Show. Apart from styling alterations, the other significant change was the fitment of a 2418 cc Fiat-built engine from Ferrari's Dino, as in 1969, the year when Fiat bought Lancia, it had also acquired a 50 per cent interest in the Maranello company.

LEFT *A pair of Lancia Stratos, with the car in the foreground revealing its Ferrari Dino V6 engine. The glass-fibre body panels conceal an immensely strong underframe. Derived from a Bertone styling exercise, the Stratos made its competitive début in 1972, although it did not move to front-line rallying events until 1974 and helped Lancia to the first of three successive World Rally Championships.*

The Stratos HF made its rallying début in the 1972 Tour de Corse but had to retire through suspension problems, and it was much the same story in the Spanish Costa del Sol event of the same year. Nevertheless, 1972 saw Lancia achieve its first International Championship (from the following year the World Rally Championship) with the well-proven Fulvia coupé.

It was clear that the highly-strung Stratos would require an expert hand to turn it into a world-beater, so Lancia secured the services of Giampaolo Dallara, who had a thorough grounding in mid-engined sports cars, having been responsible for the design of the Lamborghini Muira. He was replaced, in late 1973, by Mike Parkes, a former British racing driver, who was working for Ferrari as a development engineer following a bad crash at Spa in 1967.

During 1973 the Stratos could be run only in non-homologated events, because the firm was busy building the 500 cars within 12 months required for homologation in the Group 4 Special GT Cars class. So the Stratos took a back seat while the firm's reliable Fulvia coupés kept the Lancia flag flying. A Fulvia finished second behind a Porsche in the Targa Florio, with an important win for the Stratos in the 17-stage non-homologated Tour de France Rally.

Lancia was aiming to build the required 500 Stratos cars by March 1974 but, apparently, this was not achieved until October. In that year – the Fulvia coupé's last in competition – the older car took a well-earned third place in the Safari Rally. The first significant victory by a Stratos came in the Targa Florio, while another – fitted with special 24-valve cylinder heads – won the San Remo Rally in the face of strong in-house Fiat opposition. A turbocharged version triumphed in the Giro d'Italiana and the model was also victorious in the Canadian Rideau Lakes Rally: Lancia was now strongly challenging Fiat to win the World Rally Championship for Makes. There was a third place in the British RAC event and the team finished the year with a win in the Corsican Rally – the coveted championship was Lancia's for the second time.

The Stratos' winning streak continued in 1975–77, with a hat-trick of Monte Carlo victories as the outstanding achievement. The all-conquering Stratos was officially withdrawn from rallying in December 1978 in favour of the Fiat 131 Abarth, but the model still showed its form with a surprise victory in the 1979 Monte Carlo. These successes gave Lancia valuable publicity when it was most needed and, as a result, Fiat completely revamped the range of Lancia road cars. Production was progressively pushed up during the 1970s and in 1980 it reached an all-time high of 110,756 cars built in the year.

The modern generation

The first of a new generation of Fiat-inspired models arrived in 1972 with the Beta, the practice of naming cars after letters of the Greek alphabet having been revived. (Alpha could not be used because of confusion with Alfa Romeo, so Beta it had to be!) The Beta was a boxy four-door front-wheel-drive fastback saloon powered by a transversely mounted 1438 cc Fiat twin-overhead-camshaft engine, and it was the first Lancia to employ rack-and-pinion steering. In the following year a stylish coupé version made its appearance and was campaigned for a short while by Lancia, powered by a Fiat Abarth engine with four-valve head. One of these coupés achieved a third place in the 1975 Swedish Rally, but managed only 11th position in the RAC events of the same year. Lancia would have to wait until

LANCIA STRATOS
1972–9

ENGINE		CHASSIS	
No. of cylinders V6		Frame Unitary	
Bore/stroke mm 92 × 60		Wheelbase mm 2180	
Displacement cc 2418		Track – front mm 1433	
Valve operation Twin overhead camshafts per cylinder bank		Track – rear mm 1457	
Compression ratio 10.5:1		Suspension – front Independent, wishbones, coil springs, anti-roll bar	
Induction Triple Weber carburettor		Suspension – rear Independent, lower wishbones with vertical struts, coil springs, anti-roll bar.	
BHP 270 at 8500 rpm			
Transmission Five-speed sump-mounted all-synchromesh gearbox		**PERFORMANCE**	
		Maximum speed 230 km/h (142 mph)	

1983 and the purpose-built mid-engined Rallye before it could again win the World Rally Championship.

Nineteen seventy-five saw the appearance of two Beta derivatives – the HPE (for High Performance Estate) and the mid-engined Montecarlo. This latter model originated in the pre-1973 oil crisis days when, as the Fiat 137, it was intended to complement the X1/9 coupé of 1972. Coded X1/20, it was down-graded in the difficult mid-1970s and production targets

ABOVE *A Stratos in full cry. In 1976 and 1977 the model wore Air Italia livery. Here the Munari/Maiga car wins the 1977 Monte Carlo Rally giving Munari his hat trick. A Stratos won again in 1979.*

LEFT *In 1983 Lancia again won the World Rally Championship with the 037 Rallye, derived from the Monte Carlo and powered by a centrally mounted 325 bhp Bosch fuel-injected twin-overhead-camshaft 1995 cc supercharged engine. The top speed is 220 km/h (137 mph). Martini has been associated with Lancia's motor sporting activities for over six years.*

ABOVE LEFT *The distinctive Y10 three-door hatchback which uses the Fiat 999 cc FIRE engine or 1049 cc unit.*

ABOVE *A 1978 Lancia Montecarlo (Monte Carlo when sold in Britain), styled and built by Pininfarina. Provided by Adrian and Edmund Rudler.*

were lowered. There was talk of marketing it as an Abarth, but Lancia took the project over and launched the model as the Montecarlo, in recognition of the marque's recent successes in the event. Unfortunately the 1995 cc Fiat twin-cam engine did not give the car the performance it required, although its top speed was in the region of 185 km/h (115 mph), in keeping with its good Pinanfarina looks. Incidentally, the model sold as the Scorpion in America to avoid confusion with Chevrolet's Monte Carlo. Series Two Betas were introduced in 1976 with improved 100 bhp engines and the Montecarlo was boosted to 120 bhp. The Beta remained in production until 1985.

But the big news back in 1975 was the arrival of the first 'real' Lancia since the Fiat take-over. The Gamma reverted to the front-wheel-drive/flat-four theme of the Flavia. It had a capacity of 2484 cc and featured belt-driven twin overhead camshafts on each cylinder bank. The Gamma lasted until 1985.

The next Lancia model was, by contrast, more like a Fiat. Its forebear, the Ritmo, arrived in 1978 and the 1980 Lancia version was called the Delta. This was a crisp four-door hatchback, styled by Ital Design, with 1302 and 1499 cc four-cylinder single-overhead-camshaft engine options. Even

though the Delta carries the Lancia badge, it is manufactured by Fiat and was voted 'Car of the Year' on its introduction.

Next, in 1983, came the Prisma – effectively a booted version of the Delta. (Once again, the Greek alphabet seems to have lost favour.) The Gamma was replaced in 1985 by the Thema, which continued the front-wheel-drive theme, being available with a 1995 cc single-overhead-camshaft engine, and turbocharged option. The 2849 cc alternative power unit is, by contrast, a V6 unit, but both engines have Fiat origins. The Thema is Lancia's contribution to the so-called Type Four project in which Fiat,

LANCIA MONTECARLO
1976–83

ENGINE		CHASSIS	
No. of cylinders 4		Frame Unitary	
Bore/stroke mm 84 × 90		Wheelbase mm 2300	
Displacement cc 1995		Track – front mm 1420	
Valve operation Twin overhead		Track – rear mm 1470	
Compression ratio 9.35:1		Suspension – front Independent, MacPherson strut, lower wishbones	
Induction Weber downdraught carburettor		Suspension – rear Independent, MacPherson strut, lower wishbones	
BHP 120 at 6000 rpm		**PERFORMANCE**	
Transmission Five-speed		Maximum speed 190 km/h (118 mph)	

Lancia, Alfa Romeo and Saab have combined to pool resources.

In 1986 came yet another engine option for the Thema, the top-line 8.32, powered by the 2927 cc twin-overhead-camshaft 32-valve Ferrari V8, as used in its 308 model, and transversely mounted. Other 1986 Lancia developments included the extension of a four-wheel-drive facility to the Delta and the Prisma models. A turbocharged HF Delta won the 1987 Monte Carlo Rally, following a Delta victory in 1986.

Somewhat less conventional was the Y10 of 1985 and, although this was a Fiat project and is sold as an Autobianchi in Italy, it is badged as a Lancia in Britain. With its distinctive sloping front end and sharply cut-off tail, this two-door hatchback was the first recipient of Fiat's robot-assembled 999 cc single-overhead-camshaft FIRE engine. A 1049 cc alternative is also available in turbocharged form.

Today, as Lancia celebrates 80 years of car manufacture, it can look back on generations of inspired, distinctive and, above all, innovative designs; the Lambda, Aprilia and Aurelia. The marque has created its own unique image, and where Lancia has led the world has followed.

MASERATI

Maserati was first a racing marque, then a sporting one and, although today it caters for the prosperous executive market sector, its competitive roots remain at the core of its current appeal.

Until 1937, Maserati was essentially a family concern, but a very remarkable one indeed. There were, in all, seven Maserati brothers, born between 1881 and 1898. Their father, Rudolpho, had been an engine driver in Piacenza with the royal railway but, when he married Carolina Losi, the couple moved west to the city of Voghera, about 50 km (31 miles) south of Milan. Their first son, Carlo, was born in 1881 and was followed two years later, in 1883, by Bindo. Alfieri, who arrived in 1885, died when he was only a few months old, so the next son, born in 1887, was also named Alfieri. The three remaining brothers were Mario (1890), Ettore (1894) and Ernesto (1898). All, with the exception of Mario – who became an artist – pursued engineering careers though, as will emerge, even Mario had a role to play in the creation of the Maserati car.

Carlo set the example for the rest of the family when, in the late 1890s, he joined a bicycle maker at Affori, on the outskirts of Milan. Carlo proved an ingenious young man: in 1899, when he was only 18, he designed a single-cylinder engine which he used to power one of his employer's machines. This motorized bicycle attracted the attention of the Marquis Carcano of Anzano del Parco, who lived in the nearby city of Lecco. He decided to back Carlo in his plans for producing the Carcano motor cycle and, although the venture proved to be short-lived, young Maserati rode the machine in an inter-town race in 1900, which started and finished at the town of Brescia. There he met

LEFT *During the inter-war years, Maserati produced almost exclusively racing cars, and this 6C 34, indicating the number of cylinders and the year of its introduction, was powered by a 3.7-litre supercharged engine. In 1935 the firm dispensed with the half-elliptic front springs and replaced them with an independent torsion bar system.*

young Vincenzo Lancia, who raced F.I.A.T. cars (the firm had just opened for business that year in Turin). Lancia convinced Carlo that four wheels represented a better future than two and, enthused with the prospect of a racing career, Carlo joined the F.I.A.T. company. But he was soon on the move again because, in 1903, he returned to Milan and went to work for the Isotta-Fraschini company, which had been established only three years previously.

Racing was still in Carlo's blood. He had joined the company as test driver and technical adviser, and hoped that he would be able to drive the cars in competition. But Carlo, who must have been either ambitious or restless, did not stay long. After four years he joined the Bianchi company, which was also based in Milan. There he had his opportunities to race and was placed ninth in the 1907 Coppa Florio and 16th in the Kaiserpreis eliminating race. However, he spent only a year with Bianchi before becoming general manager of the Junior car concern, established in Turin in 1905 by Giovanni Ceirano: Giovanni was a member of that famous family whose names pepper the pages of Italy's early motoring history. This move gave Carlo the opportunity to diversify into car design, but it was while he was working on a Junior car project, in 1910, that he contracted a fatal illness and died, aged only 29.

However, Carlo had ploughed a furrow that his other brothers would follow for, soon after arriving at Isotta-Fraschini, he had managed to get his younger brother, Alfieri, a job there. Prior to this the youngster had worked in a garage but, on joining the Milan firm in 1903, he soon succumbed to the attraction of motor racing. First he served as a mechanic for Isotta's star driver, Vincenzo Trucco, but by 1908, as a 23-year-old, he took the wheel himself when he drove one of the exquisite 1200 cc overhead-camshaft FE cars in the celebrated Coupe de l'Auto race at Dieppe, when he was placed 11th. Three years later, in 1911, he and his brother Ettore, who had also joined the firm, were sent to the Argentine to represent Isotta-Fraschini, and then were transferred to London. But the pair were soon back in their native Italy and, in 1912, were sent to the city of Bologna where they organized an Isotta-Fraschini repair shop.

However, after two years, Alfieri, who was only 27, decided that the time had come to set up in business on his own account and, on 14 December 1914, only five months after war had broken out in Europe, the Società Anonima Officine Alfieri Maserati was set up in small rented premises on the de'Pepoli street in Bologna. With the help of Ettore, Alfieri intended to tune customers' engines for competition using the experience that the two men had gained with Isotta-Fraschini.

Alfieri could not have chosen a worse time to start his business for, in May 1915, Italy was drawn into the war and both brothers were drafted into the army. Bindo had followed the well-trodden path to Isotta-Fraschini and wanted to stay there, so this meant that the youngest son, 17-year-old Ernesto, had to take over the day-to-day running of the Maserati firm, which by this time employed five mechanics.

With the war still raging, Alfieri left the army to establish a business making sparking plugs, not in Bologna, but in Milan, where they were used in wartime aero-engines and, after the war, in cars. When peace came, in 1918, Alfieri, Ettore and Ernesto were reunited and set about planning their future. They decided that the small de'Pepoli building should be dispensed with as larger premises were needed. They found these in the eastern suburb of Alemanni, better known as the Ponte Vecchio

area. There, on the Via Emilia, was a two-storey building that had previously been used for the manufacture of demijohns. After the move, the three brothers not only worked at the premises, but also lived there. The building boasted a court-yard, complete with garden, which was enthusiastically tended by their father Rudolpho, who had moved in with his sons.

The brothers hoped to prepare cars for racing, and Alfieri was the first to recognize that no better publicity could be obtained than the Maserati name featuring in local races and competitions. After campaigning a somewhat dilapidated Nesselsdorf, he gravitated to a special Isotta-Fraschini, powered by one bank of that company's V8 aero-engines. He was far more successful with this car and, in a race at Mugello in 1921, he finished second in his class with a fourth overall placing.

Enter Diatto

Alfieri's competence soon attracted the attention of the Diatto company of Turin which, although known as a manufacturer of railway rolling stock, had diversified into car production in 1905. The firm had survived a number of corporate reconstructions, the most recent having been undertaken in 1919. But, in 1922, Diatto introduced its Tipo 20 with a sophisticated 2-litre four-cylinder overhead-camshaft engine and the customary Italian Rolls-Royce 'look-alike' radiator.

Diatto's management decided that valuable publicity could be gained through racing, and Alfieri Maserati was accordingly approached to produce a competition version of the Tipo 20. The company planned to give the racing car its competitive baptism at the 1922 Italian Grand Prix – the first to be held at the new Monza circuit, near Milan. Alfieri and Ettore therefore moved briefly to Turin to supervise the car's construction. Unfortunately for Alfieri, the event was dominated by the superlative Fiat 804 and both Diattos retired, one breaking down and the other crashing while trying to keep pace with Nazzaro's flying Fiat.

Diatto's fortunes took a turn for the better when Guido Meregalli won the Circuit of Garda race in 1922, and he went on to repeat the success in 1923 and 1924. There were also a 3-litre version of the design, and Maserati succeeded in winning his class in the Autumn Grand Prix at Monza in 1922. In the face of Fiat, Alfa Romeo and Ceirano opposition, the 3-litre won the 1923 Montenero Cup – the 2-litre class in the 1924 Monza 24 Hours 'Night' sports car Grand Prix. Further victories followed in 1925 and 1926.

This good showing was clouded by an incident that occurred in May 1924 when Alfieri Maserati was competing in a hill-climb at Rabassada, near Barcelona. Diatto had realized the importance of the Spanish market and asked Luigi Mora, its local agent, to supply Maserati with a 2-litre Diatto, which somehow had become a 3-litre by the day of the event. When this was discovered, Alfieri was banned from racing for five years, along with Mora and Diatto itself, although the works was subsequently reprieved.

Alfieri's sentence was later shortened, but his temporary absence from the circuits allowed Ernesto to begin his racing career. Also, despite these problems, Diatto was still aiming at the top-line Grand Prix races. Therefore Alfieri was commissioned to design a completely new, 2-litre supercharged car to conform to the current racing formula. It was an ambitious and expensive project, especially when compared with Diatto's existing racing cars which were based on production models.

ABOVE *The Maserati brothers, pictured after Alfieri's death outside their Ponte Vecchio works for a 20th anniversary photograph on 16 December 1934. From the left: Bindo, Ettore, Ernesto and Mario.*

RIGHT *The first Maserati. Tipo 26, with Alfieri at the wheel and mechanic Guerino Bertocchi, in the 1926 Targa Florio. It won its class and was placed ninth overall in this inaugural race.*

The resulting car accordingly reflected racing practice in that it had a supercharged twin-overhead-camshaft eight-cylinder engine. One example was ready for the Susa–Moncenisio race held in July 1925. Alas, it entered in a race at Maddalena in August when Onesimo Marchisio, a former Fiat racing driver, fatally crashed in the car. When the remaining racing Diatto appeared at the Italian Grand Prix later that year, it was driven by Ernesto Maserati and, on the 14th lap, when the car was holding fifth position, the supercharger bolts snapped and Maserati's race was over. Although Diatto was still committed to its racing programme, it lacked the financial resources to continue, and decided to withdraw from the competitive fray. By 1927, the firm had ceased car manufacture altogether.

The demise of the Diatto competition programme meant that the central plank of the Maserati brothers' activities had been removed. They therefore decided that, rather than rely on other manufacturers for their work, they would create their own Maserati car, using the aborted Diatto project as its basis. They had the car itself, presumably donated by Diatto in lieu of

payment. The 2-litre formula had been discontinued at the end of 1925, to be replaced by a new 1½-litre supercharged one which began in 1926.

This first Maserati, designated Tipo 26 to reflect its year of introduction, followed the general Diatto design, but differed in detail. That car had been conceived for the 2-litre formula, and neither its 65 mm bore nor 72 mm stroke was retained. Instead, the 1492 cc capacity was achieved by 60×66 mm dimensions, the resulting unit developing 120 bhp at 5300 rpm. Other departures were the fitment of roller bearings for the front, centre and rear journals, although plain, white metal ones were retained for the intermediates. At the other end of the engine the aluminium cylinder head was replaced with a cast-iron one. The Roots-type supercharger, driven off the end of the crankshaft, was kept. Alfieri followed Mercedes practice in that the twin Memini Super carburettors were located between the blower and inlet manifolds, instead of the mixture being pressurized after it had passed through the carburettor. This potent power unit was placed in a chassis that was substantially the same as Diatto's design.

Any make needs a badge, of course, and Maserati's was the work of artist brother Mario. Originally oblong in shape, replaced by an oval in 1932, the badge featured a red trident (later arising from a stylized blue sea) which bore the Maserati name. Mario's inspiration is said to have been a statue of Neptune, with a massive trident in its right hand, which was the centrepiece of a fountain in Bologna's Piazza del Nettuno.

Racing the Maserati

The Tipo 26 was ready for the Targa Florio in April 1926 and, on the car's first outing, Alfieri Maserati finished in ninth position in what was otherwise a Bugatti benefit race. He even won the 1.5-litre class: it was a good start. However, two cars entered for the Italian Grand Prix later that year suffered from carburettor and lubrication problems.

Before the start of the 1927 season, Alfieri therefore altered the carburettor layout so that a single Memini was bolted directly to the supercharger. As a result, power output rose to 128 bhp at 6000 rpm. The Tipo 26 continued to be produced with but one modification – Weber replaced the Memini in 1929 – until 1932, by which time a total of 11 cars had been built.

Nineteen twenty-seven started well for Maserati, with Alfieri being placed third in the Tripoli Grand Prix and also winning his class. In the same year a 62×82 mm 2-litre 26B derivative, in which Maserati was placed third in that year's Targa Florio event. Then, two weeks later, on 8 May, Alfieri, while competing in the Coppa Messina race at Monte Peloritani, was temporarily blinded by dust, his car left the road and overturned. As a result of his injuries, Alfieri had to have one of his kidneys removed, but he was back at the wheel again in July. The year was a successful one for the new make, which won the Italian Manufacturers' Championship title; although it should be said that successes in mostly minor events had given them the award.

The 1.5-litre formula came to an end in 1928 and was effectively replaced by *Formule Libre*, which meant that individual races could be run for almost any capacity of car. Consequently, Maserati produced yet another variant on the straight-eight twin-cam theme in the shape of the 62×70 mm 26R of 1690 cc in 1928, which was followed in 1929 by the 1078 cc (51×66 mm) Tipo 26C.

However, Maserati was beginning to feel the effects of surefooted opposition from Bugatti so, for 1929, Alfieri conceived an extraordinary V16-engined model which carried the V4 designation – no doubt inspired by the V12-engined Fiat 806 racing car of 1927. The Maserati's engine consisted of two 26B cylinder blocks, and their attendant crankshafts, geared together in a common crankcase. The capacity was therefore 3961 cc. The V4 developed 280 bhp and had a theoretical top speed of 250 km/h (155 mph).

This fearsome machine was entered in the 1929 Monza Grand Prix, when Alfieri succeeded in putting in the fastest lap, although he was placed a disappointing sixth overall. After that

event the V4, with Baconin Borzacchini at the wheel, took a new world Class C record near Cremona when, from a flying start, it achieved an average speed of 246.06 km/h (152.9 mph) over a 10-km (6.2-mile) course.

The record gave the Maserati firm vital publicity at a time when the Depression, triggered by the 1929 Wall Street Crash, had spread across the world. Maserati survived relatively untouched by the economic gloom: it was fortunate in that its production of racing cars was relatively modest. In 1926, the first year of operations, only three cars had been built, followed by five in 1927 and eight in 1928. Like Bugatti, Maserati sold its cars to private owners, usually wealthy young gentlemen of independent means who wanted to go motor racing.

In 1930, again at the wheel of the V4, Borzacchini won the Tripoli Grand Prix, ahead of another Maserati. It was the make's first Grand Prix victory and it came just in time for, from 1931 onwards, the Bologna cars were successfully challenged by Alfa Romeo which had decided to return to mainstream racing after a six-year absence. The Milan company briefly fielded, in 1931, a 3504 cc V12 Tipo A – like Maserati's V4, contrived by gearing two engines (in this instance 1750 cc units) together. But the more conventional, 2.3-litre Monza enjoyed greater success.

Meanwhile, Alfieri Maserati was at work on yet another racing car. Although it carried the 26M designation and, like its predecessors, was a straight-eight twin-overhead-camshaft unit, in reality it was a new engine with a 65×94 mm bore and stroke, and 2495 cc capacity. The crankshaft employed plain bearings, except for the centre one which was of the roller variety, and changes were made to the lubrication and carburation. But the principal departure from previous practice was the bodywork. Although mechanics had not been carried in racing cars since 1925, the two-seater bodies demanded by them had been perpetuated. But, for the 26M of 1930, Alfieri fitted bodywork which was just wide enough to accommodate the driver: this was reflected in the *M* suffix which stood for *monoposto* (single-seater). The car initially resembled a two-seater, but was narrowed in 1931 following the slim lines of the Tipo A Alfa Romeo. With the 26M, Alfieri Maserati showed greater concern with weight saving than previously, so many of the brake components, steering and differential casings were made from electron light alloy. This important work was being carried out for Maserati by Isotta-Fraschini, Alfieri's old employer.

The appearance of the 26M coincided with Maserati signing up Achille Varzi to drive for them: Varzi had left Scuderia Ferrari when they took on his rival, Tazio Nuvolari. Varzi gave Maserati, and himself, an excellent 1930, winning the Monza and Spanish Grand Prix and the Coppa Acerbo. The marque also chalked up some helpful second places and these successes gave Maserati its second Italian Manufacturers' Championship. Inevitably, Varzi's achievements made him a sought-after property and, in 1931, he signed with Bugatti.

For the following season, the 26M's capacity was increased to 2811 cc, achieved by enlarging the engine's bore to 69 mm: the model was fittingly redesignated 8C 2800. In 1931 Luigi Fagioli, who had joined the Maserati team in the previous year, pulled off a notable victory in that year's Monza Grand Prix. He maintained this success in 1932, when he was entrusted with yet another V16 leviathan, the 4905 cc V5, which he drove on its debut at the Rome Grand Prix. He won that event, but was robbed of victory in the Italian Grand Prix through poor pitwork, and had to settle for second place. Overall, however, the season was not as successful as the previous year's because of the arrival of Alfa Romeo's Tipo B monoposto, the legendary P3: when the two makes met on the race track, Alfa Romeo nearly always gained the upper hand. In 1932, Maserati also toyed with a 2.5-litre front-wheel-drive single-seater racing car, but it was not a success.

Death of Alfieri

Nineteen thirty-two was overshadowed by the death, on 3 March, of Alfieri Maserati: he was only 44. His illness arose from complications associated with that 1927 accident when he had lost a kidney. The other one began to give trouble and even the ministrations of Professor Bartalo Negrisoli, an eminent Italian surgeon, were unable to save Alfieri. His funeral took place in Bologna on the day after his death, when enormous crowds lined the route of the funeral cortège through streets still bearing signs of the winter snows.

Apart from Alfieri's death being a personal tragedy for the remaining Maserati brothers, it also represented a great loss to the firm, because he had been the company's mainspring on both the design and administrative sides of the business. Therefore Bindo, the only remaining Maserati brother not yet involved in racing (he was still a test driver with Isotta-Fraschini), assumed the presidency of the Bologna company. Ettore had no financial acumen, so the burden of administration and design fell on the shoulders of 34-year-old Ernesto: he had an unenviable task in a difficult financial climate.

RIGHT AND BELOW *Maserati's extraordinary V16-engined racing car of 1929. Designated V4 to reflect its 3961 cc capacity, it consisted of two Tipo 26B cylinder blocks on a common crankcase. Twin Roots-type superchargers were fitted, the engine developed around 280 bhp at 5500 rpm but, although its top speed was around 250 km/h (155 mph), the V4 did not enjoy much success on the race track. Only two examples were built: this one is pictured in the courtyard of the Maserati factory. There was a V5 4905 cc derivative of 1932.*

Fortunately for Maserati, financial problems overwhelmed Alfa Romeo in 1933 and, at the beginning of the year, the Milan company announced that it would be withdrawing from Grand Prix racing. Scuderia Ferrari, its competitive arm, was forced to fall back on the dated two-seater Monzas. Maserati, by contrast, had its new 2.9-litre 8CM single-seater on hand, produced in response to the 2.6-litre 215 bhp P3. With capacity increased to 2991 cc by extending the stroke to 100 mm, the engine now developed 220 bhp at 5500 rpm. The 8CM was a technological feather in Maserati's cap, as it was the first racing car to be fitted with a modern hydraulic, rather than mechanical, braking system, the layout having been pioneered on the abortive front-wheel-drive project.

Maserati scored a prestigious international success when the ample figure of Giuseppe Campari gave the company its first French Grand Prix win while Tazio Nuvolari, depressed by the uncompetitive nature of Ferrari's 2.9-litre Monza Alfa Romeos, switched alliances to Maserati and won the Coppa Ciano, and Belgian and Nice Grand Prix for the marque. This was Maserati's last successful GP season of the inter-war years as, in

1934, came a new 750 kg formula which saw the arrival of the all-conquering Mercedes-Benz and Auto Unions. Even a revitalized Alfa Romeo – government-owned since 1933 – was unable to challenge this teutonic might successfully.

From 1934 onwards, therefore, Maserati was relegated from its front-line position, despite the arrival of the company's first six – the 3.7-litre 6C 34 – in 1934, while a 4.7-litre V8-engined V8R1 of 1935 with torsion bar independent front suspension proved a non-starter. So, very sensibly, Maserati decided to turn its back on Grand Prix racing and to concentrate instead on the second-line Voiturette competition, with 1100 and 1500 cc categories, for which the 'big battalions' had no suitable cars.

BELOW *The 8C 3000 of 1932/3, still with two-seater bodywork and ready for the road. The engine is a supercharged 2991 cc twin-overhead-camshaft eight-cylinder unit with a top speed of around 233 km/h (145 mph).*

RIGHT *In Britain, young, wealthy Whitney Straight's 8CM was fitted with this heart-shaped radiator grille of his own design. In 1936 the car was bought for Prince Bira's White Mouse Stable.*

MASERATI 8CM
1933–5

ENGINE
No. of cylinders 8

Bore/stroke 69 × 100 mm

Displacement 2991 cc

Valve operation Twin overhead camshafts

Compression ratio 5.26, 6.35:1

Induction Roots-type supercharger, Weber carburettor

BHP 220 at 5500 rpm

Transmission Four-speed

CHASSIS
Frame Channel

Wheelbase 2560 mm (8 ft 5 in)

Track – front 1300 mm (4 ft 3 in)

Track – rear 1300 mm (4 ft 3 in)

Suspension – front Half-elliptic

Suspension – rear Half-elliptic

Brakes Hydraulic drum

PERFORMANCE
Maximum speed 220 km/h (136 mph)

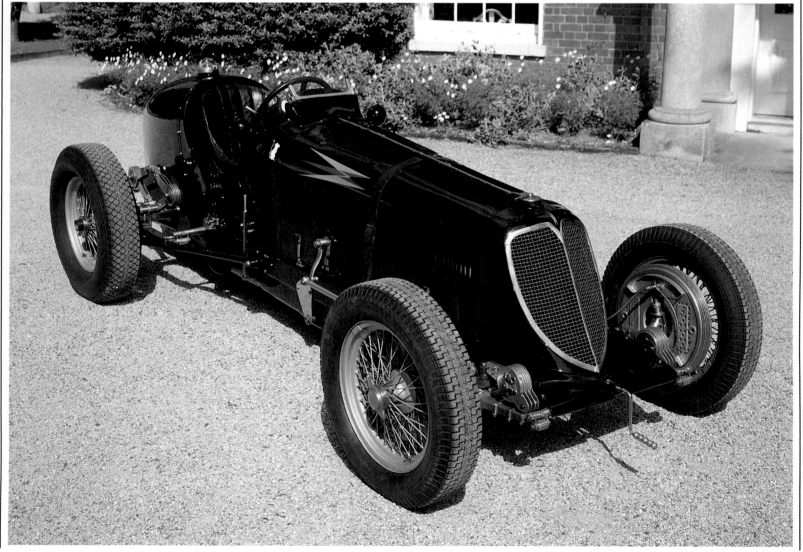

Maserati had had some presence in this formula since 1931, with their first four-cylinder racing car – the 4CTR of 1931 – and its 4CM 1100 successor, which endured until 1937. But the firm began to take the formula seriously in 1936, when it introduced the 1493 cc Tipo 6CM, with the V8RI's torsion-bar independent front suspension. The 6CM scored innumerable victories both in Italy and abroad, its only real rival being the British ERA, which had appeared in 1934. But, in 1937, Alfa Romeo decided that it, too, would find solace in the Voiturette formula, and fielded, the following year, its outstanding Colombo-designed eight-cylinder 1479 cc Tipo 158. Maserati responded with the 1490 cc four-cylinder 4CL, with four, rather than two, valves per cylinder, in the manner of the larger eight-cylinder cars. However, the new Maserati was no match for its Alfa Romeo adversary.

By this time, the surviving Maserati brothers had sold a controlling interest in the firm to the Orsi industrial combine which, with steel mills in nearby Modena, also specialized in the manufacture of agricultural implements and other machinery. In truth, Alfieri's death had shaken the brothers more than they realized and, although racing car production had picked up somewhat – 16 in 1934 and 17 the following year – in 1936 it slumped to 9. Production recovered to 14 in 1937, which was when Adolfo Orsi took over the firm. In all probability, however, it was the sparking plug business, still ticking over in Milan and helped by government contracts, that interested Orsi more. Despite this change in ownership, the Maserati brothers agreed to remain with the firm for a ten-year period.

In the meantime the 750 kg formula, although scheduled to run only until 1936, had been extended for another year and in 1937 was replaced by a 3-litre one. In response to this new challenge, Maserati produced the eight-cylinder 2992 cc 8CTF. This was the same capacity as the earlier 8CM's, but the engine in fact consisted of two 4CM cylinder blocks mounted on a common crankcase with a fixed cylinder head. The chassis also followed Voiturette practice with torsion bar suspension and quarter-elliptic rear springs.

Although the 8CTF put up some impressive performances it lacked reliability, and the best it achieved in 1938 was a fifth position in a Monza event. Paul Pietsch improved its race record in the 1939 German Grand Prix at Nürburgring, when he finished third behind Mercedes-Benz and Auto Union.

When the 8CTF eventually found success, it came from a most unlikely quarter. In 1938, across the Atlantic in America, the organizers of the famous Indianapolis 500-mile race had decided to change the rules in the hope of attracting European competitors. American Mike Boyle eagerly ordered 'the latest Maserati' from Bologna and, after the firm tried to fob him off with a 6C Voiturette, in 1939 he finally obtained an 8CTF in 365 bhp form.

Boyle reduced the supercharger pressure, so that output was down, marginally, to 350 bhp, and fitted larger Firestone-shod wheels. With Wilbur Shaw at the wheel, the Maserati set a punishing pace and won the 1939 event, two minutes ahead of the American opposition. It was the first victory of a European car in the race since Howdy Wilcox had triumphed at the wheel

RIGHT *A Maserati engine in all its glory and, like every model since 1926, with twin overhead camshafts. This is a 6C 34 unit, with its 84 × 112 mm bore and* *stroke inspired by the firm's 4C 2500 engine. The 3724 cc six employs a Roots-type supercharger and develops 270 bhp at 5300 rpm.*

of a Peugeot in 1919. Shaw repeated his success in 1940, but was robbed of the hat trick in '41 when an unbalanced wheel broke when he was a lap ahead of the field.

By this time, back in Italy, Maserati had found a new home. At the end of 1939 the firm was moved from the city of Bologna, its base since 1914, down the road the 38 km (23 miles) to Modena and the Via Ciro Menotti, where it still is today. This transfer of location allowed Adolfo Orsi to assume direction of the firm. He became president, while his brother-in-law, Alceste Giacomazzi, was managing director: for the Maserati brothers it was the beginning of the end.

War brings changes

Grand Prix racing effectively ceased with the outbreak of war in Europe in September 1939 but, on 23 May 1940, in faraway Sicily, Maserati managed to sweep the board in the Targa Florio when the make took the first three places; significantly, Alfa Romeo had no entries. Nineteen days later, on 11 June, Italy joined with Germany to declare war on Britain and a vulnerable France.

As Italy's commitment to the war effort began to bite, car production ceased, although as late as October 1940, Adolfo Orsi, using Tazio Nuvolari as an intermediary, was wanting to arrange a meeting with the Stuttgart-based Porsche company with thoughts of technical collaboration. The war put paid to such ideas and Maserati concentrated on the production of sparking plugs, batteries and other electrical equipment. A development of this business was a three-wheeled electrically powered truck, created to bypass the petrol shortage, and this was produced in limited numbers. As a result of the fuel famine even the Maserati brothers took to riding bicycles! The firm also diversified into essential machine tools such as milling machines, lathes and grinders.

The war also saw a change in the running of the firm's affairs. Managing director Giacomazzi departed to the Orsi ironworks and he was replaced by Osvaldo Gorrini, late of the Modena-based Fiat Tractors. The design side of the business was reinforced by the arrival of Vittorio Bellentani who had worked for Ferrari at nearby Maranello, and then, in 1944, Alberto Massimino joined Maserati. He was an ex-Fiat employee who,

since leaving that company, had been involved with the design of the superlative Tipo 158 Alfa Romeo, before joining Ferrari and then Maserati. Massimino was to have overall responsibility for the immediate post-war generation of Maserati racing cars.

With the coming of peace, Maserati, along with its racing contemporaries, dusted off its pre-war cars and the 4CL, fielded by the semi-works Scuderia Milano, achieved some success. The new Grand Prix formula, introduced in 1946, catered for cars with either 1.5-litre supercharged engines or 4.5-litre unsupercharged ones.

In May 1947, the Maserati brothers' 10-year contract with Orsi expired. Ettore Maserati remained with the electrical business, but Ernesto and Bindo returned to Bologna. On 1 December 1947, in premises at Via San Savena, not far from the original Via Emilia works, they established Officine Specializate Costruzioni Automobili Fratelli Maserati, which was better known by its OSCA Maserati – and later simply OSCA – acronym. Although they began by producing a small 1100 cc sports car, it was not long before they were building racing engines again, and they followed Ferrari's lead by developing a 4.5-litre unsupercharged V12 which could be fitted in the current Maserati frame. A complete Formula 1 car appeared in 1951 but, three years later, OSCA withdrew from Formula 1 to concentrate on sports car racing. In 1954 Stirling Moss and Bill Lloyd won the American Sebring 12-hour race – a faint echo of past glories. But the brothers were getting older and, in 1963, they sold out to Count Augusta's MV concern. By 1967 OSCA had vanished.

Maserati takes to the road

Nineteen forty-seven was a pivotal year in Maserati affairs. Not only did two of the brothers depart but, in addition to the mainstream Grand Prix cars, a true sports racing line was introduced and Maserati road cars also made their début. The first generation of sports racers was the A6GCS. It was usually produced with an open two-seater body, cyclops headlamp mounted in the middle of the radiator grille, and cycle wings. The engine was a 1978 cc unsupercharged six, although the single, rather than twin overhead camshafts, were a sign of the cost-conscious times. Although the model made its competition

LEFT *The first true 'production' Maserati road car was the A6-1500 of 1946–50. Only 60 were built and practically all were Pinin Farina-bodied, as is this 1947 example displayed at that year's Geneva show. Note the opening Plexiglass roof. Concealed headlamps were another advanced feature.*

ABOVE *The 4CLT/48 of 1948, also known as the San Remo Maserati, after two of them had come first and second in the San Remo Grand Prix in May 1948. A 1490 cc four-cylinder engine with two-stage supercharging was employed. By 1950, 21 of these 260 km/h (161 mph) cars had been built.*

with concealed headlights and a Plexiglass roof panel. Pinin Farina bodied practically all 60 A6-1500s, though these featured conventional headlamps. The model endured until 1950 when it was replaced by the A6G which perpetuated the single-overhead-camshaft layout, but with the capacity increased to 1954 cc. At the rear, semi-elliptic springs replaced its predecessor's coils. Again the bodies – both spiders and coupés – were by Pinin Farina, but only 16 examples were sold between 1951 and 1953.

The next car, by contrast, was rooted not in the A6G, but in the A6GCS sports car. This was the A6G 2000, whose 1985 cc engine was much the same as the competition model's, though mildly detuned to give 160 rather than 190 bhp. The other difference was the replacement of the noisy, but efficient, camshaft gear train with a cheaper, quieter chain. By the time that this new model arrived, Pinin Farina was deeply committed to Ferrari, so Allemano of Turin offered a range of stylish coupés, while Frua produced some good-looking spyders and coupés and Zagato came out with some characteristically distinctive renderings. The model remained in production until 1957, but output was relatively modest with only 59 examples built.

As always, the Maserati company's main preoccupation was with track racing and, although its cars fared reasonably well in the 1946–51 formula, they were gradually outclassed by the still highly competitive Tipo 158 Alfa Romeo, also known as the Alfetta, and by Italy's new Ferrari marque of racers, produced only 12 km (7 miles) away at Maranello.

Until 1948, Maserati had relied on its pre-war 4CL, but in 1948 a new, updated version, the 4CLT/48, was unveiled. This had basically the same supercharged, four valves per cylinder

début by winning a road race at Modena in September 1947, the car made no great impact on racing and only 16 had been produced by the time that the A6GCS was discontinued in 1950.

Its A6GCS/53 successor of 1953 was, by contrast, a much more progressive offering. The engine's bore had been increased slightly, from 76 to 76.5 mm – the capacity was now 1985 cc – and twin overhead camshafts replaced the single-cam unit, all courtesy of the current Formula 2 racing car. The quarter-elliptic rear springs came from the same source. The cycle wings were dispensed with and replaced by a more up-to-date full-width version. The first time that it was raced, in the 1953 Mille Miglia, Emilio Giletti and Guerino Bertocchi won the 2-litre class and were placed sixth overall. The model was far more successful than its predecessor: 55 were built before production ceased in 1955.

The A6-1500, the first true roadgoing Maserati, made its début at the 1947 Geneva Show. Like the A6GCS sports car, it was fitted with a single-overhead-camshaft six-cylinder engine, though of 1488 cc. The A6-1500 had a tubular chassis and rear suspension was by coil springs. Pinin Farina produced a rather unusual coupé body with the new full-width bodywork, fitted

1490 cc four-cylinder engine, with power marginally increased to 260 bhp. The coil and wishbone and quarter-elliptic rear springs were perpetuated, but changes were made to the chassis. The new car did not do particularly well in its introductory year. The 1949 season saw a marked improvement and 4CLT victories included the San Remo (the model was known by this name after a 1948 victory) Pau, Albi and British Grand Prix. Attempts were made to uprate the basic design but, rooted as it was in the pre-war years, these proved unsuccessful.

Maserati therefore turned its attention to Formula 2 events and, in 1951, introduced its A6GCM single seater, derived from the cycle-winged sports racer of 1947 vintage. However, the engine was a 1987 cc twin-overhead-camshaft six, and the car was a little more successful than its Formula 1 brother. Here again, Ferrari usually had the edge, although, in 1953, Juan Fangio drove an A6GCM to victory in the Italian Grand Prix. This success reflected the ministrations of Gioachino Colombo, one of Italy's foremost racing car designers and creator of the

fabled Tipo 158 Alfetta, who had joined Maserati in the previous October. His appointment marked a shift in Maserati's racing fortunes.

It had all begun with a change in the firm's corporate status. The electrical division was hived off, although it remained within the Orsi organization and, from 1954, produced Maserati motor cycles varying in size from 48 cc two-strokes to 250 cc overhead-valve machines, but this diversification only lasted until 1961.

Colombo pays a visit

Officine Alfieri Maserati SpA thus became the personal property of Adolfo Orsi, and his son Omer was given a much freer hand in the firm's affairs. It was in this more enlightened climate that Colombo joined Maserati from Alfa Romeo, but when he appeared, Massimino departed.

Work was already well advanced on a new car for the 2.5-litre

196

unsupercharged formula, due to begin in 1954. It was mostly the work of Vittorio Bellentani and Giulio Alfieri (the latter became Maserati's technical director in 1954). In the case of 6C 2500, as the new car was coded, Colombo was able to incorporate features that he had wanted to include on the uprated Formula 2 car but which he had been prevented from introducing due to lack of time. The weak point on post-war Maserati racing cars had long been the rigid rear axle and its associated quarter-elliptic springs. This was replaced by a de Dion rear axle, a feature Colombo had introduced on the Alfetta Alfa Romeo; but the layout was unusual on the Maserati in having the beam ahead of, rather than behind, the axle line. The suspension medium was a transverse leaf spring, located above the trans-axle unit.

The car had a completely new chassis designed by Valerio Colotti. The established twin large-diameter tubes were dispensed with and replaced by a new multi-tubular frame which was both lighter and stiffer than its predecessor, while the

The most famous of all racing Maseratis, the 250F, introduced in 1954, was a success from the outset. It enjoyed three further sensational seasons and Fangio won his fifth World Championship title in a 250F in 1957.

front suspension was carried over from the Formula 2 car. The 2493 cc engine was a straightforward six-cylinder unit with twin overhead camshaft which actuated two valves per cylinder; all of this owed much to its 2-litre forebear. With triple twin-choke Weber carburettors, it developed 240 bhp at 7200 rpm and, such was the engine's reliability, that it was eventually boosted to 270 bhp at 8000 rpm. The 6C 2500's top speed was around the 290 km/h (180 mph) mark. His work done, Colombo left Modena at the end of 1953 and went on to design the fêted 251 Bugatti of 1956.

The new car, now named 250F, was ready for the 1954 Argentine Grand Prix – the first race of the new 2.5-litre formula. With Fangio at the wheel, this outstanding car and

197

driver won the event and the Argentinian repeated the feat at the Belgian Grand Prix, before he moved to the Mercedes-Benz team. In 1954 the 250F won four Formula 1 events. Nineteen fifty-five was even better for the car achieved five Grand Prix victories, although this dropped to four in 1956. But the golden year for Maserati was 1957, when the red cars from Modena won no less than seven mainstream events, including the Argentine, Monaco, French and German Grand Prix. This also gave Fangio his fifth World Drivers' Championship victory, as he had returned to the Maserati fold after Mercedes-Benz' withdrawal from racing in late 1955.

The cars had been steadily refined since their 1954 introduction. They had been lightened and their bodywork boasted a new, sleek nose. In this form the 250F could be said to represent the epitome of the front-engined post-war racing car. The 250F was the most successful racing car in the company's history: it gave the Maserati marque an enormous fillip and an enhanced reputation which survives to this day.

This enormous success had cost Maserati dear, and the company was forced to withdraw its Formula 1 team at the end of 1957, along with a 2.5-litre V12 engine waiting in the wings, because of financial problems. These came to a head on 1 April 1958 when the receivers were called in and, while Maserati's future trembled in the balance, there was talk of German and American suitors. Fortunately, the firm's finances were put on a sounder footing when the machine tool division was sold, in 1959, to a Swiss group.

Ironically, the 250F car was not at the root of the company's difficulties. The cause lay rather in the Orsi management's decision to enter, in earnest, the highly competitive world of sports car racing. The Maserati challenge began, in 1955, with the arrival of the 300S, with a 3-litre version of the 250F's engine, while the coil and wishbone front suspension and the de Dion rear axle also echoed racing car practice. Although the first season was an encouraging one, 1956 was more successful with victories in the Buenos Aires, Nürburgring and Paris 1000-kilometre events. A 3.5-litre version of the design fared less well. In tandem with the sixes, Maserati also campaigned a second string of four-cylinder cars, although they failed to make much impact in the face of such authoritative Porsche and Ferrari opposition.

The model that effectively brought Maserati to its financial knees was the 450S of 1957, powered by a completely new

Of course, this withdrawal only related to factory entries, for the firm decided to continue to produce sports racers for private owners. The result was the legendary Tipo 60 of 1959, better known by its 'Birdcage' nickname: its chassis spaceframe was made up of a multiplicity of 1 cm ($\frac{2}{5}$ in) and 1.5 cm ($\frac{3}{5}$ in) diameter tubes. As keeping costs down was a prime concern, Giulio Alfieri incorporated the 250F's redundant coil and wishbone front and de Dion rear suspension units. The 2-litre engine – the car was intended for hill-climbing and the popular 2-litre racing class in America – was an existing 1993 cc one, previously used for sports car racing and in speed boats. To ensure a low bonnet line, this power unit was canted at a 45-degree angle which meant that a dry sump lubrication system had to be used. As this engine developed 195 bhp and the 'Birdcage' weighed a mere 561 kg (1237 lb), great things were expected

ABOVE *The Maserati 'Birdcage', so called because of its spaceframe chassis with 200 or so tubes, was introduced in Tipo 60 form in 1959 with a 1989 cc 200S-derived four-cylinder engine. There was also a contemporary Tipo 61 derivative with 2890 cc power.*

LEFT *The magnificent lines of the 250F. Note the oil tank in the extremity of the tail.*

LEFT INSET *Fangio in 1957 when he took 250Fs to victory in the German, French and Monaco GPs.*

4478 cc V8 engine with twin overhead camshafts on each cylinder bank. Although this potent power unit was reliable enough, the same, alas, could not be said of the car's other components. There were wins in the 1957 Sebring 12 Hours and Swedish Grand Prix, but the decisive blow came in that year's Venezuelan Grand Prix at Caracas, when the entire 450S team of three cars were either damaged or written off. This was a crippling blow for Maserati and with a change of the racing formula, to 3 litres, due the following year, the firm wisely took the decision to withdraw from sports car racing.

The Tipo 60 was triumphant on its first outing when Stirling Moss ran away with a sports car race at Rouen and followed this up by winning the 1960 Cuban Grand Prix with the 60's 2890 cc Tipo 61 derivative. He and Dan Gurney also won the Nürburgring 1000-kilometre event, and a Birdcage repeated this success in the following year. The Tipo 61's increased capacity had been prompted by the factory's decision to enter 3-litre American races, and this was the limit set for twin-overhead-camshaft engines. There were, however, reliability problems, which were mostly associated with the gearbox.

Formula 1 again

By the mid 1960s Maserati was fully committed to a new generation of road cars, and the chances of any further Grand Prix involvement seemed remote. Then, in 1965, Orsi received an approach from Mario Tozzi-Condivi, an old friend, and a director of the British Chipstead Motor Group which had just bought Cooper Cars. They were looking for a Formula 1 engine for the new 3-litre formula which was to come in in 1966.

Maserati had the very thing; the nine-year old V12 unit which had run in 3-litre form. The V12-powered cars, which were campaigned under the Cooper-Maserati name, were ready for the 1966 season and performed surprisingly well. John Surtees won that year's Mexico Grand Prix, while Pedro Rodriguez had a surprise win at the 1967 South African GP. Unfortunately, this promising start was not sustained.

By this time, Maserati was developing its second generation of road cars. In the mid-1950s the Orsi management had realized that, if Maserati were to survive, it would have to be committed to producing road cars in earnest, rather than in the half-hearted way it had built them in the past: between 1946 and 1958 only 139 examples had been made.

Therefore the car that Maserati exhibited at the 1957 Geneva Show represented the start of a new era for the firm. Named the 3500 GT, it was a handsome two-plus-two with Touring bodywork. Its engine was a detuned version of Maserati's 350S competition power unit of 1956, a twin-overhead-camshaft six of 3485 cc, developing 226 bhp and capable of giving the car a 209 km/h (130 mph) top speed. The chassis was tubular, while suspension was by the usual coil springs and wishbones at the front though with half-elliptic springs at the rear. By the time that the model had entered production in the autumn, Alfieri had modified the cam and porting to extract another 4 bhp.

The 3500GT was Maserati's first series-production car, if nearly 2000 examples can be so described, and was built until 1964. Front disc brakes were standardized in 1960, and a five-speed gearbox followed in 1961, while 1962 saw the introduction of a fuel-injected engine. In addition to the Touring coupé, Vignale offered a spider version on a short chassis.

Then, in 1962, Maserati introduced a supplementary model, based on the shorter 3500 chassis. This was the Sebring, named after the make's 1957 success in this American 12-hour event. Vignale produced a rather clipped two-plus-two coupé body. Although the engine was initially the contemporary 3500 unit, in 1964 a 3694 cc version became available. A Series II model arrived in 1965, and the car continued in production until 1966, though in 4014 cc form towards the end of the run.

The 3500 series was replaced in 1964 by the Frua-bodied Mistral – the name of the wind which blows over the Gulf of Lions, off the French Mediterranean coast. However, in contrast to its predecessor, this was more of a two-seater than a two-plus-two. Like the Sebring, the Mistral was fitted with the 3.5-, 3.7- and 4-litre engines, this last being the ultimate version of the twin-cam six. There was also a spider, built between 1964 and 1969. When Mistral production ceased, in 1970, Maserati's long-running six came to the end of the road.

In 1960 the firm introduced its top-line model, the limited production 5000GT, which cost 7,500,000 lire (£4305) and so was on a par with the Rolls-Royce Silver Cloud II. The power unit was a 4935 cc V8, with twin overhead camshafts per cylinder bank, of the type that had powered the ill-fated 450S sports car. Initially, practically no changes were made to the

unit but, after the first few had been built, the gears used to drive the overhead camshafts were replaced by quieter chains. This coincided with a modest capacity increase, to 4941 cc, and the fitment of Lucas fuel injection. Only 32 examples of the 257 km/h (160 mph) 5000GT had been made by the time that the model ceased production in 1964, and most of them were fitted with good-looking Allemano coachwork, although Touring, Ghia and Frua all offered their own variations on the 5000GT theme.

A somewhat more practical model was the Quattroporte Maserati of 1963, so called because it offered four, rather than

easily identifiable by its twin headlamp clusters, although less obvious was the live rear axle, replacing the costly de Dion. The engine capacity was increased to 4.7 litres at the same time, but the 4.2-litre version continued to be available until 1967. The model was discontinued in 1969.

There was also the two-seater Mexico, announced in late 1965, and given its name in 1966 after the Cooper-Maserati's victory at that year's Mexico Grand Prix. The bodywork, by Vignale, was somewhat more successful than its Quattroporte contemporary's while the 4.7-litre version of the V8 was employed and it was subsequently available with a more

RIGHT *Maserati's luxurious 5000GT of 1959–64 powered by the sports-racing-derived 4937 cc (4941 cc from 1960), four-overhead-camshaft V8. Most were bodied by Allemano but this version is by Frua and dates from 1962.*

BELOW LEFT *Maserati road-car production got into its stride with the 3500GT of 1957–64. The majority were bodied, as here, by Touring. There was also a spider by Vignale. The 3500 GT was powered by a 3485 cc twin-overhead-camshaft six-cylinder engine.*

ABOVE *The Quattroporte (four-door) of 1963 remained in production until 1969. This version endured until 1965, when the rectangular headlamps were replaced by twin circular units.*

RIGHT *The Vignale-bodied Mexico of 1966–8 had a 4719 cc V8 engine, although it was subsequently offered with a more economical 4.2-litre version. Its top speed was 217 km/h (135 mph).*

the usual two doors. Introduced at the 1963 Turin Show, it was Maserati's first unitary construction model and Frua was responsible for the bodywork. Its engine was a smaller capacity – 4136 cc – version of the 5000GT unit, and there was a de Dion rear axle; a favourite on Maserati's Formula 1 and sports racers. The model was revised for 1966 and the new Quattroporte was economical 4200 cc engine. It was heavy at 1542 kg (3400 lb) but was capable of around 217 km/h (135 mph), despite its weight. The model was not particularly successful, however, and lasted only until 1972.

Until now the Maserati management had fought shy of marketing an out-and-out sports car, but one eventually arrived, in 1967, in the form of the Ghibli – yet another wind, this time hailing from the Sahara Desert. The Ghia bodywork was by the celebrated Giorgetto Giugiaro, and had the

the French Citroën company, owned, since 1935, by the Michelin tyre concern. Citroën was intent on producing a prestigious GT version of its celebrated front-wheel-drive DS saloon, but lacked a suitable engine. They therefore approached the Orsis and made a bid for a majority shareholding in Maserati, which was confirmed by outright ownership in 1971. But to say that Citroën bought Maserati simply for its ability to manufacture high-performance engines would be an oversimplification. The purchase should be seen more in terms

MASERATI GHIBLI		
1966–73		
ENGINE		
No. of cylinders V8		
Bore/stroke 93 × 85 mm; from 1970 93 × 89 mm		
Displacement 4719, 4930 cc		
Valve operation Twin overhead camshaft per cylinder bank		
Compression ratio 8.5:1		
Induction Four Weber carburettors		
BHP 330 at 5500 rpm, 335 at 5500 rpm		
Transmission Five-speed		
CHASSIS		
Frame Tubular		
Wheelbase 2550 mm (8 ft 4 in)		
Track – front 1440 mm (4 ft 9 in)		
Track – rear 1420 mm (4 ft 8 in)		
Suspension – front Independent, coil springs and wishbone		
Suspension – rear Half-elliptic		
PERFORMANCE		
Maximum speed 265 km/h (164 mph)		

ABOVE LEFT *The Maserati Ghibli, styled by Giorgetto Giugiaro while at Ghia, appeared in 1967. A 4.7-litre V8 engine was employed.*
LEFT *Unlike the Ghibli, the Indy of 1969–74 was a four-seater GT, with 4.2-litre V8.*

distinction of being his first production design to feature concealed headlights. This handsome fastback coupé, arguably the best-looking Maserati of the 1960s, had the 4.7-litre V8 in 330 bhp form, and the firm reverted to a tubular chassis for this 265 km/h (165 mph) car although, perhaps surprisingly, the cart-sprung live axle persisted. A spider version arrived in 1969 and, subsequently, a 4.9-litre version of the V8 appeared. Production lasted until 1973 by which time 1149 had been produced, making the Ghibli the top-selling Maserati of its day.

The four-door Quattroporte was due to be phased out in 1968 and was replaced by a two-door four-seater. The Indy, a belated recognition of Maserati's 1939 and 1940 successes in the Indianapolis 500 race, was a stylish coupé by Vignale with opening tailgate, powered by a 4136 cc version of the V8, although it could be had with 4.7- and 4.9-litre power units. The Indy remained in production until 1974 and 1136 examples were built, making it the second-best-seller after the Ghibli.

The scene of the Maserati story now moves outside Italy to

of increasing Franco/Italian cooperation within the motor industry.

Citroën takes over

So, after 31 years' ownership, the Orsis bowed out. The take-over was effected in January 1968 and Citroën told Maserati the type of engine it would require for the SM. As the production V8 was too long for the DS-based SM, Alfieri was instructed to lop two cylinders off the V8 Indy engine and to have a power unit running within six months. Citroën was amazed to find that it could be produced in a mere three weeks! The 4136 cc Indy unit was suitably truncated while a one-off crankshaft was machined from solid and new camshafts were produced. This resulted in a 3102 cc engine and, as the capacity was too great, the stroke was reduced from 85 to 75 mm. This made a 2737 cc V6, but this was still too great so the bore was reduced by 1 mm to 87 mm, giving the required capacity of 2670 cc.

But the rework did not stop there. Because the engine was to be mounted back to front under the Citroën's bonnet, all the accessory drives had to be repositioned. The camshaft drives were also changed and, instead of the chains being at the end of the engine, they were transferred to the top of the unit, driving the four 'shafts, via a jackshaft, at the extremity of each one. However, a shortcoming of the design was that the primary chain lacked a tensioner, and this did present problems on the production cars.

The 220 km/h (136 mph) car entered production in 1971. Its most successful time was 1971 when 4988 examples were produced and 4036 were sold in the following year. But thereafter demand began to tail off. This was despite the arrival of the fuel-injected version in July 1972 and the addition, a year later, of a 2965 cc engine, achieved by increasing the bore from 87 to 91 mm, and with automatic transmission. Demand for the SM continued to decline and the 1973 oil crisis, sparked by the Arab-Israeli war of October, provided the final blow. In 1974, SM production was transferred to Guy Ligier's Abrest factory, which Citroën took over that year, and production ceased in 1975 after only 12,920 cars had been built. The SM's V6 engine was also used in Ligier's JS2 mid-engined model when it replaced a Ford V6 unit. It lasted until 1976.

The Citroën–Maserati association was not a one-way process, however. Maserati was able to take advantage of the French company's sales outlets but, more significantly, a new generation of Maserati chassis was planned: a mid-engined sports coupé; a front-engined GT which would incorporate some Citroën hydraulic systems, for which the French company was famous; and a new front-wheel-drive saloon, using SM running gear.

The first of this new generation of models, the 1971 mid-engined Bora, was again named after a wind: this one blew nearer home, from Trieste north towards the Adriatic Sea. The coupé was by Giugiaro's Ital Design while its aerodynamic qualities reflected Citroën expertise in that area. Purposeful, fast and capable of 257 km/h (160 mph), the Bora had a longitudinally located 4719 cc V8 engine, while a five-speed ZF gearbox was employed. Suspension, by coil springs and wishbones, was the first such on a Maserati, while the brakes were courtesy of the SM with engine-driven pump and hydraulic accumulator. A 4.9-litre V8 was available from 1976 and the Bora remained in production until 1980.

The Merak, named after the second star in the Plough

constellation, and also mid-engined, appeared in 1972. Powered by a 2965 cc version of the SM engine, it was relatively compact but still had room for two small, though hardly practical, rear seats. Again the brakes employed Citroën hydraulics, but these were dispensed with in 1978 when a more conventional system was introduced. Roadholding reflected the central engine location and the model was capable of around 225 km/h (140 mph). The Merak was the most successful Maserati of its day, as the V6 engine offered economy in those energy crisis years. About 1300 cars had been built by 1975. In that year the model was uprated, the revised SS having a more powerful version of the V6 with 220 rather than 190 bhp, a higher compression ratio and larger carburettors. It was also 45 kg (100 lb) lighter than its predecessor. In 1976 Maserati introduced a 1999 cc version intended for the Italian market, but both models were discontinued in 1981.

The final production car of these Citroën years was the Khamsin, which is an unpleasant hot, strong wind that periodically sweeps across the Sahara Desert. Unveiled at the 1972 Turin Show, the Khamsin did not enter production until 1974. The two-door coupé body was by Bertone, and was the work of the celebrated Marcello Gandini, who also has the fabled Lamborghini Miura and Countach to his credit. Concealed hydraulically operated headlamps were a feature of this Maserati, which also used the SM's brakes and power-assisted VariPower steering. The engine was Maserati's faithful V8, this time of 4930 cc. The stylish Khamsin was to enjoy a seven-year production run, remaining available until 1981.

The final model of this generation, a front-wheel-drive Citroën/Maserati hybrid, not only boasted the SM's engine but also its steering, brakes and suspension. Bertone was again responsible for this stylish four-door saloon which was aptly named Quattroporte II. It was exhibited at the 1974 shows but only a handful of these cars were built and it never entered series production.

The root cause of the Quattroporte II's demise lay in the fact that Citroën's problems, exacerbated by the energy crisis, boiled over in 1974. A Fiat deal was unscrambled in 1973 and, in December 1974, it was announced that Citroën's Michelin owners had reached an agreement with Peugeot to buy the company. The remaining problem was what was to be done with Maserati?

The answer was not long in coming. On 22 May 1975, only five months after the Peugeot take-over, Maserati was left to

LEFT *Not a Modena car, but the Citroën SM. Produced between 1970–5, the SM was powered by a Maserati 2670 cc V6 engine (2965 cc from 1973) as Citroën owned Maserati from 1968 until 1975. Unfortunately this prestigious DS-based front-wheel-drive, hydropneumatically suspended Grand Tourer never sold in the expected numbers, and the 1973 oil crisis tolled its death knell.*

sink or swim, having, according to the French company, lost a devastating £2.5 million in 1974. The people of Modena took to the streets in protest and the Italian government reacted by taking the firm over while a programme of reconstruction was put in hand. The result, announced on 8 August, was an agreement between the government and Alessandro de Tomaso, an expatriot Argentinian of Italian descent, who had lived in Italy since 1955.

De Tomaso to the rescue

De Tomaso's Italian father became Argentina's first elected prime minister, and died in 1933 when his son was only five years old. When Alessandro was 27, in 1955, he fled to Italy having been involved in a plot to overthrow the Argentine president, General Juan Perón. In 1956 he joined the Maserati brothers' Bologna-based OSCA company as a works driver, and later entered the 1958 Le Mans race. He was placed 10th and won his class. De Tomaso briefly became the firm's racing manager although he clashed with his employers and, in 1959, established Automobili De Tomaso in Modena. He began by building and selling racing cars and, in 1965, bought the Ghia coachbuilding concern. This he combined with his Automobili De Tomaso and then sold 84 per cent of the capital to the American Rowan Industries, whose president, Amory Haskell, was his brother-in-law.

De Tomaso's next acquisition, in 1969, was the Vignale body company. In the previous year he had started talks with Ford's Lee Iacocca, whose father had emigrated to America from Italy as a 12-year-old, and these meetings laid the foundations of a friendship that continues to this day. Iacocca wanted to sell an Italian-built Ford V8-engined sports car on the American market. As a result, the mid-engined De Tomaso Pantera of 1971 was born, designed by Giampaolo Dallara, late of Lamborghini.

Then, in 1970, Amory Haskell was killed in an air crash and Alessandro's companies were regrouped under the De Tomaso Industries name in America. Ford took over Rowan's 84 per cent holding and de Tomaso agreed not to work for a competitor within the motor industry for a five-year period. Consequently his next investments were in the motor cycle industry: in 1971, he bought the Benelli motor cycle company of Pesaro and, in

the following year, Moto Guzzi. Then, in December 1972, having disagreed with Henry Ford, he severed his connections with the American company which, a month later, took over his 16 per cent holding in De Tomaso Industries.

De Tomaso's agreement with Ford finally expired in 1975 when he was, once again, able to enter the motor industry, at the very time that Maserati was struggling for survival. De Tomaso told the Italian government that he was prepared to save Maserati providing that he was allowed to negotiate directly with Citroën. As a result of these talks, Maserati once more became Italian-owned. The government put up 70 per cent of the capital through GEPI (the State Capital Corporation) and also loaned de Tomaso his 30 per cent stake. The agreement was that de Tomaso could buy back the 70 per cent holding over a six-year period at a pre-arranged price of six billion lire (£4.1 million), and this is what happened.

Following the 1975 change of ownership, design responsibility was transferred to De Tomaso Automobiles, which resulted in the stormy departure on 25 August of technical director Giulio Alfieri who subsequently was to move down the road to Lamborghini. On taking control, Alessandro de Tomaso worked out a 10-year plan for the company. His strategy was to concentrate on the production of luxury, high-performance saloons to rival the top-line Mercedes-Benz, while at the same time maintaining the make's performance image. In this he has been outstandingly successful.

But, back in 1975, his first priority was to get Maserati production moving again. A record 733 cars had been built in 1968, the year of the Citroën take-over, and the figure had risen marginally to 738 in 1973. But, in 1975, annual production plummeted to a catastrophic 201, and it fell even further, to 195, in 1976.

The first visible results of the de Tomaso regime appeared in 1977 with the arrival of the Kyalami, named after the venue of the South African Grand Prix, which a Cooper-Maserati had won in 1966. The Kyalami was by Maserati out of de Tomaso – a reskinned De Tomaso Longchamps, facelifted by Frua and, in place of the Ford V8, Maserati's 4136 cc V8. The Kyalami, built until 1982, helped tide Maserati over a difficult period. Thankfully, car production crept up to 292 in 1977, and had increased to 339 a year later.

The real fruits of the new regime arrived in 1979 in the shape of a new Quattroporte, a handsome four-door saloon by Ital Design, powered by the new 4.2-litre V8 engine with the option of an alternative 4930 cc V8. The model remains in production as the flagship of the Maserati range, although only the larger capacity engine is now available.

De Tomaso sprang another surprise, in December 1981, when he unveiled the Biturbo, the first series-production road car to feature a twin turbocharged engine. Under the bonnet of this handsome sports coupé a 1996 cc V6 with belt-driven single overhead camshafts, three valves per cylinder, twin Japanese IHI turbochargers and 180 bhp on offer. The Biturbo is produced at the Milan premises of the Innocenti company – yet another business that forms part of Alessandro de Tomaso's corporate jigsaw.

The Milan-based Innocenti company had once produced British Minis and 1100s under licence, had been bought by British Leyland in 1975 and had closed, with the collapse of the Corporation, in 1976.

The Italian government approached Fiat and de Tomaso to come up with rescue plans. De Tomaso's was chosen, for he saw the Milan company as complementary to his ownership of Maserati. His intention was to merge the two, and this was accomplished in 1984. Therefore Innocenti is responsible for body production while Maserati in Modena looks after the mechanical side of production, with cars being assembled in Milan. That company, retitled Nuova Innocenti (New Innocenti) in 1976, now produces a range of front-wheel-drive Mini-derived cars, powered by Japanese Daihatsu two- and three-cylinder engines.

Nineteen eighty-two was a key year for Maserati: it moved into profit, probably for the first time in its history. This was the result of the new model strategy and a dramatic surge in output. In 1981 Maserati had built 555 cars, but in 1982 output soared to 2265, and, for the first time ever, production outstripped Ferrari's. Nineteen eighty-four's figure was 6180, with hopes for even greater things in the future.

For 1986, Maserati introduced a new model – the 228 – which was longer and wider than the Biturbo. Like the Biturbo, it has twin turbochargers, but a 2790 cc engine and four, rather than three, valves per cylinder.

And what of the future? When Alessandro's friend Lee Iacocca was summarily dismissed by Henry Ford and assumed the Chrysler presidency in 1978, he asked de Tomaso to produce a Chrysler-engined roadster. Chrysler consequently took a five per cent stake in Maserati and the model, still coded the Q Coupé, is due to be built at the Innocenti works at the rate of 5000 to 10,000 cars a year for a five-year period. So it seems as though, after spending decades in the financial doldrums, Maserati, with its distinguished competition history, is set for a more stable future. It certainly won't be a dull one, if the past is anything to go by!

LEFT *The Ital Design-styled, mid-engined Bora with 4.7-litre V8 power and 273 km/h (170 mph).*

BELOW *The current Biturbo, introduced in 1982, with a 1996 cc V6 engine for Italy, and 2491 cc elsewhere.*

206

ACKNOWLEDGEMENTS

The Publishers thank the following for providing the photographs in this book:

Covey-Gauld PR 100 above, 105, 108, 110, 111 above, 114–6; D.D.P.I. 118–119 above, 148 below; Fiat Auto (UK) Ltd 7, 119 below; Geoffrey Goddard 1 above centre, 20, 32, 46, 48 above, 53 centre, 86 below, 91, 94, 95, left, 152, 184, 190–3, 195; Chris Harvey 136–7; Haymarket Publishing Ltd (Autocar) 1 below right, 2 above right, 2 below, 3 above, 37 below, 43 below, 120–2, 147, 172, 182, 203, (Classic & Sportcar) 4 below left, 11 right, 111 below, 127, 134, 144, 177; LAT Photographic Ltd 1 below left, 51–2, 64–5, 70–2, 74–5; Lancia S.P.A. 4 right, 155–6, 161, 166 right, 170 above, 173, 175–6, 180–1; Maserati S.P.A. 5 below, 187 below, 189, 198 above, 201 centre & below; Andrew Moreland 125 below, 128, 142–3, 146, 148 above, 149; National Motoring Museum, Beaulieu 23, 26 below, 27 above, 29, 88–90, 107, 154, 166 left; Octopus Library 78 above, 153, 165; Cyril Posthumus 53 below, 86, 194; Quadrant Picture Library 4 above left, 8, 9, 54 below, 66, 73 below, 106, 124, 125 above, 138–9, 146–7, 157, 160 below, 205; Peter Roberts 1 above left, 87, 93, 95 right, 100 below, 104; Nigel Snowdon & Associates 36; Franco Zagari 2 centre, 10–11, 92, 96–9, 101, 109, 129, 140–1, 160 above, 162–5, 167, 170 below, 171, 174, 187 above, 199–201 above, 202, 204.

The following photographs were taken specially for Octopus Books Ltd:

Ian Dawson 1 above right & below centre, 2 above left, 3 below, 5 above, 8–9, 10, 12, 14, 15 below, 16, 17, 18, 19, 21, 22, 24–5, 26 above, 27 below, 28, 30, 31, 33–5, 37 below, 38–42, 44, 47, 48–9, 50, 58–9, 69 below, 73 above, 84, 102–3, 112–3, 116–7, 132–3, 135, 145, 150, 158–9, 168–9, 178–9, 182–3, 196–7, 198 below; Nicky Wright 53 above, 54 above, 55–7, 60–3, 66–8, 69 above & centre, 76–7, 78–9.